INTERNATIONAL STUDIES OF THE
COMMITTEE ON INTERNATIONAL RELATIONS
UNIVERSITY OF NOTRE DAME

Diplomacy in a Changing World. Stephen D. Keretsz and M. A. Fitzsimons, eds.

The Russian Revolution and Religion, 1917–1925. Edited and translated by Bolesław Szcześniak.

Soviet Policy Toward the Baltic States, 1918–1940. Albert N. Tarulis.

Introduction to Modern Politics. Ferdinand Hermens.

Freedom and Reform in Latin America. Fredrick B. Pike, ed.

What America Stands For. Stephen D. Kertesz and M. A. Fitzsimons, eds.

The Representative Republic. Ferdinand Hermens.

Theoretical Aspects of International Relations. William T. R. Fox, ed.

Catholicism, Nationalism and Democracy in Argentina. John J. Kennedy.

Christian Democracy in Western Europe, 1820–1953. Michael P. Fogarty.

The Fate of East Central Europe. Stephen D. Kertesz, ed.

German Protestants Face the Social Question. William O. Shanahan.

Soviet Imperialism: Its Origins and Tactics. Waldemar Gurian, ed.

The Foreign Policy of the British Labour Government, 1945–1951. M. A. Fitzsimons.

Diplomacy in a Whirlpool: Hungary between Nazi Germany and Soviet Russia. Stephen D. Kertesz.

Bolshevism: An Introduction to Soviet Communism. Waldemar Gurian.

A Search For Stability

United States Diplomacy Toward Nicaragua 1925-1933

A Search For Stability

United States Diplomacy

Toward Nicaragua 1925-1933

WILLIAM KAMMAN

UNIVERSITY OF NOTRE DAME PRESS
NOTRE DAME–LONDON

Library of Congress Catalog Card Number: 68-17060
Manufactured in the United States of America

For Nancy

ACKNOWLEDGMENT

I am indebted to many people who have made this book possible. The librarians and archivists of the Manuscript Division of the Library of Congress, the National Archives, the Naval Records Management Center, the Minnesota State Historical Society, and the libraries of Indiana, Yale, and North Texas State universities assisted me in numerous ways. The staffs of the Archivo General de la Nación (Managua) and the Biblioteca Nacional (Managua) were kind and helpful, as was Dr. Norman Ziff, cultural affairs officer, United States embassy, Managua. The Graduate Research Council of Indiana University provided funds for the initial research and the Faculty Research Committee of North Texas State University granted money to defray later research expenses and to release me from teaching duties. My colleague Professor William P. Vaughn and Mrs. Walter Prichard read portions of the manuscript and offered helpful suggestions. Miss Ann Rice of the University of Notre Dame Press saved me from many ambiguities and stylistic errors. Professor Robert H. Ferrell of Indiana University has aided me in untold ways since I started this research as a graduate student. It is impossible to thank him enough for his many kindnesses, his willingness to read and criticize several drafts of this manuscript. I owe a special debt to my wife who has acted as typist, editor, and proofreader and has been patient through it all.

W. K.

Denton, Texas
January, 1968

CONTENTS

1: NICARAGUA AND THE UNITED STATES BY 1925

During the early decades of the twentieth century, intervention was common practice in United States relations with Latin America. The Caribbean nations, whose political and economic problems often led to fear for the safety of lives and property or fear that some non-American state might intervene, most often felt the heavy hand of the United States. The U.S. occupations, notably in Cuba, Haiti, Dominican Republic, and Nicaragua, provided a measure of peace and stability but were unsatisfactory in resolving many problems. Interventions under the shibboleths of the Roosevelt Corollary or "dollar diplomacy" generated much ill will, and in the 1920's Washington began to review its policy. Although the Republican administrations did not forswear the right to intervene, they laid the groundwork for good neighborliness. The second intervention in Nicaragua, complicated in the extreme, illustrated vividly many of the problems inherent in intervention.

Relations between Nicaragua and the United States have never been so hectic as in the era 1925 to 1933—the subject of the present volume. The so-called American intervention in Nicaragua, which in those days of limited military interventions admittedly was large, became a source of enormous concern to President Calvin Coolidge and his secretary of state, Frank B. Kellogg. And in terms of what came out of the Nicaraguan revolution—the Somoza family dictatorship, which has prevailed down to the present writing—the results have been equally troublesome.

1

The present work seeks to analyze what happened, in hope that it will not repeat itself elsewhere in American foreign relations. There is also, one must add, a second purpose, which is to examine the argument, so often heard, that the United States was an imperialist nation seeking to exploit all Latin America—notably the Central American and Caribbean republics—for the purpose of what President William Howard Taft in an unfortunate phrase had termed "dollar diplomacy."

United States interest in Nicaragua did not arise suddenly during the revolutionary disturbances of 1925–26. Almost since the beginning of the twentieth century that little nation had often found its fortunes tied to the Colossus of the North. To understand these developments one must look into the background of American-Nicaraguan relations—physical, economic, and political conditions in the mid-1920's in Nicaragua and general problems of American foreign policy toward that Central American country.

For centuries, before encountering the influence of the United States, Nicaragua had belonged to Spain. On his fourth voyage, in 1502, Columbus sailed along the Caribbean coast of this future republic. The northeastern tip of the country, Cape Gracias á Dios, bears the name which early discoverers gave it after being delivered there from a series of gales. Columbus continued southward, passing the Escondido River and arriving at the San Juan River near the end of September, 1502. Unknowingly he reached the possible continental passageway of his dreams—the route of others' dreams down through the years.

Two decades later the Spaniards came again, this time under Gil González Dávila, who moved up from Panama in 1522 and was the first European to invade Nicaragua. A cacique named Nicoya courteously received him. After Nicoya's subjects accepted Christianity they gave up their golden idols, exclaiming that since they were Christians they had no need for them; the Spaniards promptly took these emblems of sin. Moving farther north Gil González met a more powerful chief, Nicaragua, who exchanged gold for some slight articles of clothing. Before baptism the native chieftain asked the Europeans some searching questions, such as, "Why did not the Christians' God make a better world?" and "Why do Christians so love gold?"[1] Answers must have proved satisfactory, for the Spaniards baptized Nicaragua.

Gold was the magic word that brought many Spaniards to Latin America, and Nicaragua had asked the right question when he inquired of Gil González Dávila about the whites' love of gold. He could not know the full meaning of it for his people. Desire for wealth, so apparent in Nicaragua's discovery, led to exploitation of the country's native population. Presence of a large Indian population in Central America forced the Spanish to imperialism. The heritage from colonial days—a small group of educated Nicaraguans, a large group of illiterate Indians and mestizos—explains much about Nicaragua in the twentieth century.

As for Nicaragua's geography, the country today forms roughly an equilateral triangle with its base on the Caribbean, one side bordering the Pacific Ocean and Costa Rica and the other bordering Honduras. It was estimated in 1925 that the country covered 49,200, square miles, the largest nation in Central America.[2] It then ranked third in population with a census of 703,540.

Physically Nicaragua divides into three areas: the Mosquito coast on the east, the central highland, and the western volcanic lands. Swamps, grassy savannahs, and pine forests which become tropical woodlands toward the central regions characterize the first area. A mountain range which is called the Cordillera de los Andes although it is not a part of the great Andean system crosses the central zone; maximum height in this area is about seven thousand feet. A volcanic chain, continuation of the one in El Salvador and Costa Rica, marks the area. The best known peak in the area is Momotombo. The western zone has no major rivers; the country's major waterways flow from highlands toward

---

[1] Hubert Howe Bancroft, *History of Central America*, 3 vols. (San Francisco, 1886, 1887), I, 485–489.

[2] Today the figure is 57,143 square miles.

the Atlantic. But, while some of these waterways are navigable, they do not form in the eastern part of the country an extensive transportation system. Up to the 1920's this fact prevented exploitation of the area and explained why revolutions began on the Mosquito coast, where government forces could not easily put them down.

Nicaragua's possible canal route was its most important geographic feature. The best way to cross the country was by this route, beginning on the Caribbean side at San Juan del Norte (Greytown), up the San Juan River to Lake Nicaragua, and from the west shore of the lake (Virgin Bay) across thirteen miles of land to San Juan del Sur on the Pacific Ocean. Here was the route Cornelius Vanderbilt's transit company had used in the mid-nineteenth century; for a while it seemed the most feasible location for any isthmian canal. The San Juan River had some rapids, but a boat of light draft, skillfully handled, could make it. Going from the east coast of the United States to the west coast, travelers on the Nicaraguan route saved about five hundred miles and two days over Panamanian transit.[3]

Close to the Pacific shore are Lake Nicaragua and its sister to the northwest, Lake Managua, both formed by a basin in a break of the Central American Cordilleras. Probably once part of the Pacific Ocean, these lakes are now inland as a result of a change in the earth's surface. Chief Nicaragua's village stood by the larger of the lakes, which attracted the attention of the Europeans who accompanied González. Their belief that the lake was close to the sea had raised the question of interoceanic communication even in the 1520's.[4]

Nicaragua's population was always concentrated around the lakes and in the narrow volcanic area along the Pacific Ocean.

[3] As late as 1900 small steamers could ply this route, but shortly thereafter the eruption of a Costa Rican volcano silted the channel of the river. See Harold Playter and Andrew J. McConnico, Nicaragua, A Commercial and Economic Survey (Washington, D. C., 1927), pp. 22, 72.

[4] Bancroft, History of Central America, I, 489.

Here were the main cities, including León, Granada, and Managua, the capital. According to the 1920 census, the largest city was León, formerly the capital, but Managua was rapidly gaining.[5] Historically León and Granada—centers for the Liberal and Conservative parties respectively—had shown some animosity toward one another, the fate of each determined by whichever party controlled the government. For a while the capital was moved back and forth according to the party in power, but in the 1850's the factions chose a compromise capital, the small town of Managua on the lake of the same name. A traveler visiting Managua in the mid-1920's described the city as dingy but pleasant and felt that it failed to make the best of its beautiful setting.[6]

Sometime in its history Nicaragua received the epithet "Mahomet's Paradise"—a strange phrase for a country which, even today, has so much illiteracy and poverty. When W. W. Cumberland made a financial survey of the country in 1927–28, he estimated annual per capita income at forty dollars and per capita wealth at one hundred forty-one dollars. On such resources people could barely have essentials. As for education, as late as 1964 an estimated 64 percent of the population could not read or write.[7] What with costly revolutions, graft and thievery of government officials, and foreign debts falling in arrears, lack of money was a constant ailment of Nicaraguan governments during the period under study. This usually meant that schooling received

[5] In 1920 the population of the country was 638,119; León had 38,318; Managua, 27,839; Granada, 16,773. By 1926 Managua had 32,536 inhabitants; León, 23,565; and Granada, 18,066. By mid-1960 Nicaragua's population had risen to over 1,593,000 and Managua was by far the largest city with 274,901 people. León had 61,649 and Granada (no longer in third place) had 40,092.

[6] Wallace Thompson, *Rainbow Countries of Central America* (New York, 1927), p. 45.

[7] S. H. Steinberg, ed., *The Statesman's Year-Book: 1966–67* (New York, 1966), p. 1292; W. W. Cumberland, *Nicaragua: An Economic and Financial Survey Prepared, at the Request of Nicaragua, under the Auspices of the Department of State* (Washington, 1928), pp. 16–17.

last consideration from the government. Nicaraguans have virtually ignored education, the usual cornerstone of any democratic
country.

Another major Nicaraguan deficiency has been transportation.
Especially in areas away from the western coast, most of the
roads are still unpaved, little more than tracks. In the late 1920's
and early 1930's the situation was, if anything, worse. The better
roads were in the western part of the country, where the one-
hundred-fifty-mile single-track railroad, El Ferrocarril del Pacifico
de Nicaragua, connected the port of Corinto with Chinandega,
León, Managua, and Granada. Until recent years transport has
been almost impossible between the Atlantic and Pacific sides of
the nation. The port of New Orleans seemed closer to the country's Caribbean ports than did Managua. To be sure, nature con-
spired to keep the opposing shores apart. A mountain range angles
generally from northwest to southeast. No rivers links the two sections, and, as we have mentioned, no rivers of consequence flow
toward the west, although some rise in the mountain highlands
and flow eastward: the Río Segovia, Río Grande, Escondido
(Bluefields), and the San Juan, which is the outlet for Lake
Nicaragua. Perceiving that the San Juan might provide too easy
a passage, nature installed rapids and sandbars, and a Costa
Rican volcano silted up the channel. Dense jungle surrounded
everything.

What kinds of people live in Mahomet's Paradise? There are
not many pure-blooded Indians; they make up only 3 percent of
the population. Mestizos are almost 70 percent. Seventeen percent are whites and 9 percent Negroes. Most people live in the
narrow strip along the lakes where weather is the most conge-
nial. The Negro population, having emigrated from the West
Indies, lives on the Mosquito coast.

Nicaragua was and still is an agricultural country whose rich
soil allows many crops. For some time the chief export was coffee, grown mainly south and west of Managua and around Matagalpa, northeast of Lake Managua. A major crop of the eastern
part has been bananas, but pests have cut down exports. Other

products are timber, gold, and cotton, which now rivals coffee as Nicaragua's chief export.

In discussing products of Nicaragua, one cannot fail to note commercial ties with the United States. Over the past thirty-five years Nicaragua has sent over half of its exports to the United States. In 1941 it was 96 percent. Nicaraguan imports have followed the same pattern, 1936 being a low year when only 46 percent came from the United States.

In regard to the relations of the United States with Nicaragua in the fateful year 1925, it is safe to say that ideas governing the great northern republic's policy for Nicaragua—indeed for all nations of the Caribbean—had not changed greatly from the first quarter of the nineteenth century. As the United States had grown in size and importance there had been some variation in these ideas, but the reasons behind its actions remained the same. Early in our relations with Central America our diplomatic representatives told the State Department of the commercial importance, for present and future generations, of Nicaragua's San Juan River and Lake Nicaragua.[8] While the State Department did not always respond with the same enthusiasm as its agents, trade was an important factor in policy toward this area. The acquisition of Louisiana with its Mississippi River outlet, the purchase of Florida, and annexation of Texas took the United States into the Caribbean geographically as well as commercially and heightened our interest there.

Concern for the independence of Latin American countries, that no Old World power should threaten United States hegemony in the New World, formed another part of our Latin American policy. Declaration of the Monroe Doctrine with its corollaries over the years, pique with France and Maximilian in Mexico in the 1860's, alarm over the pro-Communist Castro regime in Cuba a century later—all expressed this concern. At times the

[8] William R. Manning, ed., *Diplomatic Correspondence of the United States, Inter-American Affairs, 1831–1860*, 12 vols. (Washington, 1932–39), III, 176.

United States has ignored this policy, and in the early and middle years of the nineteenth century there was no aspiration to dominate the area, but there was always concern for the protection of interests, present and future.[9]

Of course, a central consideration has been the possibility and then the actuality of the Panama Canal. The canal has been so important that one historian proposed that our Caribbean policy be called the "Panama Policy."[10] It was in 1825 that the Central American minister at Washington suggested to President John Quincy Adams that Nicaragua be the site for a canal between the Atlantic and Pacific.[11] Secretary of State Henry Clay instructed the American chargé d'affaires in Central America to look into the matter. However, nothing came of this proposal. The idea of isthmian transit continued to crop up in American diplomacy, and the United States kept an eye on other nations showing interest. British activity on the Mosquito coast of Nicaragua disturbed American diplomats, who feared being shut out from a Nicaraguan canal. A treaty with New Granada (Colombia) in 1846 granted the United States free transit across Panama in return for guarantee of integrity of the isthmus. Mutual suspicion brought the United States and Britain into the self-denying Clayton-Bulwer Treaty of 1850, which provided that neither nation would act to obtain exclusive control of a canal. The treaty further stipulated that neither country would ever erect or maintain fortification near the canal nor colonize or assume dominion over Nicaragua, Costa Rica, and the Mosquito coast, or any part of Central America.

About this time (in 1848) the California gold rush excited thousands of Americans and sent them across the Central Ameri-

[9] Wilfrid Hardy Callcott, The Caribbean Policy of the United States: 1890–1920 (Baltimore, 1942), p. 20.

[10] Samuel Flagg Bemis, A Diplomatic History of the United States, 3rd ed. (New York, 1953), pp. 519–520.

[11] William R. Manning, ed., Diplomatic Correspondence of the United States Concerning the Independence of the Latin American Nations, 3 vols. (New York, 1925), II, 881.

can isthmus or around the Horn to California. Then followed a true Panama Policy. As years passed the United States grew restive and moved to abrogate the 1850 treaty. The Hay-Pauncefote Treaty of 1901 led to the Panama Canal. Afterward the United States decided to conduct itself in the Caribbean in such a way as to protect the new canal. Other nations had to tread softly in Latin America, even with United States permission, for this country would invoke the Monroe Doctrine whenever it thought nations were interfering. The Panama Policy entailed the "Roosevelt Corollary," intervention in Caribbean countries when necessary to protect the lives and property of citizens and others, or to prevent European nations from taking action. The United States would strengthen and stabilize Central American republics. Lastly, this country would acquire more property in the Caribbean, including strategic islands.

With the Panama Canal in the twentieth century, the United States still did not forget the possible canal route through Nicaragua. In the nineteenth century it had been willing to share the route on a neutral basis, but willingness changed to jealousy and a possessiveness which would allow no one to claim Nicaragua. After choosing Panama the United States refused to give up interest in Nicaragua. By the Bryan-Chamorro Treaty of 1916 Nicaragua agreed to give the United States, in perpetuity, exclusive proprietary rights for construction, operation, and maintenance of an interoceanic canal, and it granted a long-term lease on the Great and Little Corn Islands in the Caribbean and on land for a naval base on the Gulf of Fonseca on the Pacific side.

Thus Nicaragua continued to interest the United States. Because of its strategic location in the Caribbean, its nearness to Panama, and its suitability for a canal site, this Central American republic was destined to take a part in American diplomacy out of all proportion to its size.

Political conditions in Nicaragua from 1909 onward presented many challenges to American foreign policy. The country had never had much peace and quiet. The United States had been implicated in the William Walker episode of the 1850's, when

that gaunt, gray-eyed man of destiny established himself as president of the republic. In the last years of the nineteenth century a native dictator, José Santos Zelaya, became president and
threatened trouble when he sought to revoke concessions granted
American nationals in hope of regranting them for more money
or letting them out to other individuals. Zelaya also threatened
to overturn the Central American Court of Justice, which the
United States had helped establish in 1907 to keep down revolutions. He had ambitions of invading neighboring republics. By
1909 a revolt threatened. Emiliano Chamorro, a prominent Conservative, was reportedly in Bluefields masterminding a plot.[12]
The local governor, Juan J. Estrada, joined the conspirators in
return for a promise of becoming provisional president. One of
Chamorro's friends was Adolfo Díaz, who worked for an American company and in whose name large sums accrued for support
of the revolt.

When the revolt began, the United States and the Central
American nations were not displeased. The new government,
realizing the need of United States support or at least acquies-
cence, expressed friendship for the American government and
American interests. Hearing of the attempt to set up an independent republic on Nicaragua's Mosquito coast, Zelaya sent
troops to bring the area under control. Meanwhile Estrada told
the American consul at Bluefields, Thomas P. Moffatt, that he
could not give foreigners protection. Almost immediately four
hundred Marines landed and declared Bluefields out of bounds
for fighting.

In an open struggle the revolutionary forces did not seem a
match for government troops, but events gradually turned in
favor of Chamorro, Estrada, Díaz, and company. Zelaya raised
the ire of the United States government when he captured and
executed two Americans in the employ of the revolutionists,

[12] For the following brief account of political events I have relied
mainly on *Papers Relating to the Foreign Relations of the United States*
for the years 1909, 1910, 1911, 1912, and 1920. Hereafter cited as *Foreign Relations*.

Leonard Groce and Lee Roy Cannon. Secretary of State Philander C. Knox sharply criticized the Zelaya government and severed diplomatic relations with it. Realizing the futility of staying in Managua against United States wishes, Zelaya deposited his power with Dr. José Madriz and went into exile. Madriz, whom Washington considered part of the Zelaya system, also failed to receive recognition. The revolution was soon over, and the revolutionists then divided. They had been members of both Nicaraguan political parties, and their political hatreds and spites overcame the unity established in the anti-Zelaya cause.

The political situation after Zelaya's departure deserves some detailed comment. As we have mentioned, Nicaragua had two parties: Liberal and Conservative. At one time there may have been some difference in philosophy, principle, or policy, but it had largely disappeared by the turn of the twentieth century. The basis of the parties was *localismo* and *personalismo*, that is, loyalty to a town or small area and to an individual or group. Such an arrangement, which played havoc with national interests, was one of the worst evils of Nicaraguan politics. Centers for the two political parties were León and Granada. The Conservative party in Granada had such leading families as the Chamorros, Lacayas, and Cuadras. León was the Liberal city. Rivalry between the two towns dated from the early nineteenth century and had often led to killing and looting.

Though government in Nicaragua was not democratic, it usually depended on popular support. While leaders of León and Granada were party leaders, support for each faction came from other parts of the country and from the lower classes. Officials could not disregard public opinion. A spirit of being "against the government" and the disposition to do more than just talk was constantly present and evident in most of the revolutions.[13]

Alignment of the parties after the defeat of Zelaya was admittedly confusing, for while most of the dictator's opponents had

[13] Dana G. Munro, *The Five Republics of Central America* (New York, 1918), p. 73.

been Conservatives, among the rebels were many Liberals. The
provisional president, Juan Estrada, was a Liberal. General José
María Moncada was also a Liberal but a long-time opponent of
Zelaya; he had become a trusted adviser of Estrada. As minister
of war the new government appointed General Luis Mena, a
supporter of the Chamorro family and recently a hero for his
own exploits. Even the old Conservatives were not unified. The
Cuadra family opposed the party headship of Emiliano Chamorro, leader of Conservative revolts against Zelaya.[14]

Nicaragua was close to anarchy in 1910, and the United States
moved to save it from collapse. Months of fighting had almost
wrecked the national economy. The currency had depreciated;
agriculture and commerce were at a standstill. The American
government sent Thomas C. Dawson to Managua as special
agent to report on conditions and help reestablish constitutional
government with free elections, rehabilitation of finances, and
payment of legitimate foreign and domestic claims. Dawson
arrived on October 18; after ten days of talks, Estrada, Díaz, and
Mena agreed to call an election for members of a constitutional
convention. The convention was to elect a president and vice-
president for two years; leaders of the revolution agreed to
support Estrada for president and Díaz for vice-president. The
provisional government pledged to abolish monopolies, guarantee
foreigners' rights, and provide a free popular election for a president to succeed Estrada. To rehabilitate finances the leaders
planned a loan secured by customs revenues. The two governments would decide on customs collection. A mixed claims commission agreeable to both countries would examine and pass on
claims. The Dawson agreement formed the basis for United
States recognition of the new government and was the guide for
American relations with Nicaragua during the next few years. The
State Department wanted to impress on factional leaders that the
agreement bound all, not just the four signatories: Estrada, Díaz,
Mena, and Chamorro. The department hinted that without

[14] *Ibid.*, pp. 231–232.

restoration of order there would be more outside interference.

As provided in the Dawson agreement, election for members of the constitutional convention came late in November, 1910, and within a month the convention chose Estrada and Díaz as president and vice-president. Estrada promised to make his administration not a party but a national one. The new president further asserted that there would be freedom of religion, freedom of the press (within limits, of course), and no executive interference with the judiciary. Estrada also made the usual references to development of agriculture and railroads, strict economy, and currency reform. To reassure the United States, he offered his gratitude to America for its help and promised noninterference in Central American political affairs.[15]

Estrada's administration was not to have easy going. His troubles mounted, for there were too many political prima donnas trying to sing the same arias. General José María Moncada, minister of the interior (*gobernación*), was very critical of Chamorro. Moreover, Moncada and Mena "cherished for each other a beautiful hatred."[16] As minister of war, Mena had control of arms and ammunition and did not inspire the President's trust. Chamorro got out of hand. With ambition for the presidency, he gained control of the constitutional assembly and did all in his power to weaken the administration. When Estrada countered by dissolving the assembly and calling new elections, Chamorro left the country.

Events came to a crisis on May 8, 1911. In a fit of drunkenness Estrada arrested Mena for treason. The arrest excited Mena's troops and revolution was imminent. The United States minister, Elliott Northcott, believed Estrada had acted with advice of Moncada, perhaps in conjunction with a Liberal plot. Estrada resigned. Díaz became president and released Mena. Mena turned back the troops then marching on Managua.

During the next few months Díaz and Mena worked uneasily

[15] *Foreign Relations: 1911*, p. 648.
[16] Harold Norman Denny, *Dollars for Bullets* (New York, 1929), p. 95.

together. The latter was real head of the government and interested primarily in gaining the presidency. On the day that Díaz was inaugurated, he and Mena signed an agreement providing Mena's presidential candidacy for the next term. Regardless of such promises, Mena's support was at best halfhearted and the Díaz administration avoided collapse only through United States support—discouraging all talk of resignation and at one time sending the warship *Yorktown* up from Panama. Still Mena worked to have the constitutional assembly elect him president for the next term. The State Department considered the step illegal and opposed it. Mena's followers in the assembly complicated the matter by making approval of American loan contracts subject to agreement on their leader's plans.

These loan contracts and other economic arrangements provided in the Dawson agreement were important to United States policy and explain American involvement in Nicaragua during the following years. Interpreting United States moves, President Taft stated in 1911, "It needs no profuse argument to show that the financial rehabilitation of the greater part of Central America will work potential good for the stability and peace of all."[17] And Philander Knox suggested that true stability was best established by economic and social forces rather than military. Thus on June 6, 1911, the United States and Nicaragua signed a loan convention in which the Central American nation undertook to negotiate a loan for stabilizing its finances. Nicaraguan customs, to be supervised by an American-approved and protected collector general, secured the loan. Nicaragua also agreed not to change customs duties during the loan period without consent of the United States.[18] Almost immediately the Nicaraguan assembly ratified the treaty, but the United States Senate delayed and finally refused approval.

[17] *Foreign Relations: 1912*, p. 1072.
[18] *Ibid.*, p. 1075. This was the Knox-Castrillo convention which was finally defeated in the United States Senate despite strenuous efforts on the part of Philander C. Knox.

Meanwhile Brown Brothers and Company and J. & W. Seligman and Company of New York made a small advance loan of one and a half million dollars secured by customs receipts collected by a collector general who was nominated by the bankers and approved by the Secretary of State. With Knox's blessing Clifford D. Ham became the collector of customs, although Knox emphasized that approval in no way indicated the United States would grant citizens connected with this loan any aid not given other American enterprises.

The preliminary loan opened the door for further United States influence in Nicaragua. Bankers had an option on 51 percent of the new national bank. Small loans led to banker control of 51 percent of the national railway. These connections, plus the fact that there were Americans on the claims commission (provided in the Dawson agreement) and an American collector of customs, increased United States commitment to Nicaraguan stability.

But Nicaraguan politics were anything but stable. Political conditions depressed Díaz, who saw an "irreconcilable division between parties which consequently forced the government to be always in a semi-state of war against its conspiring opponents." Violent politics had economic consequences and often prevented justice in the courts. His remedy called for "more direct and efficient assistance from the United States, like that which resulted so well in Cuba." By a treaty with the American government he wanted to amend the Nicaraguan constitution to allow "the United States to intervene in Nicaraguan internal affairs in order to maintain peace and the existence of a lawful government."[19] Such a Platt-Amendment solution was certainly a horrendous suggestion to all liberals and anti-imperialists of the world—Latin American nations not least—though it would perhaps have been the quickest and most efficient route to short-term Nicaraguan peace.

General Mena could not long check his desire to head the

[19] *Foreign Relations: 1911*, p. 670.

government. The constitutional assembly had chosen him president for the term beginning January 1, 1913. Near the end of
July, 1912, after weeks of preparation, he attempted but failed
to gain control of La Loma, a fortified hill dominating Managua.
Chamorro, in charge of loyal troops, took countermeasures; full-
scale war was about to begin. The new American minister,
George T. Weitzel, interceded at the request of Díaz and obtained the resignations of both Mena and Chamorro. Mena then
fled to Masaya, where he set up a rival government. Since Americans resident in Managua feared for their lives, the minister requested a detachment of men from the U.S.S. *Annapolis*. A force
of one hundred men arrived on August 4, 1912. This date is
memorable, for it marked the beginning of a chapter in United
States-Nicaraguan relations that was not to end for twenty years.
Ten days later three hundred fifty Marines arrived from Panama.
Other battalions came later and kept communications open by
occupying towns along the railroad from Corinto to Managua.
American forces pushed through to Granada, meeting some
resistance from Mena's troops. Mena finally surrendered to the
Americans, who sent him and his son to Panama.[20]

The government wanted normal conditions as soon as possible
and hoped the upcoming elections would help. Elections of
November 2, 1912, resulted in reelection of Díaz as president.
The Liberals did not participate. Four years later the problem
of presidential elections came up again. By provision of the new
constitution Díaz could not succeed himself. His party united in
support of Emiliano Chamorro, who became president.

The Díaz administration had not been popular. It was plagued
by continued economic problems and the threat of uprisings,
which were kept in check only by the Marines. In contrast, Presi-

---

[20] Dana G. Munro, *Intervention and Dollar Diplomacy in the Caribbean, 1900–1921* (Princeton, N.J., 1964), p. 215, notes that this was the
first time United States troops had actually gone into battle in the Caribbean to stop a revolution. American Marines first appeared in Nicaragua
in 1853.

dent Chamorro was popular and felt at home in the political game. He liked politics; he liked being president. When his term was ending in 1920, he considered succeeding himself. The United States government disliked this proposed violation of the Nicaraguan constitution, so the President stepped aside in favor of his old and feeble uncle, Diego Manuel Chamorro, who received the presidency in a fraudulent election.

Under Diego Chamorro and with help from the Marines, Nicaragua gradually became orderly. The United States encouraged such peace everywhere in Central America. After the collapse of the 1907 Central American Court of Justice over canal rights through Nicaragua, the United States in 1923 supported a new conference in Washington which promised not to recognize governments brought to power by coup d'état or revolution, or a president not qualified by law. This emphasis on constitutionality and stability dominated American policy in Central America for the next several years. United States efforts for peace in Nicaragua were only beginning, for Nicaraguan politics became more and more complicated.

President Chamorro died in October, 1923, and was succeeded by Vice-president Bartolomé Martínez, who belonged to the Conservative party but not to the Chamorro faction. While Martínez showed interest in being reelected in 1924, Emiliano Chamorro also hoped for the presidency. A Conservative split followed, and the American desire, publicly expressed, to remove its "legation guard" gave the Liberals hope of coming in again.

Thus after twelve years of American intervention, 1912 to 1924, there had been little change in Nicaragua. It was still a country unprepared for democracy, with a penchant for revolution. The election of 1924 would point up the difficulties.

2: THE ELECTION OF 1924

By the year 1924 the attitude of Washington toward all Latin
America was changing. Although far from the good neighbor
policy of the future, neither was it the bombast of Theodore
Roosevelt. The State Department had not given up intervention;
Secretary of State Charles Evans Hughes was willing to employ
what he described as "temporary interposition" when the interests of the United States called for it. Yet intervention was undesirable. Forces could stay no longer than necessary and would
withdraw when political stability prevailed. The State Department hoped that the 1924 Nicaraguan election would bring conditions which would allow withdrawal of the legation guard
from Managua. The United States hoped that by orderly, fair,
and democratic methods the Nicaraguan people could elect a
true-representative for president. The North American nation
believed an honest election and hope of others in the future
would cancel the attraction of revolutions. Up to this time rebellion had been the only way to throw a Nicaraguan party out of
power. However, if a man could become president without trickery and with popular support, the department believed he would
stay in office a full term without danger of revolt.

But the Nicaraguan election of 1924, conducted little better
than preceding elections, was a saddening affair—no exception
to the country's political axiom that the candidate of the party in
power always won. Nicaragua was not ready for free elections,
and the plan of the United States failed. The interests of the two

governments, American and Nicaraguan, thwarted one another
and produced a sort of mutual defeat.

The first step had been to draft an election law that would
insure free elections, and so in December, 1921, the Nicaraguan
government had engaged a young college professor of political
science and secretary of the National Municipal League, Harold
W. Dodds, to come to Nicaragua to help write a new law. Early
the next year Dodds arrived. As might be expected, Conservatives were not enthusiastic over this project, while Liberals,
aspiring for power, welcomed the American's proposed reforms.[1]
Dodds found several things wrong with the law then in effect.
It was poorly drafted; it was ambiguous; precincts were too large;
there were possibilities for repetitive voting; officials of the majority party controlled ballot boxes; many persons on the voting lists
were dead or disqualified.[2] Dodds would have to make changes.

The resultant "Dodds law" gave suffrage to males over twenty-
one; those able to read or write or who were married could vote
at eighteen. Both parties were to have representatives on election
boards, central and local. The law set up small election cantons.
It provided prior registration of voters, posting of registration
lists, government-printed ballots, dual party supervision of voting,
prompt reporting of returns.[3] Since the Conservative-controlled
congress understandably hesitated to embrace the proposal, the
State Department instructed the American minister, John E.
Ramer, to remind President Diego Manuel Chamorro of the
Nicaraguan government's promise to employ an American expert
for revision of the electoral law and to inform Chamorro that the
State Department believed this implied acceptance of the expert's recommendations.[4] After two months and several attempts

[1] Virginia L. Greer, "State Department Policy in Regard to the Nicaraguan Election of 1924," *Hispanic American Historical Review*, XXXIV
(Nov., 1954), 448. Hereafter cited as *HAHR*.
[2] *Ibid.*
[3] *Ibid.*
[4] *Foreign Relations: 1923*, II, 605.

at modification, Congress passed the law on March 16, 1923, with some changes Ramer considered of no importance.[5] The new legislation was assuredly an advance over the old. But since the government appointed chairmen of election boards, the party in power still had much control of the polls and everything would depend on who put the law into operation.[6]

Passage of the bill was the beginning of the State Department's plans for fair elections and removal of the Marines. Next came putting the law into effect and training a constabulary to keep peace after the Marine withdrawal. Washington was under no illusions about Central American elections. It was convinced that Americans should observe the Nicaraguan hustings and that Dodds or other electoral experts should help Nicaragua set up machinery and put it in motion. The department, of course, wanted a request from the Chamorro government for United States aid, since such an invitation would avoid charges of unsolicited interference in Nicaraguan domestic affairs. If Nicaragua failed to ask assistance, however, some individuals in the State Department felt that observers should go anyway.[7] Hopefully, our obvious determination to send observers would push Nicaragua into accepting our plan, or at least it would put the United States in a position to act intelligently after the election if one side should claim fraud. Either way the American purpose was retirement of the Marines when the new government came into office in January, 1925.

Secretary Hughes revealed his proposals to the homebound Emiliano Chamorro, then Nicaraguan minister to Washington. Chamorro had doubts about American commissioners putting the law into effect. He felt a supervised election would injure the prestige of the Conservative party and cost it thousands of votes.[8]

[5] Ibid.

[6] H. N. Denny, Dollars for Bullets (New York, 1929), p. 191.

[7] Francis White to J. Butler Wright, third assistant secretary, Sept. 26, 1923, 124.1718/77. Citations followed by file numbers refer to State Department records in the National Archives.

[8] Foreign Relations: 1923, II, 606–607.

After hesitation, the minister did agree that commissioners might serve some purpose if they withdrew before the election. Hughes, however, felt State Department ideas were sound. He sent the Nicaraguan government a note embodying the same suggestions he had made to Chamorro: Marines would stay in Managua during the preelection period if the Nicaraguans felt their presence would secure a free election and would leave after inauguration of the new government. The note suggested that the United States help to implement the electoral law. Dodds and some assistants, the department stated, could do the job. Before the Marines left, the United States would, if Nicaragua desired, train a constabulary. The State Department would be glad to ask the American Congress for members of the Marine Corps to serve the Nicaraguan government as advisers.[9]

Bartolomé Martínez (who became president on October 12, 1923, after Diego Chamorro's death) made a counterproposal. He agreed that Dodds and two or three assistants should come to Nicaragua some months before the election, perhaps February to April, 1924, to help install the new electoral system; the poor Nicaraguan economic situation did not permit a longer stay, that is, through the October election. The President also agreed to a national guard but said his budget prevented it at that time. He suggested an intermediate measure—that some Nicaraguans receive instruction from officers of the legation guard.[10] The two governments seemed in accord. Perhaps the constabulary would not come along as fast as the United States wished, perhaps there would not be as complete a supervision of the election as was desirable, but at the beginning of the year 1924 events were going fairly well.

Outside the Department of State some individuals were not entirely happy. Among them were New York bankers, concerned about the proposed withdrawal of American Marines. J. & W. Seligman and Company intimated that Washington was paying

[9] *Ibid.*, pp. 607–612.
[10] Ramer to Department of State, Dec. 14, 1923, 124.1718/84.

no attention to banker interests. Acknowledging State Department responsibility in inducing bankers to invest in Nicaragua,
the department took pains to explain its policies to the bankers
and to assure them that their interests were considered—pointing
out, for example, that Nicaraguan debts to them would be small
by withdrawal time.[11]

Harold W. Dodds, too, was unhappy. Conservatives were
reluctant to allow Liberals to register; communication with the
east coast was bad; election materials were not ready. Dodds
became convinced that supervisors needed to watch the polls.
Registration had given neither major party a majority and a few
votes either way would make the difference. Extreme party loyalty combined with inefficiency, bad communication, and illiteracy, made fraud likely unless Dodds had seventy-five to a hundred poll supervisors.[12]

Washington, desiring a free election yet reluctant to force
supervision on Martínez, held back. Knowing Dodds's difficulties the department was anxious and suggested that Martínez
retain one of Dodd's assistants until after the election. Martínez
agreed. Later in the summer the United States urged that Dodds
be asked to return and have at least one assistant in each of the
thirteen electoral districts, but Martínez declined to accept this,
stressing the futility of supervision with so few people. The
American chargé, Walter C. Thurston, asked if more complete
supervision at United States expense was desirable. Nicaragua
absolutely refused the offer. It was obvious the government could
control the election.[13] Those political groups, then, that expected
the government's benevolence applauded Martínez's stand, while
the opposition correctly anticipated many difficulties. One León

[11] Dana G. Munro to White, Nov. 23, 1923, 124.1718/79; Dec. 3,
1923, 124.1718/81; see also 124.1718/95 in which a United States businessman with interests in Nicaragua expressed fear of Marine withdrawal
and suggested that this country should control Nicaragua for ten or fifteen years.
[12] Dodds to Munro, May 21, 1924, 817.00/3075.
[13] Foreign Relations: 1924, II, 496.

newspaper did not see in the refusal an evil attempt to control
the election, for the Nicaraguan government was capable of
guaranteeing the voting; acceptance of the offer would have been
humiliating while rejection was a dignified attitude worthy of
the country's support. Those—the Chamorristas—who called for
electoral intervention, so the charge went, simply wanted to perpetuate themselves in power by means of American troops, such
as in 1916 and 1920.[14]

Nicaraguan politics meanwhile had become more muddled
than usual. A split in the Conservative party had appeared as
early as 1922, when a faction seized La Loma fortress, overlook-
ing Managua, as a move against their fellow Conservative, Diego
Chamorro (uncle of Emiliano). Dissension had arisen over who
would control the party—Chamorro of Granada or the anti-
Chamorristas of Managua.[15] The attempted coup d'état did not
succeed, because of quick and decisive action by the American
legation. Then, shortly after this political disorder, the aged Diego
Chamorro died in office, bringing Martínez to the presidency.

The approaching election produced new confusions. Emiliano
Chamorro returned from Washington to look after his family
interests. He had plans for becoming president as head of the
Conservative party, and in March, 1924, he announced his candidacy. Martínez, of course, wished to continue in office, and
shortly after Chamorro's return (but before his announced candidacy) the President had a conversation with Chamorro in

---

[14] El Centroamericano (León), Aug. 13, 1924, p. 2; Aug. 19, 1924,
p. 3. El Centroamericano, Sept. 21, 1924, p. 2, condemned the Chamorro
Conservatives for their flirtations with intervention; the paper asserted
that even though the Chamorristas had influence in the electoral machinery and had money for corrupt purposes they were still weak; they had
everything but popular support. Thus in the anguish of imminent defeat
they were counting on the bayonets of the Americans to tie the hands
and feet of popular will.

[15] V. L. Greer, "State Department Policy in Regard to the Nicaraguan
Election of 1924," HAHR, XXXIV (Nov., 1954), 460.

which the chief executive suggested that the Nicaraguan Supreme Court be called to render a declaration that the constitution did not prohibit his reelection. This announcement would then be communicated to Washington. Chamorro, expressing fear that the State Department and Supreme Court might not agree on the constitutional interpretation, foresaw an extremely awkward situation and disapproved the idea.[16]

The President's desire to be a candidate in 1924 was not unusual, but the Nicaraguan constitution forbade a president to succeed himself. The constitution, Martínez found, was not difficult to circumvent. One plan called for his being elected to the presidency, admitting disqualification, and handing the office over to the vice-president, who would call a special election at which Martínez would be a candidate to succeed not himself but the newly elevated vice-president.[17] Another scheme was to retire from office six months before the election and then run as a candidate for the next term.

It was difficult to dissuade Martínez. As early as January, 1924, the American minister told him the department understood that Article 104 of the Nicaraguan constitution prevented any president, however he obtained office, from running for that position during the next term. In the next few weeks Dr. Salvador Castrillo, the new Nicaraguan minister to Washington, tried to convince the department to change its interpretation of Article 104. In addition, the minister's cables to Managua gave erroneous impressions of Washington's views and rumors of Mar-

---

[16] Emiliano Chamorro, "Autobiografía," *Revista Conservadora*, II (Aug., 1961), 142. Article 104 of the Nicaraguan constitution stated: "The term of the office of the President and Vice President of the Republic shall be four years, and shall begin on the first of January. No citizen who holds the office of President either as the duly elected incumbent, or accidentally, shall be eligible to the office of President or Vice President for the next term."

[17] Walter Thurston, chargé in Managua, to Department of State, June 1, 1924, 817.00/3079.

tínez's candidacy continued to plague the State Department.[18] Finally, at the end of May, 1924, it told the President privately that on January 1, 1925, the United States would decide whether to recognize the new government and hoped there would be no question about eligibility of whoever was elected president.[19] Still, Martínez continued his candidacy.

A week later the department spoke with plainness: "It would regard his election as unconstitutional, and upon the expiration of his present term would be highly indisposed to extend recognition to him as Constitutional President." To assure that Martínez had no illusions, the Secretary of State threatened to make the department's views public.[20] Martínez withdrew.

He did not withdraw interest in the election, for he turned to defeat his arch rival Chamorro, the Conservative choice for president. Thus he broke with the Chamorro Conservatives. Looking toward a fusion ticket, the Martínez group, calling themselves Republican Conservatives, got together with a Liberal faction known as the Liberal Nationalists. In the summer of 1924 these groups arranged a pact in which they nominated a Conservative, Carlos Solórzano, as president and a Liberal, Juan Bautista Sacasa, as vice-president; they divided the nominations for congressional seats and made arrangements for judicial and cabinet positions as well as *jefes politicos* (governors of departments).[21] Before the fusion was concluded the Nicaraguan minister of foreign affairs, acting under Martínez's instructions, quizzed Washington about its attitude toward such an alliance. After Washington disclaimed any preference, the political pact was announced in Managua amid much celebrating and with care-

[18] Memorandum from Department of State to Ramer, Jan. 28, 1924, 817.00/3029; memorandum from Munro to White, Mar. 3, 1924, 817.00/3032; Ramer to Department of State, Mar. 25, 1924, 817.00/3045.

[19] Department of State to Thurston, May 29, 1924, 817.00/3078a.

[20] Department of State to Thurston, June 5, 1924, 817.00/3079.

[21] For this pact signed in Managua on July 17, 1924, see *El Diario Nicaragüense* (Granada), Feb. 18, 1926, p. 1.

fully worded statements conveying the impression that the
United States approved the ticket.

The major segment of the Conservative party remained loyal
to Chamorro. He, too, tried to gain United States backing. The
chief Chamorrista spokesman in Washington was Chandler P.
Anderson, who had been a special counsel for the State Department under Root and Knox and had served as counselor from
1910 to 1913. As early as April, 1924, Chamorro had told his
friend Anderson about the dangers of Nicaraguan politics and
had sought his "most valuable assistance which may prove practically decisive in enabling us once more, with the friendly
action of the United States of America, to clear the breakers. . . ."
Chamorro's letter (sent before Martínez had given up his own
candidacy) warned that Martínez was courting Zelaya elements
which might be harmful to American interests and that Martínez
himself, regardless of appearances, was strongly anti-American.
What did Chamorro want done? "The only way to check further
aggravation of the situation is for the Department of State to take
positive and effective action toward maintaining constitutional
order and guaranteeing liberty, and it is in that sense that I seek
its intervention."[22] Writing to Charles Evans Hughes in August,
1924, Anderson told the Secretary that Chamorro's party was
pro-American while the opposition groups were strongly anti-
American. He further warned that if the anti-Americans gained
control of the government they would favor Great Britain in
financial and commercial arrangements and would probably grant
some concessions to British interests in order to place them in a
preferential position relative to the Nicaraguan canal route.[23]
Regardless of Anderson's pleadings, Hughes did not move to
favor Chamorro.

Meanwhile the rump Liberal group, having refused to join

[22] Copy of letter from Chamorro to Anderson, Apr. 28, 1924, Library
of Congress, Charles Evans Hughes papers, box 51, Anderson folder.
Hereafter cited as Hughes papers.

[23] Letter from Anderson to Hughes, Aug. 20, 1924, Library of Congress, Chandler P. Anderson papers, box 42. Hereafter cited as Anderson
papers.

the new coalition (known as the National party), selected Luis
Corea as their candidate.

Such was the state of affairs. And President Martínez did
not intend a free and honest election. In preelection months the
candidates outside the coalition were fighting uphill against
Martínez's choice, Solórzano. There were the usual arrests and
annoyances. Chamorro recalls a fracas involving throwing of
rocks at his supporters on the day he proclaimed his candidacy.
The Conservative leader then concluded that Martínez was not
going to allow free elections and that it was necessary to seek
aid from the Department of State.[24] Martínez used executive
decrees to nullify guarantees of the Dodds law. He created a
large armed security force to watch the polls; he allowed impro-
vised ballots and voting urns; if registration books were lacking,
recognition of a voter by an election official would be enough;
challenged voters could deposit their ballots anyway; as a last
measure, opposition candidates were deprived of quick communication between parts of the country.[25]

What would the State Department do? Recognizing the need
for American approval of any candidate, or at least not dis-
approval, the Nicaraguan minister for foreign affairs, José Andrés
Urtecho, inquired. The State Department again disclaimed
preference for any candidate: the United States "supports no
candidate and is hostile to no candidate; it desires only that free
and fair elections may be held in order that the will of the people
may be expressed without hindrance at the polls."[26] Hence the
United States would recognize anyone not prohibited by the
Washington treaty of 1923 who became president by fair election
in accord with the laws and constitution. The department was
aware that the government party would control the election, but
it did not feel justified in helping with the vote unless Nica-

[24] Chamorro, "Autobiografía," loc. cit., p. 144.
[25] Thurston to Department of State, Sept. 20, 1924, 817.00/3154; Sept.
27, 1924, 817.00/3156; Sept. 30, 1924, 817.00/3162.
[26] Department of State to Thurston, July 16, 1924, 817.00/3101.

ragua desired aid. Washington did send a warning to Martínez in case the President contemplated coercing the electoral boards: If the boards failed to perform according to law, the United States would have difficulty considering the election expressive of wishes of the Nicaraguan people.[27]

Martínez now took a new course. After refusing help of American experts, he approached Chargé Thurston to ask if Marines from the legation guard might "observe the elections and examine the election returns submitted to the departmental boards of election before these boards make the count of the votes." But when the legation received written confirmation of the request, Martínez had distorted his original presentation. He now suggested that the chargé meet representatives of all political parties and ask unanimous consent for a few Marines to observe the election unofficially. This would make it appear that Americans had taken the initiative on the supervision question. Thurston advised the department against this course.[28]

And so election day came. The government party took full advantage of its privileges. The Solórzano home was the scene of much celebration as favorable election returns steadily arrived by telegrams all bearing the frank sign. At the same time the office of the national board of elections and the other party headquarters were ignorant of electoral trends. Solórzano won easily.

The Nicaraguan government claimed that the election of October 5, 1924, took place with admirable liberty and impartiality. A pro-administration newspaper proclaimed that for the first time from independence to the present the people of Nicaragua had made use of the right freely to elect their supreme authorities.[29] Admittedly there was a disturbance in Chontales, which the authorities had put down immediately. Chargé Thurston thought this latter remark interesting, for the government

[27] Department of State to Thurston, Sept. 2, 1924, 817.00/3145.
[28] Thurston to Department of State, Sept. 27, 1924, 817.00/3158.
[29] El Centroamericano, Oct. 7, 1924, p. 2.

had declared a state of siege in some departments, which remained for two weeks after the election.

The Conservatives were unhappy with the outcome and protested voting in several cantons. The defeated Chamorro later recorded that in spite of all impediments the election was favorable to him and he lost only because the election figures were changed.[30] Still, Conservatives did not want new elections for fear the government would control them even more drastically. Thurston cited, for example, San Juan del Sur and San José de los Remates, where the government candidates had lost initially but after new elections won substantial victories.[31]

Strangely, even the victors of 1924 were far from jubilant. They feared extralegal action from the Conservatives, especially Chamorro. Even before the election this crafty Conservative was intimating he might lead a revolt. After returns were in, such a course seemed more likely. Solórzano was plainly worried, and while making a courtesy call at the United States legation he tried to enlist United States aid. He promised a conservative and pro-American administration. While urging Thurston to warn the Conservatives about disturbances, he requested help in reconciling Chamorro. The President-elect also secretly offered high cabinet posts to the Conservatives.[32] Chamorro disclaimed revolutionary intent, but the declarations always seemed to leave the door ajar enough to keep nearly everyone, including the Department of State, uneasy.

Under the circumstances, the United States feared revolutions more than questionable elections.[33] The 1924 election was disappointing. Foreign policy toward Nicaragua was predicated on fair elections, the will of the people. With popular government in control in Nicaragua the Marines could withdraw with some assurance of political stability. Such government could meet

---

[30] Chamorro, "Autobiografía," loc. cit., p. 144.
[31] Thurston to Department of State, Nov. 7, 1924, 817.00/3201.
[32] Thurston to Department of State, Nov. 20, 1924, 817.00/3216.
[33] Department of State to Thurston, Dec. 16, 1924, 817.00/3242.

its economic and political obligations; a fairly elected government, free from revolt, could save money and make internal improvements. Nicaragua could become a Mahomet's Paradise. But, in spite of the fondest hopes of the State Department, the elections had not been free; still, peace was better than disturbance and nonrecognition would surely encourage disturbance.

After much consideration the United States decided to recognize the Solórzano government upon its inauguration in January, 1925. Yet recognition was awkward for several reasons. For one, the department had to delay it until almost the last moment, for fear it might affect the touchy electoral situation in Honduras (where another unfair election threatened). Political leaders there might feel that the department would accept two accomplished facts. Moreover, in the Nicaraguan case the department felt it might get a quid pro quo if it kept its decision secret. Plans for 1924 had been thwarted, but perhaps it could salvage something by 1928; the department wanted assurance that the next presidential election would be honest, in accord with the Dodds law. It wanted formation of a constabulary and solution of Nicaragua's economic problems. The United States desired that Solórzano obtain cooperation of as many political elements as possible but believed it impractical to impose a coalition.

Eager for United States approval, Solórzano agreed to all suggestions and signed a document giving assurance on each point —1928 elections in full freedom and fairness, a constabulary upon taking office, solution of Nicaragua's economic problems, cooperation of as many political elements in Nicaragua as possible.[34] Four days after the State Department received these promises, it instructed the Managua legation to explain to Chamorro that Washington disapproved of revolution and that its moral support would be on the side of the constituted government in any effort to keep order.

Then followed the next step in department plans—withdrawal of the Marines. This was to come after the election and forma-

[34] Thurston to Department of State, Dec. 13, 1924, 817.00/3242.

tion of a constabulary. The latter had not yet begun, despite American efforts. But shortly after passage of the Dodds law, in 1923, the United States had informed the Nicaraguan government that it planned to withdraw the Marines, and it intended to go ahead.

Soon after taking office Solórzano begged that the Marines remain.[35] The State Department was piqued at this sudden panic of the Nicaraguan government. The department felt justified in removing the Marines at once and that responsibility for any unfortunate results would belong to Nicaragua, but the fact remained that Uncle Sam was over a diplomatic barrel.[36] The Marines had come to bring peace and order; yet, after thirteen years of intervention, things might revert to the chaos of 1912. United States citizens in Nicaragua (including the commander of the legation guard, national bank officials, the Nicaraguan director of the Rockefeller Institute, the high commissioner, and the collector of customs) urged retention of the Marines. The American government acceded to Solórzano's request but for only three to six months. The United States expected Nicaragua to hasten constabulary development and to obtain constabulary instructors in time to get training under way before the Marines withdrew. Before withdrawal the Marine unit would aid in the training.

However, Nicaragua continued to move haltingly in regard to the Guardia Nacional, and the United States had to prod it along with threats of immediate evacuation. In early January, 1925, Solórzano had asked the legation for a constabulary plan, which was then prepared. The United States proposal included specific requests for Marines' services in the formation and training of the four hundred-man force until permanent instructors, suggested by the United States, could be obtained by Nicaragua. Other provisions lessened political influence in the guard by making the commander answerable directly to the Nicaraguan

[35] Thurston to Department of State, Jan. 3, 1925, 124.1718/104.
[36] Memorandum from White to Hughes, Dec. 15, 1924, 817.00/3247.

president, rather than to a cabinet official.[37] After weeks of delay and irritation, Nicaragua finally unveiled, by mid-May, its own version of the constabulary plan. The act as passed was not pleasing to the United States, for it omitted reference to the temporary services of the legation guard and allowed too much political control of the Guardia at the hands of the minister of *gobernación*.[38] Chargé Thurston felt there had been too much equivocation in the negotiations and that Nicaragua was not serious in establishing a national guard. That government, he asserted, wanted only to find means to retain United States forces. He advised immediate American withdrawal.

Besides the dilatoriness of the government, press attacks also peeved Thurston. There were charges that the constabulary was another step in the scheme of American imperialism, and one paper even suggested that the United States desired to build up armies in Central America for the defense of North America in event of war with some great power, such as Japan.[39]

Nonetheless, Washington decided to cooperate until instructors employed directly by Nicaragua arrived. By the end of June, Major Calvin B. Carter of Elgin, Texas, had agreed to head the constabulary and was in Nicaragua. The United States Marines now prepared to leave. The Solórzano government made last-minute requests for help in training, but the department turned down the requests. Although Marines had been in Nicaragua for thirteen years, the United States had never considered their stay anything but temporary. It had never liked military intervention but felt it could not tolerate political and economic chaos in a country geographically so important to the United States. The intervention had been light. For the most part, relations between

[37] *Foreign Relations: 1925*, II, 618, 624–627.

[38] Thurston to Department of State, Apr. 7, 1925, 124.1718/131; Thurston to Department of State, June 20, 1925, 124.1718/137; *Foreign Relations: 1925*, II, 630–632.

[39] *La Tribuna* (Managua), Feb. 15, 1925, p. 2; Mar. 6, 1925, p. 1; Mar. 17, 1925, p. 3; May 5, 1925, p. 2; Thurston to Department of State, June 20, 1925, 124.1718/137.

American forces and the population had been good.[40] Marines who got into trouble were punished. The Marines and the Nicaraguans had mixed feelings about each other and about withdrawal, but policy called for removal of troops and the time was at hand. Some Nicaraguans seemed to find it difficult to believe the Marines were actually going. In late July one reporter asked a Marine officer if it were a fact that the detachment was leaving, and a few days later a news story carried the declaration: "definitely, the Marines will be going on Monday."[41]

What the average Nicaraguan felt about the intervention and withdrawal is difficult to assess. Perhaps those outside of Managua gave it little thought; probably the few times they did consider it their national pride was wounded. One Managua newspaper interviewed a number of prominent Nicaraguans about the evacuation. Most expressed pleasure with the departure, and some evidenced bitterness toward the North Americans. One interviewee considered the withdrawal a third independence, the first being independence from Spain, the second from William Walker; another asserted that the great majority of the Nicaraguan people were not, nor would they be, friends with the United States or any other nation which intervened in the internal affairs of Nicaragua. His people, he declared, rejected intervention in 1912 and it was only gradually tolerated because the political leaders destroyed or benumbed Nicaragua's virility. A third person regarded the Marines' presence as a major factor in keeping peace and regretted their departure; another felt it was peace paid for at the high price of great depression of Nicaraguan patriotic sentiment.[42]

---

[40] During the last few months of intervention, however, there were a number of incidents—knifings, beatings, and a stoning. Thurston to Department of State, July 8, 1925, 711.17/42.

[41] La Noticia (Managua), July 30, 1925, p. 1; Aug. 1, 1925, p. 1.

[42] Ibid., July 31, 1925, p. 1; Aug. 1, 1925, p. 3; Aug. 2, 1925, p. 3; Aug. 6, 1925, p. 3; Aug. 7, 1925, p. 3; Aug. 8, 1925, p. 3; Aug. 14, 1925, p. 3. See also El Comercio (Managua), Aug. 5, 1925, p. 2, which editorialized: "It is said with certainty that the great people of the United

Generally, in 1925, the Conservatives—particularly the Chamorristas—spoke favorably of intervention, while the Liberals expressed more nationalistic sentiments. One cannot infer, however, that this division of opinion remained constant. Much depended on who would benefit from the presence of American troops, and in the period 1925 to 1933 neither Conservatives nor Liberals offered much criticism of intervention. The greatest opposition, as will be seen, came from outside the regular parties.

Withdrawal came on August 3, 1925. With flags and music the Marines left the Campo de Marte and entrained for Corinto, where they boarded the U.S.S. *Henderson*. The occupation was at an end. The Nicaraguan government expressed patriotic satisfaction with its new status. President Solórzano, his predecessor Martínez, and a large group of citizens went to the Campo de Marte, where the blue and white flag was raised to the tune of the national hymn. An official government publication headlined proudly that the national colors fluttered supreme in Nicaragua; the republic had returned to full enjoyment of its sovereignty; it was Nicaragua's day.[43]

Despite understandable national pride, the Nicaraguan administration was fearful. Solórzano begged all Nicaraguans to preserve peace and make the nation worthy of independence and civilization. Upon the Nicaraguans themselves, said the President, depends the future of the nation. "The lessons of yesterday are sad and ought to be long lasting. To return to the old errors

States, being occupied in their productive labor and in the accumulation of millions of dollars, do not know the use being made of their force in the neighboring lands, do not know of the injustice which is committed in their name and do not suspect that there has opened in Latin America an era of hostility, an inextinguishable antagonism produced by their politicians. The government of the United States cannot contain the avalanche of hate caused by the occupation of Nicaragua which reaches as a mountain from the pampas of Argentina up to their own borders, and in order to calm this raging sea they have ordered the evacuation."

[43] *La Gaceta* (Managua), Aug. 5, 1925. See also *La Tribuna*, Aug. 7, 1925, p. 2.

. . . would not only provoke old situations, but perhaps others more grave. . . ."[44]

Observers did not believe the plea would have much effect. Solórzano himself considered moving to the Campo de Marte with the constabulary close by, thus hoping to assure his security.[45] Although the United States was hopeful, there was nothing on which to base optimism. Nicaragua was, indeed, spoiling for a revolution.

[44] *La Prensa* is quoted in *La Noticia*, Aug. 8, 1925, p. 1; *La Tribuna*, Aug. 8, 1925, p. 2.

[45] *New York Times*, Aug. 3, 1925, p. 1; *La Noticia*, July 30, 1925, p. 1.

3: CHAMORRO'S COUP D'ETAT

Solórzano's first eight months in office were not easy. The president, who was vacillating by nature, fell under control of the stronger personalities around him. Desiring physical as well as political survival, he wanted Marines to remain, yet he hoped to avoid antagonizing the more nationalistic groups. There was pressure from the American minister concerning the constabulary and complaints about anti-American associates of the President.[1] Offsetting United States advice was that of some members of the cabinet, including former president Martínez, who desired to reduce American influence. Many problems arose from the coalition nature of the new administration, with Liberals and Conservatives eyeing each other jealously to insure equal distribution of spoils. Early in the year one Liberal editor complained that there was a president but no government—that that which had been done in thirty days of national administration was no more than a shameful partition of power in which those who were most clever had grasped consulates and legations; moreover the Chamorristas were exercising too much power.[2] Always in the background was Emiliano Chamorro. After the inauguration he retired to his hacienda, "Río Grande," but whether the President slept more comfortably after reading reports that the general was now solely interested in agricultural chores—making new pastures and sowing corn—is doubtful.[3]

[1] Thurston to Department of State, Jan. 1, 1925, 817.00/3266.
[2] La Noticia (Managua), Jan. 30, 1925, p. 1.
[3] Emiliano Chamorro, "Autobiografía," Revista Conservadora, II (Aug., 1961), 145; La Noticia, June 17, 1925, p. 1; July 19, 1925, p. 1.

On August 28, 1925—little more than three weeks after Marine withdrawal—a Managua newspaper carried a front-page story with picture about a reception and ball to be held that evening honoring Dr. Leonardo Argüello, minister of public instruction.[4] Perhaps the story caused more than usual interest among a certain group of men, for about eleven o'clock that evening a comic-opera coup d'état interrupted the gala reception at the International Club. A motley band of insurgents, armed and slightly drunk, were led by a Conservative political leader, Gabry Rivas. Coatless, booted and spurred, a large hat with turned-down brim drawn well over his head, he had come to arrest some political enemies. Striding through the party of formally dressed ladies and gentlemen, which included the American minister, Charles Eberhardt (President Carlos Solórzano had already left), Gabry Rivas hazardously fired into the air and roared that he had come to liberate Solórzano from domination of the Liberals. General Alfredo Rivas, brother-in-law of the President and commander of La Loma, had sent him to carry off the offenders, he said. After several minutes of shouting and frenzied importunities directed at the American minister, the intruders chose several individuals, among them Dr. Roman y Reyes, minister of finance, and General José María Moncada. They then departed.

Behind this incident were the recent convolutions of Nicaraguan politics. The Conservative party had believed itself cheated by the election of 1924. The head of the aggrieved party, Emiliano Chamorro, was not of the temperament to allow an electoral defeat to pass quietly. Solórzano, who was new at politics, had formed a cabinet of both parties in an attempt to bring order. But this move satisfied no one, least of all the Conservatives. After the Marines had gone, they felt able to do something, and the affair of August 28 was the result.

Many observers saw Chamorro behind this breach of the political peace. Extremely partisan and ambitious, he enjoyed

[4] *La Noticia*, Aug. 28, 1925, p. 1.

politics and wished to be at the center of authority. If denied power he plotted to recover it, and he was no tyro in revolutionary pursuits, for he reportedly had participated in all the uprisings against the old dictator, José Santos Zelaya. While Chamorro was friendly toward the United States, where he had supporters, he often ran afoul of America's peace-keeping policies in Central America. Outwardly, however, he was not involved in the International Club incident; General Rivas appeared as the mastermind.[5] Rivas explained that there was too much Liberal influence around Solórzano. The Liberals, he said, were planning a revolt the following week and he was acting to prevent bloodshed, to aid rather than embarrass the President.[6] The day after the incident, Rivas made his demands. He desired some Liberals dismissed from the cabinet and Conservatives appointed in their places.

Solórzano hesitated while politicians and friends gave advice. Finally the President conferred with the commander of the national guard, Major Calvin B. Carter, who gave Solórzano an extra guard and advised him to have a showdown. He offered to accompany the President and shoot the President's brother-in-law if the latter misbehaved, but Solórzano declined.[7] Afraid of Rivas, the President gave in—to avoid, he said, further disorder. The United States minister, Eberhardt, took Solórzano's acceptance to the commander of La Loma, and on the evening of August 29 the hostages were free.

In spite of promises to resign after the cabinet changes, the insurgent general kept control of the fortress garrison. Solórzano continued to vacillate. The fortress commander agreed to come to the President's house; but, not trusting his sister's hus-

[5] Chamorro records in his "Autobiografía," loc. cit., p. 145, that he was at his hacienda during the affair and learned of it one morning (he gives no date) at breakfast when some of his friends came from Managua to tell him.

[6] Eberhardt to Department of State, Aug. 29, 1925, 817.00/3303.

[7] C. B. Carter, "The Kentucky Feud in Nicaragua," The World's Work, vol. 54 (July, 1927), 318.

band nor apparently caring for her safety or that of her child, Rivas brought several carloads of troops with machine guns and gave them orders to fire on the house if he did not reappear within a half hour. He returned in time, after reaching an agreement. Rivas promised to give up La Loma within a week (by September 10), and this he did. Reportedly he received forty-five hundred dollars and a promise of the Nicaraguan consulate in Los Angeles. The other Rivas, Gabry, leader of the raid of August 28, received twenty-eight hundred dollars, and the International Club elected him to membership.[8]

September, 1925, was a troubled month, for Solórzano came under all sorts of pressure. A wealthy businessman in his early sixties, the President had no political or military experience, and his wife's family—mainly Alfredo and Luis Rivas, who held important commands in the army—dominated him. While the ambitious Chamorro and his Conservative followers threatened, the Liberals urged him to assert authority. Conservatives desired more positions in the national guard, but Major Carter was unmovable about keeping it free from politics.[9] Faced with such conflicts, Solórzano appealed to the American minister for a warship at Corinto and one at Bluefields, because he believed this sort of demonstration would stabilize the country and improve his position. Washington was hesitant unless American lives were in danger, but it sent the light cruiser *Denver* to Corinto and the *Tulsa* to Bluefields, under orders not to land troops unless in emergency.[10] At least temporarily these ships stayed the revolutionary hand. The President, revealing to friends that troops were at his disposal in an emergency, emphasized United States support for peace and order in Nicaragua.[11] Some Liberal writers, regardless of past sentiments on American intervention, urged

[8] Eberhardt to Department of State, Sept. 26, 1925, 817.00/3330.
[9] Carter, "The Kentucky Feud in Nicaragua," *loc. cit.*, p. 318.
[10] *New York Times*, Sept. 13, 1925, p. 14. The ships stayed until Sept. 20, 1925.
[11] *La Noticia*, Sept. 17, 1925, p. 1.

the President to make use of this power to strengthen the administration and lessen Conservative influence.[12]

Even if most United States citizens in Nicaragua, including Minister Eberhardt, felt that the vessels had helped the President out of a difficult situation and halted a trend toward revolution, the crisis was far from over. Eberhardt informed the State Department that much depended on a stand by Solórzano, and here the minister had doubts. He foresaw that pressure would increase and believed that the Chamorro elements might achieve control.[13]

Meanwhile Chamorro, originator of revolutions both real and imaginary, returned to Managua to see what use his party could make of the intranquillity.[14] The nervous President did not know what to do. He ordered Carter to expel the Conservative leader, then changed his mind and ordered a guard at Chamorro's residence. Rumor had it that Chamorro planned to attack La Loma. At two o'clock one morning the President sent Carter to Chamorro's house to break up a demonstration by Chamorro supporters. Carter delivered Solórzano's message and threatened to use the national guard if Chamorro would not send the crowd away. Liberals urged Solórzano to put the guard in charge of La Loma, and Eberhardt advised him to do so, but Conservative press opposition kept him from following that advice.[15] Chamorro and the President held conferences in which they sought to reconcile their differences. The general was interested in strengthening the Conservatives in the government and increasing his own influence. But the talks accomplished nothing, and Chamorro, believing that Solórzano had reestablished control of

[12] *Ibid.*, Sept. 17, 1925, p. 1; Sept. 18, 1925, p. 1; Sept. 22, 1925, p. 1.
[13] Eberhardt to Department of State, Sept. 21, 1925, 817.00/3317.
[14] Chamorro, "Autobiografía," *loc. cit.*, p. 145.
[15] There was a Nicaraguan belief that whoever controlled this fortress controlled Managua and thus the country. Carter felt, however, that properly equipped troops could easily take the fortress and that it need not have had such an effect on Nicaraguan politics if the government had availed itself of loyal, efficient, and well-equipped troops.

the armed forces, went home to wait. Soon realizing that affairs were far from settled, the general plotted a coup for September 25, which he cancelled at the last hour. When finally Chamorro abandoned hope of agreement with the President, he decided to strike and informed Adolfo Díaz, leading Conservative, who approved the plans.[16]

In the early morning of October 25 the general seized La Loma, where Colonel Padillo, a supporter who was an officer in the fortress, allowed the general to take control.[17] The garrison welcomed its new commander. Major Carter probably expressed common Nicaraguan opinion when he remarked that there was nothing unusual about this proceeding. "It simply was a matter of making a bargain with an opposing politician."[18]

Having gained the heights of Managua, Chamorro telephoned the President, warning him about military moves which would bring fire from La Loma and advising him to surrender peacefully the Campo de Marte, which eventually was done.[19] Chamorro also talked with Eberhardt by telephone and said his purpose was to drive all Liberals from the cabinet and restore Conservatives to the power they had enjoyed before the "fraudulent elections" of 1924. Solórzano could remain as president but must appoint Chamorro minister of war or at least give him control of the army.[20]

Now that he was in control of La Loma and its troops, Chamorro naturally was interested in the attitude of the national guard and its commandant, Major Carter. When approached by phone, Carter said he would take orders from the President. Chamorro jokingly inquired whether the major would call him if he were ordered to attack the fortress but with a laugh hung up before receiving an answer.[21] He knew that members of the

[16] Chamorro, "Autobiografía," loc. cit., pp. 145–146.
[17] Carter, "The Kentucky Feud in Nicaragua," loc. cit., pp. 318–319.
[18] Ibid., p. 319.
[19] Chamorro, "Autobiografía," loc. cit., p. 146.
[20] Eberhardt to Department of State, Oct. 25, 1925, 817.00/3333.
[21] Carter, "The Kentucky Feud in Nicaragua," loc. cit., p. 319.

guard had no machine guns and only thirty rounds of ammunition per man. Carter had asked for more, but Solórzano, fearing a full-scale fight, had put him off. Already there had been sporadic firing in the city and some skirmishes in which a few members of the constabulary were killed. Chamorro probably knew that most of the Conservative party leaders supported him and that Solórzano could not move without their backing.

During the hot autumn day the parleys went on and on. Crickets chirped in the dusty houses; the sun boiled down on the roofs and unpaved streets. That night there was firing and then quiet until another slow day began with more political talk. Eberhardt conferred with Liberal leaders, Solórzano, and Chamorro's spokesman, Adolfo Díaz. The Liberals were reluctant to give up posts in the government and urged the President to resist. While Solórzano dawdled, Chamorro's partisans reportedly killed two men in front of the presidential palace.[22] Then, about noon on October 26, the President signed a document which acceded to the general's wishes. Solórzano was to break the coalition pacts and the government was to be Conservative. The President would grant amnesty to all participants in the coup d'état; the government was to pay troops involved in the rebellion, as well as 10,000 cordobas for General Chamorro, and Chamorro was to become general-in-chief of the army.[23] Under this agreement Solórzano remained titular head of the government, but the real power lay with the general. Thus Chamorro maintained a semblance of constitutionality without limiting his control.

The successful *golpe de cuartel* was not difficult to understand. Both major parties had expressed dissatisfaction with the regime, and since the Conservatives felt greater grievances, they acted. One newspaper suggested that the decomposition of public power justified Chamorro's act; he did only what the Liberals would have done had they reckoned with the military contin-

[22] Eberhardt to Department of State, Oct. 25, 1925, 817.00/3333.
[23] Eberhardt to Department of State, Oct. 26, 1925, 817.00/3334. See also *El Diario Nicaragüense* (Granada), Feb. 18, 1926, p. 3.

gencies and the traditional ties of conservatism. The editor concluded it was necessary to accept accomplished facts.[24]

While events moved back and forth in Managua, all on this fairly small political stage, the scene shifted imperceptibly to Washington, where in these old days of American imperialism the decisions supposedly were made. The wily Chamorro kept one eye on Washington, for Eberhardt had told Chamorro that the United States would support constitutional government.[25] Knowing that an edict from the State Department and a few Marines could break his power, Chamorro wrote to explain his actions to his friend and supporter in the American capital, Chandler P. Anderson, a former counselor for the State Department and at the time a private Washington lawyer. Anderson was hopeful of inside influence with the Department. After receiving Chamorro's telegram he talked with Secretary Kellogg, sounding out the Secretary and presenting Chamorro's side. Anderson found that the bustling, seventy-year-old Secretary had

[24] El Diario Nicaragüense, Oct. 28, 1925, p. 3.
[25] Eberhardt to Department of State, Oct. 25, 1925, 817.00/3333; Department of State to Eberhardt, Oct. 26, 1925, 817.00/3333. Chamorro states in his "Autobiografia," loc. cit., pp. 146–147, that he went to see Eberhardt on Oct. 26; during the conversation the American minister allegedly asked what would be done with Carlos Solórzano. Chamorro answered that his plans were to remove from government only the Liberal element while allowing the President to finish his term. Eberhardt commented that the executive was difficult to understand and very changeable—in the morning he thought one thing, at midday another, and by night still another. Chamorro interpreted the minister's remarks as approval for Solórzano's removal, and when asked who might replace the President, Chamorro answered Adolfo Díaz. Before the general left, Eberhart asked him if he wanted the legation to consult the State Department about these matters; Chamorro was agreeable. Three days later the general returned to the legation where, according to his account, he learned Washington would accept Díaz. But in the following days Solórzano's removal was slowed because of the legation's growing coolness toward the plan. State Department records do not corroborate Chamorro's account.

On the afternoon of Oct. 25, Eberhardt sent the department a tele-

not yet given the problem much thought, although the Latin American division had, in Anderson's opinion, filled him with half-truths and prejudice. Before he left the interview Anderson expressed hope that Kellogg would not support the anti-American element in Nicaragua.[26] Anderson kept Chamorro informed.

As Chamorro spun his revolutionary web, the 1923 Central American treaty offered some embarrassing questions. That instrument had embodied the wish of the United States for political stability in Central America by requiring nonrecognition of any government coming to power by other than constitutional means. United States recognition or lack of it had meant success or failure for a government in that area. Were Chamorro's acts a violation of the 1923 treaty? The Liberals, removed from their government posts, resolved that the United States should act in their behalf. The party claimed Chamorro had violated the constitution, that Liberal Vice-president Juan B. Sacasa was in danger, and that the 1923 treaty obligated the United States to cooperate for constitutional order.[27] But the department felt it could do little except inform Chamorro to keep his hands

gram which, in part, reads: "I have been in communication with General Chamorro and have advised him this Legation had no other course to pursue than to support the Constitutional Government and that any government assuming power by force would not be recognized by the Government of the United States." *Foreign Relations: 1925*, II, 639. On Dec. 3, 1925 (817.00/3354) Eberhardt informed Washington that there was talk of Solórzano's resignation and possible replacement by Adolfo Díaz. "Most Nicaraguans, other than Liberals, and virtually all foreigners here, hope for election within the law of Díaz whose judgment is considered generally sound and his well known stability in economic matters is particularly desirable in present unsettled conditions." And on Dec. 9, 1925 (817.00/3354) the department replied that "should President Solórzano resign, the Government of the United States would accord recognition to any successor who had been elected or appointed by constitutional means."

[26] Entry of Oct. 31, 1925, diary of Chandler P. Anderson, MS. in the Anderson papers of the Library of Congress. Hereafter cited as Anderson diary.

[27] Eberhardt to Department of State, Nov. 5, 1925, 817.00/3340.

off the presidency. Thus, through the autumn of 1925 the United States concern in Nicaragua was to keep a semblance of constitutionality.

Meanwhile Chamorro strengthened his army and equipped the national guard. He needed both groups, for the Liberals were not accepting the coup d'état. In some towns, especially around León, feeling turned violent and (as the American minister reported) it seemed a question of only a few months before the Liberals would organize an army and begin a counterrevolution.[28] Chamorro sent troops to León, where he hoped to collect some money—the old Nicaraguan custom of forced loans—and capture Vice-president Sacasa, who had prudently left Managua before Chamorro finished the coup. Chamorro much desired Sacasa's resignation, but Sacasa escaped by horseback to the Gulf of Fonseca and crossed by launch into El Salvador, en route to Washington to plead his case. The Conservative leadership even offered the Vice-president a ministership to Washington or any other place he might desire in return for his resignation, but Sacasa's wife (in the absence of her husband) indignantly rejected the proffer, which "would cast on the immaculate name of Doctor Juan B. Sacasa the blackest stain."[29]

During November, December, and the early new year, Nicaraguan politics were in flux; few could doubt the final result, but the questions of how and when remained. One rumor forecast the resignations of both Sacasa and Solórzano, with Adolfo Díaz succeeding to the presidency. While this was an unusual political turn, even for Nicaragua (an editorialist wrote, "there is . . . in this plan something abnormal and illogical, but when a situation is presented with the complications of the present one, everything absurd is tolerable"), it was not far from the final solution.[30] As the rumors of Solórzano's pending resignation mounted, the National Liberal and the Republican Conservative parties—the

[28] Eberhardt to Department of State, Nov. 7, 1925, 817.00/3342.
[29] El Diario Nicaragüense, Nov. 5, 1925, p. 1; Chamorro, "Autobiografía," loc. cit., p. 148.
[30] El Diario Nicaragüense, Nov. 13, 1925, p. 2.

fusionists of 1924—urged him to stay in office, but resolution of the problems remained for the Nicaraguan Congress which assembled in December.[31] Solórzano outlined for it the situation. He praised the conduct of the Liberal party toward him, and expressed the desirability of fuller interpretation of the fusion pacts which might have avoided dangers then confronting the nation. The Conservative party, he said, was impatient and distrustful. Having the power of compact, disciplined ranks, it changed the political direction. Although he had remained loyal to the political promises of 1924, the President now felt the maintenance of peace and constitutional order was of supreme importance:

> This does not mean that I abandon or lose faith in the ideals of concord and cooperation of all the parties for the common good of the country, nor does it establish for a moment that these ideals are utopian or contrary to the credo of the Conservative party and its historic practices. It has demonstrated, only, that our public men have not yet been able to break the old habits of partisan politics. . . . Perhaps the *golpe* will bring new reflections from the leaders of various groups and help in rebuilding on a firmer foundation. . . .[32]

During the congressional session Chamorro continued his plan, which was assuming an almost artistic proportion. Since the country had become fairly quiet, the general determined to become president, though he knew he must have United States recognition for his government. He could not openly turn out Solórzano.

According to Article 106 of the Nicaraguan constitution, Congress could designate a successor from among its members if there were neither president nor vice-president. Chamorro assured his control of Congress by having that body disqualify many of its members because of illegalities in the election of 1924—no difficulty, as almost any Nicaraguan received election

---

[31] *Ibid.*, Nov. 17, 1925, p. 1; Dec. 10, 1925, p. 4.
[32] *Ibid.*, Dec. 17, 1925, p. 3.

only after methodical fraud. He brought charges of conspiracy against Sacasa for obtaining arms in Guatemala to start a revolution and gave the absent Vice-president twenty-five days to return to answer the charges. The Chamorro rump Congress then declared Sacasa's office vacant on January 12 and banished the former Vice-president for two years. A senator from Managua now resigned and his replacement—appointed in early January, 1926—was Chamorro. Legally the new senator, who remained as general-in-chief of the army, could not simultaneously be a member of the legislature, but he decided to ignore that technicality. As a senator, Chamorro became first designate of the Congress according to Article 106.

Meanwhile Solórzano, too, received Chamorro's attention. The general offered him the position of Nicaraguan minister to Washington, which he refused. There followed various threats, including one of having him declared insane. Under extreme pressure Solórzano became ill and desired to leave the country. Following this lead, Chamorro obtained his resignation but did not immediately present it to Congress.[33] Early in 1926 Congress granted Solórzano a leave of absence, and two months later, on March 13, 1926, accepted his resignation. Thus Nicaragua acquired a new chief executive, General Emiliano Chamorro.

Here, then, was a familiar situation in Latin American politics, where a revolution proceeded by superficially constitutional means. While Sorlózano's resignation simply formalized what had been fact since October, there was advantage in maintaining a

---

[33] Carlos Solórzano, "Mi Vindicación ante la Historia," *El Centroamericano (León)*, Jan. 24, 1932, p. 2; Jan. 30, 1932, p. 1; *La Noticia*, Nov. 5, 1927, p. 6. See also Chamorro, "Autobiografía," *loc. cit.*, p. 148. Chamorro explains why he, rather than Adolfo Díaz, succeeded Solórzano; in the Conservative party there was a division created by the friends of Carlos Cuadra Pasos and the friends of Chamorro. Chamorro's friends feared that Díaz would favor Cuadra Pasos. Thus Chamorro changed his support from Díaz to his father, Salvador Chamorro. The Senate nonetheless picked Emiliano Chamorro for the Senate seat and ultimately for the presidency.

facade of legitimacy. Without it there would be no United States recognition, which, as one observer commented, "involves everything, including the conservation of order and public peace."[34] The United States government, which had no essential interest in the outcome so long as Nicaraguans generally were happy and there was a decent regime in Managua, now found itself looking mildly foolish. Moreover, in this present case the Nicaraguan dissidents were preparing for a counterrevolution. The last thing the government of the United States wished in the golden year 1925, one of the years of peace and prosperity before the country was to plunge into the Great Depression, was a full-scale revolution in Nicaragua, in which American troops might have to participate. The issues were so small, the stake even in dollar diplomacy so insignificant. It was ludicrous if one compared Nicaraguan problems to those of the rest of the world, where, after all, there had been recently a world war in which, only eight years before, the United States had intervened to make the world safe for democracy. The Mexican government was also threatening to get out of hand in this period, and that was a much more difficult prospect, for American nationals had large investments in Mexico.

The United States did not want to intervene in Nicaragua. When the Marines had left in August, 1925, the department had hoped it was for good. America's position in support of constitu-

---

[34] *El Diario Nicaragüense*, Mar. 16, 1926, p. 1. In a memorandum of a conversation between Stokeley W. Morgan, assistant chief of the State Department's Latin American division, and Salvador Castrillo, Nicaraguan minister, dated Jan. 6, 1925 (1926?), Morgan had given as his personal opinion (in no way committing the State Department) that the only proper and safe course was for Solórzano to finish his term; Chamorro could remain as the President's right-hand man and chief of party. There could be no objection to Chamorro's exerting a legitimate influence on the Nicaraguan government, providing he did not use force or unconstitutional means. Morgan noted that the department had the highest opinion of Chamorro's ability and character and if, after the present constitutional term, Chamorro were elected to the presidency by the Nicaraguan people, the department would extend congratulations. (817.00/3397.)

tional governments in Central America was clear. The American minister told Chamorro on the day of the coup d'état that the United States would not recognize him if he took over the government in the manner it then appeared he would. But in December, 1925, the department told Eberhardt that it would not place Sacasa in office should the President resign and that, even though the United States would not recognize the usurping government, this act did not oblige us to oppose such a regime with force.[35] Interestingly, the department was not willing to make its policy clear to the Nicaraguans. The same telegram instructed the American minister not to "say anything to members of Congress which might predispose the followers of Chamorro to seize the government even at the risk of not being recognized." The department did not feel it necessary to give out any statement that the United States did not contemplate armed force or interference in the domestic affairs of Nicaragua. Kellogg expressed the same feeling when he asserted that the department desired to help Central American republics solve their problems but that regeneration should come from within, through desire of the people for constitutional government.[36] The sooner people felt responsible for their affairs, orderly government would develop.

In the days preceding his take-over, Chamorro was not content to work through diplomatic channels, nor did he believe Washington meant to adhere to nonrecognition. Latin Americans believed the department prone to bluff, that it would bow before a fait accompli. The Nicaraguan election of 1924 was an example of the department's pushing hard but accepting far less when presented with facts. Chamorro kept in touch with Chandler Anderson and instructed the legation in Washington to consult Anderson on all problems.[37] Shortly afterward Manuel Zavala, first secretary of the legation, expressed his and Anderson's im-

---

[35] Department of State to Eberhardt, Dec. 14, 1925, 817.00/3358.
[36] Department of State to Eberhardt, Dec. 21, 1925, 817.00/3361.
[37] Anderson diary, Dec. 10, 1925.

pression that the department was reluctant to interfere.[38]

Chamorro apparently considered these observations from the Potomac quasi-official, nullifying Minister Eberhardt's contrary advice. The minister complained to Kellogg, who cautioned Anderson not to speak for the department. Notwithstanding the warning, Chamorro moved ahead with some encouragement from his friends in Washington. Two days before Christmas he reported to Anderson on Eberhardt's doubts about recognition of a new government and wanted Zavala to discuss the matter with the department. Anderson thought such a discussion would be a mistake. If Nicaragua asked the department's attitude, there was danger of an adverse opinion, which would be difficult to change; better to act and ask later. Chamorro, as noted, seized presidential power in January, 1926.[39]

In conformity with the General Treaty of Peace and Amity of 1923, the United States government refused recognition and felt that the treaty signatories should make their position clear to Chamorro, who had signed the pact in 1923 when he had been minister to the United States. The governments of El Salvador, Guatemala, Honduras, and Costa Rica agreed and cited Chamorro's acts as a treaty violation.

Chamorro could not ignore the Washington treaties of 1923 and mentioned them in his inaugural address. He asserted that theoretical appreciation of the treaties might have influenced the

[38] These two men suggested that Chamorro proceed, using the appearance of legality. In their opinion the simplest course was to treat the 1924 election as a coup d'état in which the third party (Solórzano) returns were fraudulent while Conservative (Chamorro) returns were valid. Chamorro would only right the wrong of the previous year. Copy of cable from Zavala to Chamorro, Dec. 16, 1925, Anderson papers, correspondence, box 43; Anderson diary, Dec. 21, 1925.

[39] Chamorro in his "Autobiografia," *loc. cit.*, p. 148, acknowledges the warning of nonrecognition from Washington. He notes that for several days he had been making a popular campaign for taking the presidency and he thought the last-hour warning improper and not in accord with political reality. He felt secure with support of his party and the Nicaraguan people.

United States "but that only constituted a diplomatic contingency which could be explained in the future, when the events should be carefully examined and the situation analyzed."[40] His government wished guarantees for citizens and full liberty within the law. These statements in defense of his coup were, of course, in contrast to his words of other years. Of the conventions signed in Washington in 1907 (similar to those of 1923) he once had said: "They dried many tears at the source, and more than once they stopped the hand of a brother raised to strike another brother."[41]

Chandler Anderson visited the department and talked with Kellogg. At one meeting Kellogg promised not to do anything about recognition until the general could present whatever he wished on the problem. When withdrawal of recognition came soon after, it surprised Anderson, who tried to put business pressure on the department by showing Chamorro, friend of American interests, as the only man available to ensure stable government. Urging businesses to write or call the department, he noted that a failure to recognize Chamorro would probably bring revolution and destroy American influence. In Nicaragua, Chamorro tried the same approach by granting concessions to American businesses, hoping to secure recognition through influential Americans and also revenue from the price of the concessions.[42] He sent to Washington Señor Carlos Cuadra Pasos, who

[40] Walter Scott Penfield, "Emiliano Chamorro, Nicaragua's Dictator," Current History, XXIV (June, 1926), 350.

[41] Ibid. Joseph C. Grew, undersecretary of state, sometimes speculated about the correctness of American policy under the pact of 1923, since occasionally a good and strong man like Chamorro was the only one capable of holding the nation together. Yet he recognized that lifting restrictions and recognizing anyone regardless of how he came to power would open the door for revolutions. Joseph C. Grew (Walter Johnson, ed.), Turbulent Era: A Diplomatic Record of Forty Years, 1904–1945, (London, 1953), I, 668.

[42] Anderson diary, Jan. 16, 1926; Anderson to Bradley Palmer, Jan. 17, 1926, Anderson to J. Gilmore Fletcher, Jan. 17, 1926, J. Gilmore Fletcher to Anderson, Jan. 21, 1926, B. W. Palmer to Anderson, Jan. 22,

hoped to get United States approval by selling the Nicaraguan railroad and the national bank. But at the same time Sacasa was in Washington warning off buyers.

Chamorro's argument for recognition was ingenious in demonstrating his concern for the constitution and the 1923 Washington treaties. By the terms of these documents, he contended, the affair of October 25 had not been a revolution or *golpe de estado*, for Solórzano had continued as executive; there was no complete disorganization of the country. Actually, the argument went, Solórzano's resignation and Sacasa's removal were of such internal nature that from no point of international law could they be discussed or objected to. Referring to the constitutional provision prohibiting a man exercising high military command from election to the presidency, Chamorro distinguished between normal, regular elections and occasional ones provided by Article 106 whereby Congress had to act. The prohibition reasonably applied to regular elections to avoid pressure on voters but not to the type which brought Chamorro to power, because the Congress was not elected ad hoc; besides, the Conservatives had a majority in the legislature and there was no military pressure. These men reflected Chamorro's policies, and he was the only one with enough popularity and prestige to keep peace. After citing other examples of revolutionary governments that had been accepted in Central America, Chamorro concluded that his case was surrounded by circumstances of legality which would usually receive recognition.[43]

Despite these elaborate arguments and such special missions as that of Cuadra Pasos, the United States withheld recognition. The Conservatives tried hard to convince the Nicaraguan people that it was not essential to good, stable government. The recently created Conservative paper, *La Prensa*, assured its readers that

1926, all in Anderson papers, correspondence, box 43; Eberhardt to Department of State, Apr. 8, 1926, 817.00/3537; Eberhardt to Department of State, Apr. 26, 1926, 817.00/3570.

[43] *El Diario Nicaragüense*, Feb. 12, 1926, p. 3; Feb. 14, 1926, p. 1; Feb. 16, 1926, p. 1; Feb. 17, 1926, pp. 1–2.

the party's immense prestige compensated for nonrecognition, and, besides, lack of recognition did not mean United States hostility.[44]

At this juncture came a fateful change, for Minister Eberhardt left his post the first week of June, 1926, on leave of absence. Lawrence Dennis, secretary of the legation, became chargé in Managua.[45] In short order he would turn things upside down, as Chamorro had done some months before.

[44] *Ibid.*, Mar. 4, 1926, p. 2; Mar. 6, 1926, p. 1.

[45] Announcing his departure, the State Department reaffirmed its attitude and said the minister's departure had no political meaning. *Foreign Relations: 1926*, II, 787. Eberhardt was gone until Dec., 1926. The State Department was annoyed by Eberhardt's long absence and it was suggested he feared violence against his person. L. Ethan Ellis, *Frank B. Kellogg and American Foreign Relations, 1925–1929* (New Brunswick, N. J., 1961), p. 256, n. 12.

4: THE CORINTO CONFERENCE

Chamorro's coup d'état thoroughly confused Nicaraguan politics and upset United States policies. Despite American opposition Chamorro's hold seemed to tighten, until by June, 1926, he appeared as firmly entrenched as at any time since his take-over. At this time Lawrence Dennis became the spokesman for the United States in Nicaragua. A thirty-two-year-old Harvard graduate and veteran of the A.E.F. of World War I who had been in the foreign service in Europe as well as Latin America, Dennis undertook his new duties with youthful directness.[1] He decided that Chamorro should resign, that he, Dennis, could bring the usurper to this way of thinking by a confrontation. Dennis told Chamorro to quit; the suggestion at first amused the dictator, but later he became annoyed by its repetition in early morning telephone calls or at otherwise pleasant social events. Dennis also intended to educate the Nicaraguan people to the State Department's attitude, for he felt that Chamorro was distorting the

---

[1] Dennis, later an advocate of fascism in the United States, wrote *Is Capitalism Doomed?* (New York, 1932), *The Coming American Fascism* (New York, 1936), and *The Dynamics of War and Revolution* (n.p, 1940), For a synopsis of these later views of Dennis see Arthur M. Schlesinger, Jr., *The Politics of Upheaval* (Boston, 1960), pp. 74–78.

Writing in the 1930's Dennis was critical of our earlier Latin American policies. He did not believe it necessary for the maintenance of our supremacy in the Western Hemisphere to follow the "stupid and unnecessary adventures of Presidents Theodore Roosevelt, Taft, Wilson, and Coolidge, and Secretaries of State Root and Hughes, in dollar diplomacy, loans, military interventions, financial interventions, political meddling

United States position. He spread information that his government hoped the Nicaraguan people would return to consitutional government and make recognition possible. He conferred with Conservatives, including members of Congress and the cabinet. The dictator's fellow party members, who flocked to the United States legation, worried lest their leader damage their party. Capitalizing on this fear, Dennis urged them to oppose Chamorro.[2]

There is evidence of Dennis' success in the strong protests which the Chamorro people sent to the State Department, charges that the American diplomat's actions were compromising public peace, forcing Nicaragua to anarchy. Chamorro emphasized that Dennis was intervening in purely domestic matters and sought to arouse public indignation by arranging publication of the charges and by interesting the anti-imperialist Senator William E. Borah in the Nicaraguan affair.[3] The Con-

to insure free elections, sound financial control, or protection, of American capital in the Caribbean republics." (*The Coming American Fascism*, p. 287). A few years later he referred to this episode as a chapter in American imperialist history and remarked that as the American chargé in Nicaragua he had asked, at the direction of the State Department, for Marines to land. (*The Dynamics of War and Revolution*, p. 108).

Contemporary records do not reveal such antipathy toward a policy of protecting lives and property. In a dispatch from Dennis to Department of State, Aug. 23, 1926, 817.00/3730, Dennis states, "We should be prepared to intervene to protect American life and property and prevent further fighting. I fully appreciate objection to such a course and favor it only because the alternative is to allow the ruin of Nicaragua. I consider presence of war vessels at Bluefields and Corinto desirable to meet emergencies."

[2] H. N. Denny, *Dollars for Bullets*, (New York, 1929), pp. 221–222, gives a good description of Dennis' tactics. See also "Big Brother or Big Bully," *The Nation*, vol. 123 (July, 1926), 25; Dennis to Department of State, June 7, 1926, 817.00/3607, 3609; Chamorro to Minister Castrillo, June 12, 1926, found in Anderson papers, correspondence, box 43.

[3] Department of State to Dennis, June 14, 1926, 817.00/3635; memorandum of a conversation between Castrillo and Stokeley W. Morgan, June 28, 1926, 817.00/3657; *The United States Daily*, June 18, 1926, pp. 1, 5.

servative newspaper *La Prensa* called for party members to rally behind their leader to maintain the dignity and traditions of the party as well as the independence and worthiness of the nation.[4] Commenting on a convocation of Conservative leaders at the United States legation—to publicize the American position— *La Gaceta* (a government publication) attempted to downgrade it and dismissed it as revealing nothing new in the attitude toward Chamorro. Obviously Dennis was *"el hombre de actualidad"* (the man of the hour) in Managua, and the Chamorristas did not like it.[5]

Meanwhile the Liberals had started a compaign of their own. Ever since the Chamorro take-over there had been a threat of Liberal counterrevolution. At first the Liberals were patient, and whatever the reason—lack of arms or funds, disorganization, or a willingness to wait and see—had held off for six months. As weeks passed and Chamorro seemed more secure and had funds and arms despite nonrecognition, the Liberals began to question American policy. In early March, 1926, Sacasa complained at the State Department. He knew the United States did not want to intervene but felt there ought to be encouragement and permission for constitutional authorities to assert themselves. Stokeley W. Morgan of the Latin American division, quoting from the 1923 Central American treaty, opposed fitting out expeditions in neighboring Central American nations and told Sacasa that the department would not favor any new revolution. Give moral pressure a chance to work; Chamorro would fall; remember, so Morgan philosophized near the end of the meeting, that public affairs move slowly. Upon leaving Sacasa voiced little faith in the

---

[4] Quoted in *El Diario Nicaragüense* (Granada), June 15, 1926, p. 4.

[5] *La Gaceta* (Managua), June 16, 1926, quoted in *El Diario Nicaragüense*, June 19, 1926, p. 1; Chamorro, "Autobiografia," *Revista Conservadora*, II (Aug., 1961), 151. In perusing some of the Nicaraguan newspapers of 1926, this position of the American representative in Nicaragua is apparent; often statements or interviews were given prominence on front pages.

department's policy but agreed to advise his supporters to wait.[6] Finally the Liberals began a military campaign.

Liberal forces raised their standard on the sparsely inhabited east coast—the usual locale of Nicaraguan revolts. In May, 1926, Liberal troops led by Luis Beltrán Sandoval attacked and took the town of Bluefields, after much firing and few casualties. The governor and the director of police fell into insurgent hands, as did the national bank, from which the rebels obtained $161,642.06. The American manager of the Nicaraguan-owned but Connecticut-incorporated bank protested. The Liberals also took the customs house and demanded the receipts—again treading on United States toes, because an American citizen collected Nicaraguan customs. Within a week they controlled a large portion of the east coast: Rama, La Cruz, Río Grande, Bragman's Bluff. The Chamorro Congress declared the country in a state of war and authorized the President to assess citizens for $500,000. Chamorro called up three thousand men, reinforced most of the Pacific coast garrisons, and arrested over two hundred prominent Liberals.[7]

Both the American and British consuls at Bluefields requested war vessels from their governments. Washington dispatched a light cruiser and indicated that it preferred no British war vessel in Nicaraguan waters at this time.[8] On May 6 the *Cleveland* arrived and Marines occupied the town, declaring it a neutral zone. Armed Nicaraguans either had to leave the area or turn over their arms to American troops. Marines protected the customs house and the customs collector.

Marines were back in Nicaragua only to protect American

[6] Memoranda of conversations between Morgan and Sacasa, Mar. 2, 1926, 817:00/3490; Mar. 16, 1926, 817.00/3506; Apr. 2, 1926, 817.00/3532.

[7] *El Diario Nicaragüense*, May 4, 1926, p. 2; May 5, 1926, p. 1. See also Humberto Osorno Fonseca, *La Revolución Liberal Constitucionalista de 1926* (Managua, 1958).

[8] Memorandum of conversation between Henry Chilton of British embassy and Morgan, May 4, 1926, 817.00/3546. See also 817.00/3542.

lives and property. The State Department was eager to stress this point, for as officials including the secretary of state asserted, the people of Nicaragua should learn to accept political responsibility and settle domestic issues themselves. Naval forces were to maintain a strict neutrality; as long as no American lives or property were in danger, the Marines were not to hinder operations of either Liberals or Chamorro followers. Washington cautioned Americans not to interfere with Liberal authorities in areas where they had control.[9]

The Chamorro government proceeded with its military plans. Cavalry reconnoitered Rama, and troops approached. By mid-May, 1926, General José Solórzano Díaz led three thousand men to the Atlantic coast to attack Liberal forces around Bluefields, who numbered about twelve hundred.[10] Although anti-government troops continued their activity along the coast and captured Cape Gracias á Dios near the Honduran border, the Chamorro army was able to suppress these first uprisings. By May 20, Rama fell, then Bluefields, El Bluff, and Cape Gracias á Dios. Conditions were approaching normal as revolutionaries dispersed to Puerto Limón, Costa Rica, or toward the Nicaraguan interior.[11]

During almost three months of the summer of 1926—between the end of May when Chamorro squelched the first outbreak, and August when fighting began anew—both sides attempted to get their houses in order. Chamorro was having money trouble. The full treasury which the dictator had acquired when he eased himself into the presidency was now nearly empty. His nonrecognized status hurt, for he could not negotiate foreign loans. He could not even find takers when he proposed to sell the Nicaraguan railroad and national bank. Working behind the scenes, the State Department effectively stopped possible financial assistance

[9] Department of State to Andrew J. McConnico, consul at Bluefields, May 15, 1926, 817.00/3561.

[10] New York Times, May 16, 1926, p. 7.

[11] Osorno Fonseca, La Revolución Liberal Constitucionalista de 1926, p. 23, 26.

for Chamorro. When the department heard that the general was seeking $500,000 from the Anglo-South American Bank, Washington voiced objections to the British embassy. And when Chamorro pressured the National Bank of Nicaragua to pay an extra dividend of $80,000, the department encouraged the American president to refuse.[12]

In August, 1926, rumors circulated in Nicaragua that Sacasa and his followers were plotting revolution with aid from Mexico and Guatemala and, seemingly in support of such rumors, the government did find a quantity of arms hidden right under its nose in downtown Managua.[13] Late in the month Liberals attacked an important sugar center, San Antonio. They cut the telegraph wires along the railway from Managua to Corinto and dynamited a troop train, injuring a few soldiers. As resistance began all over the country, the government announced it would show the insurgents no mercy. Chargé Dennis believed Nicaragua was in for a cycle of revolutions unless Chamorro agreed to a settlement acceptable to the Liberals. The United States again sent warships to Bluefields and Corinto, and on August 28 Marines and bluejackets were in Bluefields in response to the governor's statement that his forces were unable to protect Americans there.

There was mounting evidence that the rebels were receiving outside help. Former Vice-president Sacasa had found a friendly reception in Mexico City. Reports stated that Mexican ships were landing arms and supplies and nationals were participating in the revolution. The garrison at Corinto claimed to have seen one such supply ship, the *Concón*.[14] American aviators, then part of the Nicaraguan constabulary, reported attacks on a ship flying

[12] Memorandum of conversation between Sir Adrian W. M. Bailie and J. H. Stabler of the Latin American division, Sept. 7, 1926, 817.516/142; memorandum of conversation between C. F. Loree and Stabler, Sept. 8, 1926, 817.516/141.

[13] *El Diario Nicaragüense*, Aug. 10, 1926, p. 1.

[14] *New York Times*, Aug. 26, 1926, p. 2; Osorno Fonseca, *La Revolución Liberal Constitucionalista de 1926*, p. 30.

the Mexican flag and landing guns at Consequina Point near the
Gulf of Fonseca. The ship proved to be the *Tropical*, under
Mexican registry. Its captain, shortly before going to Nicaragua,
was in La Unión, El Salvador, where he talked with an American naval officer. The latter learned that the vessel was carrying
thirty-two machine guns, small arms, and ammunition. The captain denied the ship was operating under the Mexican government but refused to say who had leased it.[15] Chamorro sent a
large force to Consequina Point to engage the rebels and captured many men along with arms and ammunition. The letters
"F.N.C.," the national cartridge company of Mexico, were on
the ammunition containers. Rifles bore the Russian coat of arms;
a United States firm had made the rifles for a Russian order but
after being rejected they went to filibusters. Major Carter of
the national guard talked with some Mexican captives and learned
"that leaves of absence had been granted so they might come to
Nicaragua and make their fortunes by helping place Sacasa in
power. . . ."[16] The crew of the tugboat *Foam* attested that aid
was coming from Mexico; while on its way from New York to
San Diego, the *Foam* had stopped at a port in Mexico where it
loaded arms and Nicaraguan revolutionists. The new passengers
took charge of the ship, using it to bombard cities along the
Mosquito coast, capture strategic points, and transport troops
and supplies. Only after the tug went aground and the captors
departed was the crew able to ask for help from the United
States Navy.

The Chamorro government denounced Mexican aid and even
complained of it to Sir Eric Drummond, secretary-general of the
League of Nations, accusing Mexico of violating sacred rights

[15] Dispatch from U.S.S. *Tulsa* to naval operations, Sept., 1926 (no date
given), National Archives, naval records collection of the office of naval
records and library, subject file, 1911–1927, WA 7 Nicaragua, record
group 45, box 641. Hereafter cited as naval records collection.
[16] C. B. Carter, "The Kentucky Feud in Nicaragua," *The World's
Work*, vol. 54 (July, 1927), 321.

of sovereignty by attacks which would destroy the bonds of brotherhood.

The State Department now faced a widespread civil war in Nicaragua. Patience, moral suasion, nonrecognition were no longer adequate. How to return the Nicaraguan ship of state to a constitutional channel? The division of Latin American affairs considered possible solutions. Solórzano could take back the presidency, but there was doubt that Chamorro would accept this answer and the United States did not want responsibility of returning a weak president. The State Department did not consider Sacasa's ouster legal; he thus could become chief executive. Again, Washington would have to use Marines to put him in Managua, for to Conservatives he was less acceptable than Solórzano. Recognition of Chamorro was out of the question, yet keeping aloof from Nicaraguan affairs would encourage Chamorro to stay in power and open the way for prolonged fighting to unseat him. Another possibility was to continue nonrecognition, discourage business and financial dealing with the de facto president, and do nothing to prevent arms shipments to revolutionists. This possibility was as unacceptable as the others, for it would encourage revolutions and probably wreck the financial program evolved during the first intervention. After eliminating these possibilities J. H. Stabler of the Latin American division presented one more suggestion to Kellogg: bring withdrawal of Chamorro by negotiations with the Conservative general and leaders of the other political parties.[17]

Stabler's last point became department policy. About two weeks later—August 23, 1926—Chargé Dennis recommended a communication to Chamorro calling for immediate steps toward a constitutional settlement. The United States offered a warship for a conference and planned for American naval forces to neutralize Corinto during the meeting. By mid-September Dennis and Admiral Julian Latimer, commander of the special service squadron, met with the opposing sides to arrange for the Corinto

[17] Memorandum from Stabler to Kellogg, Aug. 11, 1926, 817.00/4823.

conference.[18] Latimer talked with the Liberal General Moncada while Dennis opened talks with Chamorro. The factions agreed to a fifteen-day armistice beginning September 23, subject to extension.

Although Dennis denied any direct participation in or control of the conference, refusing initially to attend except as a spectator, many Nicaraguans felt the United States would use the conference to dictate a settlement.[19] Former President Bartolomé Martínez, interviewed in Costa Rica, even supported intervention. Never a friend of interference, Martínez now saw no other remedy but the return of Solórzano supported by Americans, and Solórzano, now living tranquilly in San Francisco, voiced readiness to return if needed.[20]

After Dennis agreed to preside, the talks began October 16 with skirmishing over credentials and wording of the conference's purpose.[21] Soon the main problem appeared. Conservatives wanted an executive of their party and a government with Liberal participation, while Liberals insisted upon Sacasa as president. They argued over what returning to constitutional ways

[18] The special service squadron was a naval force, generally made up of five light cruisers, with headquarters in the Panama Canal Zone. Its mission was to protect American lives and property in the Caribbean. At times of unusual turmoil (as in Nicaragua in 1926–27), the Navy Department increased the squadron's strength.

[19] El Diario Nicaragüense, Sept. 22, 1926, p. 2; Sept. 28, 1926, p. 1.

[20] Ibid., Sept. 30, 1926; El Comercio (Managua), Sept. 26, 1926, p. 3; Sept. 29, 1926, p. 1. The State Department considered the return of Solórzano, but Dennis thought the plan impracticable. Department of State to Dennis, Sept. 25, 1926, 817.00/3832; Dennis to Department of State, Sept. 29, 1926, 817.00/3831.

[21] See José Barcenas Meneses, Las Conferencias del "Denver," actas autenticas de las sessiones, con introduccion y lijeros comentarios (Managua, 1926), pp. 6, 8, 9, 11, 12, 18. Hereafter cited as Las Conferencias del "Denver." Dennis accepted the offer to preside if he would not be a party to nor sign any agreements reached and if his comments would not form part of the minutes. Dennis to Department of State, Nov. 1, 1926, 817.00/4094.

meant: reestablishment of the way things were before the nation wandered from the narrow path, or a form of restoration not necessarily the same as before? Liberals held they could not assent to a new formula when an individual already existed who ought to assume the presidency. Conservatives reported that the Vice-president did not have any power, therefore did not exist. Liberals rejoined that the situation was not yet ended.[22] Positions hardened and the Liberals threatened to carry on their struggle with aid of Mexico, denying at the same time that such aid put obligations on them.[23] Dennis felt the conference would deadlock.

The following day the Liberals proposed that the conference submit the question of constitutional government to arbitration by the American secretary of state and representatives of the four Central American countries. Dennis demurred, telling the delegates that the problem was not subject to arbitration of foreign governments but was a domestic political problem which Nicaraguans must settle. Feeling that Central American governments would be partial, Conservatives also opposed arbitration. At another time, in reply to a Conservative offer that both Chamorro and Sacasa withdraw claims in favor of Adolfo Díaz, Liberals suggested that Sacasa might relinquish the presidency to Manuel Antonio Carazo. Conservatives refused. Finally Liberals announced they were obliged to withdraw.[24]

The Chamorro group offered to reinstate congressmen and magistrates, to give Liberals posts they had held, to hold elections, in return for resignation of Sacasa and Liberal acceptance of Adolfo Díaz. The Liberals declined. Dennis was convinced that the Liberals' inclination to break the conference was either bluff or came from support by Mexico. He felt the Conservatives were conciliatory and ready to compromise, while the Liberals

---

[22] Barcenas Meneses, Las Conferencias del "Denver," pp. 20–21.

[23] Dennis to Department of State, Oct. 19, 1926, 817.00/3943; Barcenas Meneses, Las Conferencias del "Denver," pp. 32–33.

[24] Barcenas Meneses, Las Conferencias del "Denver," pp. 43, 64; Dennis to Department of State, Oct. 21, 1926, 817.00/3946.

were holding out for all or nothing. He advised the State Department to take prompt measures if the Liberals refused to modify their attitude. The chargé reasoned that a strong declaration would smash, once and for all, the doctrine of constitutional restoration by means of foreign aid to revolution. But to the policy makers in Washington, Chamorro still appeared the major problem and the Mexican threat might make him more reasonable toward a settlement.[25]

Nonetheless the department instructed its chargé in Guatemala to interview Sacasa (then in Guatemala) and explain the United States position, while at the same time learning his. The American government voiced anxiety about foreign intervention in Nicaragua; it wished no interference in that country's internal affairs and would oppose interference by any other nation: "any faction or party which solicited or accepted such aid or assistance could count upon the firm opposition of the United States Government." Sacasa evasively claimed he was not a member of the revolution but "an independent worker for the maintenance of the treaties and a constitutional order in Nicaragua." He said he had no information from Liberals at the conference about their attitude toward revolution and refused to discuss Mexican participation in the revolt.[26]

The Denver conferees held their final session on October 24. The Liberal delegates admitted they could not agree to a Conservative president, since that would mean abandoning their Mexican allies. Failing agreement at the conference, Chamorro intended (Dennis reported) to deposit the presidency with some Conservative in the near future.[27]

----

[25] Dennis to Department of State, Oct. 19, 1926, 817.00/3943; Oct. 21, 1926, 817.00/3946; Department of State to Dennis, Oct. 22, 1926, 817.00/3943.

[26] Department of State to Leon Ellis, Oct. 22, 1926, 817.00/3943; Ellis to Department of State, Oct. 23, 1926, 817.00/3954.

[27] Dennis to Department of State, Oct. 23, 1926, 817.00/3958. Chamorro in his "Autobiografia," Revista Conservadora, II (Sept., 1961), 156, says that despite the Denver conference failure he could have continued to fight against the revolutionaries and won if it had not been for

Thus, on the evening of October 30, 1926, Chamorro deposited the presidency with Senator Sebastián Uriza, second designate of the Chamorro-controlled Congress. Before making this move Chamorro exacted from leading Conservatives a written pledge signed in the American legation that they would support his presidential candidacy in 1928; apparently the caudillo also desired a statement from Dennis that he was withdrawing to meet urgings of the United States government, but the chargé refused.[28] Chamorro's passing was unavoidable in face of Liberal revolt and American opposition; *El Comercio* commented that it could not be held off for many days because of the vigorous hand of Tío Sam.[29]

The whole affair had been extremely complicated. So much had been required, in terms of talk and insignificant but vexing military actions, to produce action of a pacific sort in Nicaragua. How convenient it would have been had the United States in previous years never been under the injunctions of the Roosevelt Corollary, never had any feeling that its strength and power as the largest and richest nation of the hemisphere placed it under obligation to act as policeman of its weaker neighbors. It was easy for President Taft in the old days to speak of substituting dollars for bullets, but neither seemed to solve problems in the sensitive Latin American countries close to the Panama Canal. Now, although Coolidge and Kellogg found Nicaraguan problems an enormous bore, they had to hope that the factions there would produce peace.

Uriza was to be president for only a few weeks. The Conservatives planned to reinstate excluded members of the Solórzano Congress and secure from that Congress designation of Adolfo Díaz as president. The department liked this plan. If Conserva-

growing opposition within the Conservative party which he feared would cause a deep split. At the center of this opposition, he notes, was Dennis, who encouraged animosity against his government.

[28] Dennis to Department of State, Oct. 30, 1926, 817.00/3992; Nov. 1, 1926, 817.00/4095.

[29] *El Comercio*, Nov. 2, 1926, p. 1.

tives restored the Congress elected in 1924, or at least made an honest effort to restore it, the United States might recognize de jure a *designado* chosen by Congress, since Solórzano and Sacasa were both absent.[30] In the department's view Díaz had not been closely involved in the Chamorro coup d'état and could qualify under the treaty of 1923. He was strong enough to handle internal problems and avoid domination by such men as Chamorro. (For this latter reason, incidentally, many Conservatives did not favor Díaz.)

It took maneuvering and threats to bring Díaz's appointment, but Dennis was successful.[31] The Congress that designated him on November 11, 1926, was not entirely as elected in 1924, but the United States chose to consider it a sincere attempt to reconstitute the 1924 Congress.[32] Díaz took office three days later in

[30] Department of State to Dennis, Nov. 2, 1926, 817.00/3992.

[31] Denny, *Dollars for Bullets*, pp. 234–235.

[32] Because of Washington's insistence on a semblance of constitutionality in Nicaragua and a desire to answer critics of recognition of Díaz, the State Department showed considerable interest in the reconstituted congress. Trying to answer the questions from the Potomac, Dennis discovered a morass of confusion. The department wanted to know (1) the names of senators and deputies elected to Congress in 1924; (2) the names of senators and deputies who attended the opening session in Jan., 1925, plus the names of those who, for any reason, did not attend; (3) the names of those expelled from Congress during the Chamorro regime and who took their places; (4) the names of those who attended the session electing Díaz. Dennis despaired of answering intelligently. He asked the Nicaraguan minister of foreign affairs and a prominent Liberal congressman and attorney to furnish data; their lists disagreed. An example of the problem was how to determine the status of an individual declared elected by the electoral council but afterwards refused admission by Congress. Or what was the status of a person declared elected by Congress and later declared not elected by Congress? The official records of Congress were inadequate or contradictory.

Dennis concluded, as a sound principle of constitutional law, that Congress was judge of its own elections and that a foreign government should simply accept official statements by another government. The lists which Dennis sent provided occupation for someone in the Latin American

the presence of the Nicaraguan Congress, government officials, and the diplomatic corps, including Dennis. The new President expressed hope for the continued friendship and good offices of the United States and deplored Mexican interference in Nicaraguan affairs. On November 17, much to the chagrin of the Sacasa people, the American government was happy to recognize Díaz.

affairs division. Placing the names on graph paper and using a code of numbers, there was an attempt to determine status; the material was duplicated for others to try, various symbols being employed, but there is no indication of conclusions reached.

In the congressional vote picking Díaz, he received forty-four votes, Solórzano received two, and six Liberals refrained from voting. While not all Liberals attended the session, Washington believed they had opportunity to do so. See Dennis to Department of State, Nov. 6, 1926, 817.00/4103; Nov. 13, 1926, 817.00/4054; Nov. 19, 1926, 817.00/4205; Dec. 11, 1926, 817.00/4233; Dec. 11, 1926, 817.00/4355; Department of State to Dennis, Dec. 7, 1926, 817.00/4209a. Note also Department of State, *A Brief History of the Relations Between the United States and Nicaragua, 1909–1928* (Washington,1928), p. 36.

5: BOLSHEVISM

The inauguration of Díaz and his recognition by the United States did not end the Nicaraguan trouble; within two weeks Sacasa, the rival presidential claimant, returned to Nicaragua. On December 1, 1926, at Puerto Cabézas on the east coast, he announced he had assumed the presidency of the republic. Mexico quickly recognized the Sacasa government. Thus the revolution was no longer "ins" versus "outs" but a struggle for prestige between the United States and its neighbor just below the Rio Grande.

For some time United States-Mexican relations had been troublesome. The Mexican Revolution had raised questions of expropriated hacienda lands, the position of the Catholic Church, and, perhaps most important, title to oil lands acquired after 1876. Under the presidency of Alvaro Obregón (1920–24) the two nations moved toward an understanding through the Bucareli Conferences. Much of the new-found goodwill was based on a gentleman's agreement known as the Extra-Official Pact which, after Plutarco Elías Calles succeeded Obregón, no longer seemed to have much meaning. Portions of the United States press and groups with interests in Mexico clamored for action, while public officials increased the tension by openly expressing fears of Bolshevik activity south of the border.

The difficulties in Nicaragua increased the strain. Reportedly Mexico was backing Sacasa to embarrass the United States and to spread revolutionary doctrine into Central America. One account arriving in Washington from Mexico City noted a forensic attack on the United States delivered before an audience including supporters of Sacasa. The Mexican speaker was credited with the statement that after establishment of a Liberal government in Nicaragua that government would denounce the canal treaty and would cancel various concessions and agreements with private American interests.[1] Some United States diplomats who were not friends of the Mexican Revolution and who felt that Washington had not appreciated their alarm over Mexican events now sensed a change, particularly in Kellogg. In November, 1926, the American ambassador to Mexico, James R. Sheffield, informed Chandler P. Anderson that Kellogg was very much stirred up by the intrigue in Nicaragua and that his (Sheffield's) position was strengthened thereby.[2]

Thus in December, 1926, and January, 1927, there was a flux of statements and charges among the governments in Nicaragua, Mexico City, and Washington. For the United States it was a time of uncertainty. While Chamorro was in power there was little doubt about the State Department's policy of nonrecognition; after Washington had helped bring a constitutional settlement and incurred responsibility toward the Díaz government—much greater than the department was willing to admit—there arose among the American people many supporters of alternative settlements.

By recognizing Díaz the department found only an incomplete answer to the Chamorro problem. The United States allowed Conservatives to retain the presidency because it feared using force to seat Sacasa. But to disallow a coup d'état by an individual while at the same time letting benefits accrue to his party was harmful to stable government and did not satisfy the Liberals. Not unnaturally they set out to regain power just as Chamorro had gained it in 1925.

At the end of 1926 nothing yet was clear-cut. The United

[1] H. F. Arthur Schoenfeld to Department of State, Oct. 29, 1926, 711.17/46.

[2] Anderson diary, Nov. 13, 14, 1926.

States maintained a stance of nonintervention while the Mexican-supported Liberals menaced the government. Díaz was willing to concede some points. He would allow Liberal participation in the government, reforms in favor of minorities, reorganization of the national guard, but Liberals did not want any agreement which did not guarantee that Díaz would carry out the arrangements. Some of Sacasa's supporters feared Díaz could not keep his promises and that Chamorro might return. Liberals had in mind American intervention to reestablish order on a reasonable basis. They said they would accept no peace terms without prospect of United States intervention and as long as they could count on Mexican aid.[3]

In this situation the United States faced an awkward choice. Contending with Díaz, Liberals, Mexico, and Bolshevism, the United States moved toward a second Nicaraguan intervention. The slow beginning in December, 1926, gained momentum, until by spring of 1927 the Coolidge administration was up to its neck in Nicaragua.

The day after his inauguration Díaz showed political acumen by addressing a note to the American legation in Managua relating that his country was in a bad way because of Mexican hostility. His feeble nation could not meet the forces of that government. Knowing the source of many American fears in regard to Nicaragua, the President suggested that sovereignty of his country was in jeopardy; this, he said, would imperil interests of North Americans and other foreigners. He wanted State Department support in stopping Mexican hostilities.[4] This first communication of the new administration with Chargé Dennis revealed Nicaraguan policy. Díaz wanted to use the fears, prestige, and, if necessary, force of the United States to gain a full term. The United States was not blind to this fact and told Díaz

[3] Dennis to Department of State, Nov. 12, 1926, 817.00/4050; Eberhardt to Department of State, Dec. 24, 1926, 817.00/4303; Eberhardt to Department of State, Dec. 19, 1926, 817.00/4275.

[4] Dennis to Department of State, Dec. 8, 1926, 817.00/4197.

he was counting on too much; the State Department regretted
that the new administration was relying upon the United States
to protect it from revolutionists. Dennis told Díaz that recognition did not mean armed assistance.[5]

Unabashed, Díaz in an interview reportedly said he had
accepted the presidency "expecting the United States would aid
Nicaragua to restore order and secure peace."[6] He issued a manifesto accusing Mexico of armed expeditions against Nicaragua; if
successful these expeditions would deny religious freedom, con-
fiscate property, and bring disorder and communism.[7] He called
for peace and repeated his terms—general amnesty, compensa-
tion for revolutionary losses on the basis of political fair play,
and a national government in which Liberals would have a fair
share.

Mexico and the Liberals denied Díaz's charges. A spokesman
for the Mexican foreign office asserted that the manifesto was so
absurd it did not deserve comment. As for the Liberals, their
agent in Washington described the charges as laughable and a
play for outside help. He charged Díaz with exploiting the
people of Nicaragua and added that if the Díaz regime were left
to the Liberals it would not last long. Attempting to parry the
accusations, Sacasa promised to guarantee property rights of
Nicaraguans and foreigners, and, knowing the Conservative President's aims, he accused Díaz of trying to excite American opinion
against the Liberal cause. Some Liberals believed the American
State Department had written the Díaz manifesto.[8]

At this point General Chamorro thoughtfully left the scene—
at least that incubus was out of the way. When he gave up
the presidency Chamorro had retained headship of the army,
but this arrangement was unsatisfactory to many—perhaps Díaz
most of all. In mid-December, 1926, the general resigned. Díaz

[5] Department of State to Dennis, Dec. 8, 1926, 817.00/4227a.
[6] H. N. Denny, Dollars for Bullets (New York, 1929), p. 242.
[7] New York Times, Dec. 12, 1926, p. 1.
[8] Ibid., p. 2; Dec. 14, 1926, p. 20; Dec. 15, 1926, p. 32.

appointed him minister on special mission to Great Britain, France, Italy, and Spain. When an American asked a Nicaraguan official about Chamorro's duties, the reply was that his only duty was to be absent from Nicaragua.[9] On December 20, Chamorro departed for his new post, leaving the complexities he had created. Some people hoped his departure would bring Costa Rican and Guatemalan recognition, but it did not. Probably it gave Díaz a freer hand to negotiate with the Liberals.

Still, the various peace efforts from November through December, 1926, accomplished nothing. A conference between General Moncada and Rear Admiral Julian L. Latimer, commander of the special service squadron, came to nought. So did offers of mediation from Guatemala and Costa Rica.

Meanwhile requests for protection were coming from American interests along Nicaragua's east coast; as Liberal activity increased, pleas increased. In answer Washington instructed the commander of the special service squadron to protect American lives and property along the Mosquito coast. Reports of Mexican aid to the Liberals brought the United States to lift its arms embargo in favor of Díaz. The American government was supporting Díaz and coming to believe that those opposing him—the Liberals and Mexico—obstructed peace and justice. In view of the requests of Díaz, the seeming intransigence of Sacasa, Mexican attitude toward America in Nicaragua and elsewhere, the United States response to the Nicaraguan problem was not strange.

As mentioned, there was the problem of Bolshevism, perhaps the most interesting factor in the hardening of American policy toward the Nicaraguan revolution. Apprehension over communism was widespread in the United States in the 1920's. Refusal to recognize the Soviet Union, and the Red scare of the early 1920's, evidenced the feeling. When there was suggestion of communist activity in Central America near the Panama Canal, Americans worried. The President and the Secretary of State

[9] Munro to Department of State, Sept. 28, 1927, 711.17/203.

worried aloud, causing much comment in the United States and knowing glances among Europeans.

The specter of Bolshevism came partly from United States relations with Mexico. President Calles had expropriated land-holdings, and his attitude toward American oil companies, conflict with the Catholic Church, and support of the employer-baiting labor boss Luis Morones caused much criticism in the United States. To many persons it looked Red. Even members of the State Department felt the Calles regime was at least semi-Bolshevik, bad enough in Mexico and dangerous if spreading south. Reports came that Mexico was trying to influence Central America, and Mexican activity seemed to confirm its intention to dominate first Guatemala and then her small sister republics. In late September, 1926, a department official, believing a timely word would make other Western Hemisphere governments think before acting against the United States, spoke about Mexican influence to the Guatemalan minister, Francisco Sánchez Latour. He told the minister that Washington was not ignorant of the general plan for setting up Liberal governments throughout Central America under Mexican sway, preliminary to establishing semi-Bolshevik regimes such as existed in Mexico.[10] Chandler Anderson, James R. Sheffield, and, of course, Adolfo Díaz encouraged this apprehension.[11]

Díaz shrewdly emphasized Mexico's role in the Liberal revolu-tion; facing this aid his government could not end the fighting and the only recourse was United States help. The Coolidge administration hesitated to give support but did show alarm over Mexican meddling in Nicaragua.

The Mexican government professed surprise, denying assistance to Nicaraguan rebels. If rebel sympathizers smuggled material to Nicaragua, the government was not responsible; patrolling every

[10] Memorandum of conversation between Stabler and Francisco Sán-chez Latour, Sept. 30, 1926, 817.00/3952.

[11] Anderson diary, Oct. 29, 1926, box 7; Oct. 30, 1926, box 7; Nov. 2, 1926, box 7; Nov. 13, 1926, box 7; Nov. 14, 1926, box 7.

inch of the coasts was impossible. As if to silence all argument, it recalled that the United States had not always restrained filibusters.[12] Unofficially Mexican officials declared their country had the same interests in Central America as did the United States. Naturally Mexico wanted a sphere of influence and desired close relations with Central American countries; but these desires did not warrant criticism by the United States, for America had them too.[13] Calles was reticent but stated that propaganda about Mexican Bolshevism was "a new lie to discredit Mexico." General Alvaro Obregón, a former president and close to President Calles, asserted that Nicaragua was shameless in requesting the American government to intervene. At the same time Mexican newspapers fired broadsides at the "exhibition of dollar diplomacy," "spurious Díaz Government," "absurdly irritating farce," "rabid exhibition of hypocrisy," and "puppet of American capitalism in Nicaragua."[14]

Charges and countercharges continued. Representative Fiorello LaGuardia, of New York, on December 12 introduced a resolution to determine whether the State Department was inspiring propaganda concerning communism in Mexico and Mexican activities in Nicaragua. A St. Louis reporter had stirred his suspicion by charging the State Department with propagating news

[12] To American knowledge, gun-running ships were the *Tropical, Foam, Jalisco, Star,* and *Palonita.* See *New York Times,* Nov. 18, 1926, p. 1. In 1932 Salomón de la Selva, a supporter of Sandino and Nicaraguan labor leader, reported that "Mexico aided Sacasa, took him from the waiting rooms of the State Department, carried him to Mexico, and sent him to Puerto Cabézas, Nicaragua, to organize a government which it recognized immediately." *New York Times,* Dec. 4, 1932, sect. 4, p. 7. Hubert Herring in *A History of Latin America,* 2nd rev. ed. (New York, 1961), pp. 465–466, n. 4, notes that the activities of Sacasa's representative in Mexico and the labor boss Luis Morones, who was detailed by Calles to help the Nicaraguan Liberals, were known to all observers, including Herring, in Mexico at the time.

[13] *New York Times,* Nov. 19, 1926, p. 2.

[14] Denny, *Dollars for Bullets,* p. 245; *New York Times,* Nov. 21, 1926, p. 2.

about Bolshevism. Kellogg denied that the department or any of
its officers had used any news agency to put out information concerning Mexico without assuming responsibility for it.[15] He
declined to discuss whether the department had information
about Bolshevik activities in Mexico or Nicaragua.

Other events confused American opinion. Díaz issued the
manifesto in which he predicted all sorts of dire things. Shortly
afterward, a Mexican refugee and former provisional president,
Adolfo de la Huerta, accused the Calles regime of Bolshevistic
tendencies. Then American troops, on December 24, 1926,
landed at Puerto Cabézas, seat of the Mexican-recognized Sacasa
government.

Charges of communism and the landing of Marines kept
United States-Nicaraguan-Mexican relations on the front pages.
Some editors felt this country had concern about any government
in Central America and that the course of the State Department
was "fully justified by all precedents and experience." This argument contended that "a spread southward of the peculiar form of
radicalism represented by the Calles Government would spell
trouble at Panama." America's canal rights seemed the center of
support for the government. The New York Herald Tribune saw
the Panama Canal and Nicaraguan canal rights as "national
assets of vast importance, which the Bolshevization of Nicaragua
would endanger." And there was a large amount of hostile editorial opinion. The Newark News believed talk about Bolshevism
was nonsense. Other papers saw the charge of communism as
propaganda, the State Department trying "to build up a background for future action, either in Nicaragua or Mexico, or
both."[16]

Senator Borah, chairman of the Foreign Relations Committee,
said he did not feel troops were necessary in Nicaragua. Talking

---

[15] "Mexico and Central America," Current History, XXV (Feb., 1927),
763–764. See also New York Times, Jan. 4, 1927, p. 3.

[16] All quotations in this paragraph are taken from "Mexico's Hand in
Nicaragua," The Literary Digest, vol. 91 (Dec. 4, 1926), 14.

with Kellogg he softened his remarks and admitted the United States should protect its people, no more. Senator Burton K. Wheeler announced that American troops should withdraw from Nicaragua; otherwise he would introduce a resolution for withdrawal. American forces were there, he said, in violation of the United States Constitution and disregard of American principles. As to charges of Bolshevism, only simple souls who believed in Santa Claus would swallow such hypocrisies.[17] Early in January, 1927, Wheeler introduced his resolution. He declared that American lives were not in danger and that Sacasa was rightful president; only United States aid could keep Díaz in office. The resolution received little attention, as the Coolidge administration continued to protect Americans in Nicaragua.

With hundreds of Marines entering Nicaragua, the White House announced they were going in not only because of American lives and property but to protect the canal route. The State Department spokesman refused to say which interest was paramount. To a direct question he replied the department could not assert that a Sacasa victory would threaten America's right to build a canal and establish naval bases, but such might be the result.[18]

The administration turned also to history to justify its policies. Department researchers discovered a half-century-old idea—the Evarts doctrine. William M. Evarts, secretary of state from 1877 to 1881, once had told the American minister to Mexico that the first duty of a government was to protect life and property. A government even had the duty to protect nationals who were in jeopardy by neglect of another government in whose territory they lived.

Then there was the American goal of preserving peace and stability in Central America. Charles Evans Hughes, pointing the way, had hoped to squelch Central American revolutions by

[17] The United States Daily, Dec. 29, 1926, pp. 1, 11; Dec. 30, 1926, p. 3.
[18] New York Times, Jan. 4, 1927, p. 1.

refusing recognition to any government brought to power by a coup d'état. Under Hughes's aegis the Central American countries signed at Washington in 1923 a General Treaty of Peace and Amity, which included this provision. Reviewing the 1923 treaty, President Coolidge now contended Díaz should have recognition, for in administration eyes Díaz was the constitutional president and attempts to oust him were illegal.

President Coolidge came forward "unexpectedly, diplomatically, with a Rooseveltian suddenness" on January 10, 1927, and asserted in a message to Congress that although conditions in Nicaragua and his government's policies were known, he felt it time for a statement. Reviewing events from the election of 1924 to January, 1927, he said that Sacasa had been out of the country from Chamorro's coup d'état until December, 1926, remaining in Mexico and Guatemala most of the time even though revolution had broken out against Chamorro during the period. The United States therefore was correct in recognizing the president designated by a congress which was about the same as that elected in 1924; the Nicaraguan constitution provided such a course in the absence of both president and vice-president. As for Mexican help for the revolutionists, Coolidge said he had evidence that Nicaraguan Liberals were receiving Mexican arms and munitions.

The President turned to protection of American lives and property. Americans were in Nicaragua developing industries and business, and the local government encouraged their activity. Revolution endangered people and industries. The United States, Coolidge continued, had owed them protection and in crisis had taken measures at the request of the Nicaraguan government. He spoke of the United States' "peculiar responsibility." The United States had rights in the Nicaraguan canal route, along with obligations from investments of citizens in Nicaragua. There was no desire to intervene in internal affairs of Nicaragua or any other Central American republic. The American nation had interest in order and good government. Stability, prosperity, independence of all Central American countries were not matters of indifference. The United States could not fail to view with concern any threat to stability and constitutional government in Nicaragua which jeopardized American interests, especially if outside influences or any foreign power contributed to it or brought it about. Coolidge pointed out the policy of the United States in such circumstances—to take steps for the protection of lives, property, and the interests of its citizens.[19]

The administration was not through with explanations. Kellogg appeared on January 12, 1927, before the Foreign Relations Committee with a memorandum on communism, an interesting compilation of Red intent. He pointed out that Bolshevik leaders had ideas concerning Mexico and Latin America and one of their goals was to destroy American "imperialism." He quoted from the third congress of the Red International of Trade Unions, from the executive committee of the Communist International, and from the Workers' Party of America, all about anti-American goals in Latin America. There was, he said, an All-America Anti-Imperialist League, founded by communists and taking orders from Moscow, whose purpose was to organize Latin America against the United States. Under questioning, Kellogg stressed keeping the Nicaraguan government friendly toward the United States, if only because of America's canal rights. The Secretary believed the United States would begin constructing the waterway in a few years. Defending quick recognition of Díaz, he said that the quicker a nation recognized a constitutional government the quicker it could make adjustments and settlements.[20]

Reaction to the Coolidge and Kellogg pronouncements was mixed in the United States, hostile in Latin America, generally hostile with amused sarcasm in Europe. Mexico repeated its denials of interference in Nicaragua and disclaimed trying to establish a Bolshevik hegemony. Newspapers south of the border

[19] *Foreign Relations: 1927*, III, 288–298.
[20] Testimony of Kellogg before the Committee on Foreign Relations of the Senate, Jan. 12, 1927, Minnesota State Historical Library, Frank B. Kellogg papers, box 19; testimony of Kellogg to Senate Foreign Relations Committee, Jan. 12, 1927, 817.00/5304a.

editorialized that Kellogg's charge of communism was mere
bugaboo, arousing people of the United States to support his
policies. European comment spoke of how America was discover-
ing the slipperiness of the imperialist slope. In the United States,
Borah continued attacking administration policy—which he
described as "mahogany and oil policy." He proposed that the
Foreign Relations Committee go to Mexico and Nicaragua to
investigate.

Hostile congressmen did not believe the Díaz presidency constitutional or that Marines should be in Nicaragua to support a
usurper. Like Senator Borah, most of them felt Díaz was involved
in the Chamorro revolution and thus disqualified for the presidency under the Washington treaty of 1923. They contended
the administration's policies were not only illegal but leading the
country to war with Mexico.

Strangely—and while the Nicaraguan problem was far from
settled, and with trouble between the United States and Mexico
increasing during December, 1926, and January, 1927—by the
end of January the sense of trouble had passed. There had been
no large reason for conflict with Mexico. No one, least of all Coolidge and Kellogg, wanted a conflict. The talking probably served
to stop some of the more extreme allegations and accusations.

To individuals friendly to the United States, Coolidges's statement to the Nicaraguan minister on January 20 was reassuring.
The President expressed hope that Nicaragua's internal dissension would end. He spoke of American forces in the minister's
country and referred to their presence at Nicaragua's request.
They should not stay longer than necessary. "The United States,
as I know your Government and the people of Nicaragua fully
appreciate, has no selfish aims or imperialistic designs to serve."
Further, Coolidge continued, the United States did not want to
interfere with Nicaragua's internal affairs but desired independence and prosperity for every Central American country.[21]

Administration charges against Mexico were partly a lashing

[21] *Foreign Relations: 1927*, III, 301–302.

out against a despoiler of the fruits of victory. The United States had held out against Chamorro in the interest of Central American stability and had thought to untie the Nicaraguan knot by recognizing Díaz. When the plans went awry, injured pride and prestige looked for reasons. From that time Washington would not look on Sacasa's movement as anything but a revolution against a rightful government.

6: THE MARINES RETURN

The Latin American policy of the United States has seldom won many friends south of the Rio Grande. Often there has been too much of the "big stick," perhaps too much condescension, and frequently a clash of civilizations. The post-World War I period, while not bringing a bright new era to our relations with the southern continent, seemed however to presage a slight change toward the better. The obvious desire to get out of Nicaragua in 1925 was evidence of this change. On the other hand, the return of American troops about a year later did extreme damage to American prestige. With the probable exception of Roosevelt's role in the Panamanian revolution, the second intervention in Nicaragua caused more ill will in Latin America than any other event in our diplomacy with that area during the first sixty years of the century.

In face of mounting revolution in Nicaragua, establishment of neutral zones by American Marines seemed the best way to protect American lives and property. The second Marine intervention began haltingly in late spring 1926 when Liberals first unfurled the flag of rebellion; by the first few months of 1927 Marines had spread out to cover most of the important towns of Nicaragua. Although Washington at first sent these forces to protect Americans, they could not help becoming involved in the revolution. Their presence shored the tottering Díaz government. The occupation thus returned the United States to the position it held vis-á-vis Nicaragua prior to the ill-planned 1925 withdrawal.

From the outset, landing the Marines had a clear political meaning. In late August, 1926, after the Nicaraguan government told American nationals that in case of fighting it could not guarantee their safety, American forces landed at Bluefields. When fighting increased in December, 1926, Marines landed at Río Grande Bar and Puerto Cabézas. The latter town was important politically, for it was the seat of the Sacasa government.

To land Marines at Puerto Cabézas seemed an affront to Sacasa's dignity. The Liberals reported that landing officers had given Sacasa a violent verbal warning and had told him that all territory within rifle range of American property was a neutral zone. The Liberals could leave with their arms by four o'clock the next afternoon or stay without arms; in addition they could not send radio messages bearing on the war. Sacasa reportedly was astonished and strongly protested such treatment, to no avail. His capital was disarmed and occupied. The insurgents naturally felt that American action was political, aimed at defeating the Liberals.

The State Department, of course, denied this, reiterating that the neutral zone was only to protect American and foreign lives and property. American fruit and lumber companies and mines with properties at or near Puerto Cabézas had asked for protection. Americans had interests in Bluefields and more in Puerto Cabézas. The latter locality, in fact, was almost a company town of the Bragman's Bluff Lumber Company. This company had protested conditions around its holdings. Shortly thereafter Marines arrived.[1] Admiral Latimer was to prevent revolutionists from interfering with American citizens and companies in lawful discharge of commercial duties.[2]

The State Department, facing criticism for intervening, hoped to make its pressure as light as possible. It wanted to assure that American forces followed their avowed purposes, and that they

[1] Anderson diary, Dec. 24, 1926, box 7; H. N. Denny, *Dollars for Bullets* (New York, 1929), p. 262.
[2] *Foreign Relations: 1926*, II, 818–819.

preserved strictest neutrality. Nonetheless at the beginning there was confusion of aims between the State and Navy departments. The latter, after consultation with Stokeley W. Morgan of the State Department's Latin American division, sent instructions to Latimer concerning neutral zones. The Navy Department expressed hope that the zones, in addition to giving needed protection to Americans, would also control Liberal bases on the coast and cut off supplies from outside. The message gave Latimer discretion to choose places and measures for neutral zones and even suggested that the Navy's action might make the Liberal bases untenable.[3] When a paraphrase of these instructions came to Kellogg's attention ten days later, it disturbed him, for he felt the message could mean intervention in hostilities. The Secretary of State asked that explicit instructions be sent to the admiral not to intervene in the internal affairs of Nicaragua.

Kellogg, Secretary of the Navy Curtis D. Wilbur, and President Coolidge then drafted a telegram to Latimer making clear what the administration wanted:

> The following instructions for your guidance; neutral zones should be of local nature only and solely for the protection of lives and property of Americans and foreigners. There should be nothing in the nature of intervention or interference with the internal affairs of Nicaragua. Arms and ammunition found in the neutral zones at Río Grande and Puerto Cabézas should be returned to owners. . . . But in the future no arms or ammunition or armed forces of either party should be allowed to pass through the neutral zones.[4]

Regardless of these instructions, it still seemed that the United States was discriminating against the Liberals. Although intended for regulation of neutral zones, the new instructions hurt the Liberals more than they hurt the Díaz government. Equally

[3] Secretary of Navy to secretary of state, Dec. 18, 1926, Navy branch, National Archives, record group 80, secretary's files, folder 117–24. Hereafter cited as secretary's files.

[4] Secretary of Navy to secretary of state, Dec. 29, 1926, 817.00/4366.

damaging were two messages sent out a few days later. One directed the commander of the special service squadron not to allow use of Puerto Cabézas and Río Grande for revolutionary operations; the other authorized the admiral, if asked by Díaz, to seize arms and ammunition brought into Nicaragua by unauthorized persons.[5]

Whatever the purpose of American Marines in Nicaragua, there was no easy way to explain their presence. Secretary Kellogg had trouble with fine distinctions between protection of foreigners and intervention in the internal affairs of Nicaragua. Americans had established neutral zones only where a Liberal attack seemed imminent and Conservative defenders had declared themselves unable to protect foreign interests, or at Liberal-controlled areas where revolutionists might interfere with American citizens or companies. Thus Washington relieved the Díaz regime of responsibility for protecting such areas and gave Díaz' troops a haven in case of defeat. At the same time the Díaz government continued to receive taxes from the neutral zones. Taxes belonged to the legal government—which to the United States meant Díaz. When Sacasa attempted to collect an export tax on mahogany logs, Latimer instructed United States-owned companies to pay taxes only to Conservatives.[6]

Other actions created friction between Americans and the insurgents. After the Marine landing at Puerto Cabézas, Liberals charged radio censorship of their messages. The State Department first denied the charge but then admitted that American forces had imposed censorship and now had lifted it. There was also the question of two million rounds of Liberal ammunition which a Marine detachment had lost. Again the State Depart-

[5] Secretary of Navy to secretary of state, Jan. 5, 1927, secretary's files, folder 117–24; office of naval operations to commander, special service squadron, Jan. 5, 1927, secretary's files, folder 117–24.

[6] New York Times, Dec. 26, 1926, p. 1.

ment was confused but finally admitted that it had lost some ammunition.[7]

Yet the Coolidge administration tried to avoid enforcing peace by a large American detachment. This aloofness bothered one other Central American government besides Nicaragua. The representative of El Salvador in Managua commented to Díaz and Eberhardt that his government regretted hasty recognition of Díaz in view of unchecked Mexican aid to the revolution. The Salvadorian feared Mexican displeasure might result in a decision to overthrow his own government, "since it was generally understood that the United States was not disposed to check Mexican armed expeditions against Central American republics, thereby leaving Mexico a free hand."[8]

Such a statement naturally helped Díaz, who since his inauguration had tried to gain the all-out backing of the State Department. Díaz well knew that his government rested on the support of Washington, and, understandably, he spent much of his time keeping the United States interested in him and suspicious of his enemies. Near the end of December, 1926, he broached the matter of support again, in the form of some questions to which, he said, he wanted definite answers. Was the United States government disposed to take measures which would check Mexican

[7] *New York Times*, Dec. 20, 1926, p. 3; Dec. 31, 1926, p. 3; Mar. 9, 1927, p. 1; Denny *Dollars for Bullets*, pp. 265–266. American landings caused much hostile comment in the foreign press. Latin American editorial writers, smarting at intrusion in a sister republic, waxed vehement. Perfidy, hypocrisy, illicit interest characterized the "modern Phoenicians, temple money lenders, and atavistic slave drivers" of Washington. Another, more justly, noted Roosevelt's big stick was in the hands of Kellogg, who was creating intense feeling against the United States in Latin America. From Canada to France, Norway to Italy, newspapers reported interference, imperialism, trickery, swashbuckling. Department of State records contain clippings of the press comment. See for example file numbers 711.17/55, 711.17/56, 711.17/57, 711.17/60, 711.17/61, 711.17/66, 711.17/69, 711.17/70, 711.17/76, 711.17/99, 711.17/102.

[8] Eberhardt to Department of State, Dec. 31, 1926, 817.00/4334.

aid to Liberals? Did the United States consider it possible for the
Nicaraguan government, with the means at its disposal and no
outside assistance, to resist the Mexican-aided revolution? Did
the United States feel that Nicaragua should carry on the struggle down to defeat, involving destruction of life and property, or
should Nicaragua surrender at once to the Mexican-aided revolutionists? Disclaiming complaint, desiring only information, Díaz
explained that he thought recognition implied that the United
States would not allow revolution.[9] These were embarrassing,
not to say loaded, questions, and the department held off giving
answers. Nevertheless, the wait would be only a short one.

Presence of American forces on the east coast did not halt the
Liberal campaign. At Pearl Lagoon on Christmas Day, 1926,
Conservative forces lost a fight and had to retire to the El Bluff-
Bluefields area. Victory gave Liberals access to the Escondido
River. Díaz ordered his troops to defend the river, but at the
same time turned to the United States with the familiar "I can-
not guarantee protection of foreign interests." In quick succes-
sion, on January 8, 9, and 10, 1927, United States naval forces
created neutral zones at Pearl Lagoon, Prinzapolca, and Rama.
All important points on the east coast were in American hands.

At the turn of the year military activity therefore switched to
the west. As General Moncada made plans for leading his troops
out of the Mosquito coast, another Liberal army was forming in
the northwest. These developments caused anxiety for Díaz and
his supporters.

American interest now turned to the Pacific side of Nicaragua.
Reports came to the State Department that conditions in Managua were serious and American citizens were receiving threats.
The cruiser *Galveston* appeared at Corinto, and by January 7,
1927, a force of one hundred sixty American troops had settled
in barracks of the Campo de Marte in Managua. Díaz, hard
pressed by dwindling finances and rebellious troops, was delighted by this prop to his regime.

[9] Eberhardt to Department of State, Dec. 29, 1926, 817.00/4326.

Soon after the legation guard returned to Managua, Kellogg instructed Minister Eberhardt to encourage Díaz to find a way to end disaffection and bring peace to the nation. Measures to protect American lives and property might, the Secretary admitted, stabilize Nicaragua and enable Díaz to reestablish order, but they would not bring a lasting peace. No matter how constitutional a government might be, it could not maintain itself by relying upon support from the government of the United States. Nicaragua's government should lay its own foundations for stability.[10]

To forestall complete intervention Washington pressed for mediation, but mediation was difficult to arrange. President Ricardo Jiménez of Costa Rica had offered his assistance, which Sacasa accepted; Kellogg, too, made clear that he would be glad for Costa Rica to mediate.[11] But Díaz refused the offer, asserting that Jiménez had expressed prejudice against his regime. Suggesting, perhaps, that Jiménez was not knowledgeable about the actual conditions in Nicaragua, Díaz countered with an offer to send a delegation to inform him of them.

In mid-January, 1927, Díaz announced his own plan for ending Nicaragua's difficulties. He proposed to finish his term but to bring Liberals into executive and judicial posts and permit their election to Congress without opposition in districts where the revolution had prevented elections. Looking to 1928, he suggested that the United States supervise the election. He wanted American troops to train a national police force. The President also recognized the need for economic rehabilitation and indicated he would seek a large loan from the United States for construction work.[12]

Shortly after Díaz made known his peace offers, a Liberal delegation met with the President and revealed that while Sacasa was sympathetic toward most of the Díaz proposals, he thought the presidency should go to someone outside the Conservative and

---

[10] Department of State to Eberhardt, Jan. 10, 1927, 817.00/4394a.
[11] New York Times, Jan. 16, 1927, p. 1.
[12] Ibid.

Liberal parties. Eberhardt opposed such a solution; he felt it
was impractical, certain to lead to another Solórzano-Sacasa fiasco,
meant a Mexican triumph, and would eliminate Díaz, who was
the only person who could and would carry out a conciliatory
program.[13]

The department agreed with its minister. Morgan of the Latin
American division looked on Sacasa's plan as a last attempt to
gain a partial victory by eliminating Díaz. In a memorandum
Morgan wrote that no doubt Mexico was encouraging the Liberal leader because it could save some face by bringing about the
fall of Díaz. Morgan also thought it would hurt the United States
policy of according moral support to recognized governments.
Throughout his memorandum ran the theme of United States
prestige. America must avoid any appearance of fearing Mexico
or of backing down in face of anti-American criticism. The assistant chief of the Latin American division explained that there was
a feeling below the Rio Grande that this country could be controlled, in large part, by propaganda, criticism, and appeals to the
Senate over the head of the secretary of state; retreat now would
confirm belief in these tactics. Apparently Morgan accepted ill
will as a natural part of United States-Latin American relations.
To him the Nicaraguan affair did not change anything; it simply
provided an opportunity for "irresponsible elements such as student and labor organizations and professional journalists whose
living depends on the sensational character of their writing" to
bring the hostility to the surface. After Mexico interfered in
Nicaragua, Morgan could see only two possibilities for United
States policy—suffer criticism or suffer a serious loss of prestige.[14]
Of these choices the State Department preferred the former.

Within a few days Secretary Kellogg spoke out on the Nicaraguan problem with the intention of making his position clear
to Sacasa. It was not the department's intention to urge Díaz to
accept foreign mediation based on withdrawal of both Díaz and

[13] Eberhardt to Department of State, Jan. 23, 1927, 817.00/4456.
[14] Memorandum prepared by Morgan, Jan. 24, 1927, 817.00/4868.

Sacasa. The United States would not recognize a government headed by Sacasa or anybody else if based on armed force or insurrection; the Díaz government was the only government which, under the Nicaraguan constitution, the United States could and would recognize until the next regular election.[15]

Notwithstanding United States backing, Díaz considered his burdens heavy. He was weary of financial and revolutionary troubles, and he indicated to a newsman that he was ready to give way to someone if that course seemed best to the United States. It did not, and five days later Foreign Minister Cuadra Pasos denied that Díaz would resign. Reports of willingness to step down were, he said, misinterpretations.[16]

Meanwhile the war resumed ominously in the west. Fighting had broken out around Chinandega, not far from Corinto and on the rail line from that port to Managua. Several blocks of the town caught fire during the Liberal attack, which at first went well for the revolutionists. The government troops, however, gained their positions, although the Liberal danger in the area remained. The importance of Chinandega was obvious. The battle there temporarily cut the capital's main communication and supply lines with the coast. People in Managua were extremely uneasy; American troops there would also be in an awkward position if Chinandega fell to the insurgents.

The Nicaraguan government, now seeking to emphasize the unsuitability of halfway intervention, used its minister in Washington to intimate that the United States should help in the emergency. Interestingly, while facing the adverse trend in the revolution, proclaiming loudly against Sacasa and Mexican intervention, and covering Nicaragua with troops, the United States still thought it could avoid fighting. This government informed the minister that his own government was responsible for order

[15] Secretary of state to secretary of Navy, Jan. 27, 1927, 817.00/4496a; Department of State to Arthur H. Geissler, minister in Guatemala, Jan. 27, 1927, 817.00/4438.
[16] New York Times, Feb. 10, 1927, p. 5; Feb. 15, 1927, p. 2.

and communications. United States forces would not engage the revolutionists. Should the latter be successful, Kellogg cabled Eberhardt, they too would be expected to protect American lives and property and maintain communications for American forces in Managua.[17]

But as likelihood of attacks on Chinandega or other cities continued, Admiral Latimer received permission on February 14 to use his forces to keep the railroad open and establish neutral zones along the railroad where he deemed it necessary to safeguard lives and property of American and foreign citizens. Six days later Marines and bluejackets were patrolling not only the railroad but also Chinandega and León to make sure there would be no fighting within two thousand yards around the railway or around the cities of Corinto, Chinandega, León, and Managua, as well as smaller places scattered along the line.[18] In addition twelve hundred more Marines prepared to leave Hampton Roads for Corinto.

Mild warnings came from the Liberal camp. Earlier Sacasa had asserted, no doubt partly to impress his American sympathizers, that he had done everything possible to avoid trouble with Marines but that in due course Marines would have to open fire against Liberals, as in 1912. Beginning on March 1 incidents occurred in which Americans were fired upon and Marines sometimes returned fire.

Then came an unexpected diplomatic démarche. In the midst of America's increasing intervention in Nicaragua, Great Britain took concern for the safety of its citizens. As early as the first few days in January, 1927, before American forces had arrived in Managua, both the British and Italian chargés d'affaires believed their fellow citizens in imminent peril, but within a couple of days the legation guard was ensconced in the Campo de Marte

[17] Foreign Relations: 1927, III, p. 309.
[18] Office of naval operations to commander, special service squadron, Feb. 14, 1927, secretary's files, folder 117–24; El Diario Nicaragüense (Granada), Feb. 24, 1927, p. 2.

and things looked safer. On February 19, after rebel activity had increased in the west, the British government reminded Kellogg that it hoped the United States would protect British subjects and property in Nicaragua. Not receiving what it thought was a satisfactory answer from either Managua or Washington, it informed the State Department on February 23 that the cruiser H.M.S. *Colombo* was on its way to Corinto. The ambassador to Washington, Sir Esme Howard, explained that his government felt the war vessel might have a moral effect and be a refuge for British subjects. He assured Kellogg that the British government had no intention of landing troops.[19]

The United States did its best to reassure the British. The department told Sir Esme that American forces would be pleased "to extend to British subjects such protection as may be possible and proper under the circumstances." This answer was not unexpected, since one of the long-standing arguments for American intervention in Latin America had been that it prevented action from other countries. Nonetheless, the *Colombo* went to Corinto to protect two hundred Britishers and two and a half million dollars invested in Nicaragua. The Coolidge administration's reaction was tranquil. Acting Secretary of State Joseph C. Grew acknowledged the British decision, noting the stated intention not to land troops. The United States did not consider the affair any violation of the Monroe Doctrine or any opposition to American policy in the area.[20]

Because British action came when there was criticism of American policy and since the administration was calm in its response, speculation arose about collusion between the two governments. The Liberal agent in Washington ridiculed the excuse for sending the *Colombo* and charged that the two governments had staged the event to make Americans believe Nicaraguan con-

[19] Eberhardt to Department of State, Jan. 4, 1927, 817.00/4352; Sir Esme Howard to Department of State, Feb. 24, 1927, 817.00/4610.

[20] Memorandum of conversation between Howard and Joseph C. Grew, Feb. 24, 1927, 817.00/4615; *New York Times*, Feb. 25, 1927, p. 2.

ditions justified Latimer's activities. A few senators added their
gibes. Senator Borah, leader of Nicaraguan critics, mused that
little Nicaragua, 600,000 people, was trying to maintain its duly
elected president. It was already surrounded by a naval force
sufficient to reduce it to ruin overnight. "In addition we are
informed the British Navy may move to the scene of conflict.
There are a few Italians there. I suppose the Italian Navy will
cease its watch upon the Mediterranean Sea and move to Caribbean waters."[21] Even the Washington bureau of the New York
Times saw evidence of some quiet prior agreement between
Britain and the United States.[22] Despite the many charges, there
was no proof they were any more than speculation. Whatever
Britain's reason for sending the Colombo, it obviously was not
needed to protect British lives. It left a few days after it arrived.

Meanwhile the United States buildup continued. Over two
thousand American bluejackets and Marines were in Nicaragua,
but there was still no indication of any lessening of revolutionary activity. The war-weary regime in Managua blamed its lack
of success on America's limited intervention. Díaz wanted more
support; a neutral-zone policy was inadequate. The United
States should guarantee the sovereignty and independence of
Nicaragua—which until the next general election meant the
Díaz government.

In late Febraury, 1927, Díaz proposed a treaty of alliance
between the United States and Nicaragua.[23] The Díaz treaty—a
Nicaraguan Platt Amendment—would have made Nicaragua a
protectorate. The pact would have allowed the United States
to intervene to maintain a government for protection of life,
property, and liberty. Nicaragua would pledge not to contract
financial obligations without consent of the American government. Nor would the country sell or lease territory or perform
any act which would impair its independence. Díaz suggested

[21] Charles W. Hackett, "United States Intervention in Nicaragua,"
Current History, XXVI (Apr., 1927), 106.

[22] Ibid.; Denny, Dollars for Bullets, p. 284.

[23] The State Department did not officially receive the Díaz proposal
until Mar. 16.

three conventions to the proposed treaty—a financial plan, sanitary plan, and plan of security and national tranquillity.[24] It was a sweeping proposal which he felt ought to bring peace, prosperity, and happiness to Nicaragua, albeit at the cost of strict independence.

The American minister, Eberhardt, liked the proposal, and he reported that most Nicaraguans, regardless of party affiliation, approved it.[25] General Latin American criticism, he believed, would be less than for any other plan of intervention; and intervention, he assumed, was the only solution for the Nicaraguan problem. In fact, intervention under such a treaty would allow the United States to withdraw Marines in a short while, since the pact would pave the way for a large loan, an adequate constabulary, and political stability.[26]

The United States government was not prepared to accept the Nicaraguan proposal and cautioned Eberhardt not to encourage Nicaraguans to believe such a treaty was acceptable. Even if the treaty were favored by the State Department, it was unlikely that the Senate would ratify such an agreement.

In early 1927 there was another attempt to resolve the conflict. A Liberal party caucus in Managua commissioned a group of leaders to visit General Moncada and hold talks for an armistice and settlement. In the meeting Moncada refused to commit himself on the grounds that he would have to consult Sacasa but stated willingness to negotiate for peace if this were done through the American minister. He opposed Díaz as president but was

[24] Foreign Relations: 1927, III, 472–475.

[25] On Feb. 25, 1927, the Nicaraguan Congress supported the Díaz proposal by a vote of forty-five to ten; the Conservatives unanimously in favor, while the Liberals opposed it. Eberhardt interpreted opposition as largely a matter of form. (711.1711/2). Nonetheless, a representative of Sacasa filed a protest against the treaty. T. Seydel Vaca to Department of State, Mar. 26, 1927, 711.1711/10. The editor of El Diario Nicaragüense, Feb. 26, 1927, p. 1, believed such a treaty would establish order and prosperity.

[26] Eberhardt to Department of State, Feb. 25, 1927, 711.1711/1.

willing to accept a government administered by the United States until the election of 1928.[27]

Moncada's attitude toward the United States was surprisingly friendly and trusting. He indicated that the U.S. could help bring fair elections. The general had heard of Díaz's proposed treaty and approved of a defensive-offensive pact with the United States, although he opposed the loan proposal.[28] He did not question American motives or believe them the cause of the war. He indicated that fighting might continue until the United States intervened or fired on Liberal forces. In the latter case it would end for him, because he was unwilling to fight the United States.[29] Reports from the Moncada camp gave evidence the United States might be able to bring a negotiated peace. These reports also came at a time when the American government was examining its policy.

For the State Department the Nicaraguan situation had reached an unsatisfactory state, perilously close to involving American troops in the fighting. The United States had acted with expectation that Díaz would succeed. Never having decided what its policy would be if this appeared unlikely, by mid-March, 1927, the department began to consider the possibility. The Latin American division saw two courses. The United States could continue as before—establish neutral zones but insist that the contenders themselves must find a solution to the revolution —allowing loss of life and property and perhaps eventually bringing intervention to save Díaz. The other course was immediate intervention, preferably before the revolution overthrew Díaz.[30]

The Coolidge administration decided to negotiate. Coolidge now sent down Henry L. Stimson, the onetime secretary of war, with instructions to investigate and report and, if a chance were presented, straighten matters out. Stimson and his party left New York aboard the Chilean steamship Aconcagua on April 9.

[27] Eberhardt to Department of State, Mar. 7, 1927, 817.00/4640.
[28] El Diario Nicaragüense, Mar. 8, 1927, p. 2.
[29] New York Times, Mar. 7, 1927, p. 2; Mar. 8, 1927, p. 27.
[30] Memorandum prepared in division of Latin American affairs, Mar. 18, 1927, 817.00/4849.

7: THE STIMSON MISSION

For Henry L. Stimson it was a fascinating experience to go to Nicaragua and try to set things straight, for he had not done much government service in recent years—indeed, not since he had been mustered out of the Army at the end of the World War. In the dreary Harding years Stimson felt unwelcome in Washington and shared "the oblivion which overtook most of the younger eastern Republicans during the early 1920's."[1] Even during the early years of Coolidge's administration, he failed to establish a connection with the White House. For nearly a decade Stimson had been outside of things. Although he was busy with his law practice and community affairs, these were probably not the happiest years of his life. In 1926 Stimson's retirement from public service came to an end when he worked briefly on the Tacna-Arica dispute between Chile and Peru and made an unofficial trip to the Philippines. Afrer returning from the Far East he enjoyed two friendly visits with Coolidge, and from then on opportunities for service were more frequent. With gusto he prepared to take himself and Mrs. Stimson off to Nicaragua to see what was wrong and how he could put it aright.

Before leaving, the "Colonel" conferred with Coolidge at the White House and asked the President whether he was to have full powers. Coolidge told Stimson to go down and settle things, doing whatever was necessary. The President was tired of the Nicaraguan mess and wanted to get it off his hands. On April

[1] Henry L. Stimson and McGeorge Bundy, *On Active Service in Peace and War* (New York, 1948), p. 107.

97

17, 1927, Henry L. Stimson arrived in Managua with the task of investigating, reporting, and—perhaps—settling Nicaragua's problems. His instructions offered latitude; he could do almost anything he pleased if it would end the Nicaraguan war and extricate the United States.

For some Nicaraguans, Stimson's arrival was long overdue. After the fighting had started the previous summer, the United States had expressed concern for the revolution and had established neutral zones, but the war continued. Nicaraguans were perplexed, since from experience they knew that a hint from Washington often settled otherwise insoluble problems in Central America. Now the appearance of a prominent American had significance for their poor country, for "the powerful American government does not manifest its interests in vain."[2]

The Nicaraguan problem had begun with a constitutional question: Who was rightfully president? Any solution would have to answer this, or at least include agreement on who should hold office until the 1928 election. Such an agreement would have to be coupled with satisfactory guarantees that the election would be fair; otherwise there would be little hope for the conceding party. But to get the contending armies to agree to a cease-fire would be the most difficult part of Stimson's duties. Of course any agreement here would depend again on who should occupy the presidency.

While political and military factors held the fore, there were other issues. Disruption of the nation's economy and depletion of its finances, as well as the inhuman aspects of the fighting, made an end to the situation the more necessary. The Nicaraguan trouble also involved the United States-Mexico conflict. Would the Mexicans approve of whatever arrangements the United States made?

When he accepted the task of mediation, Stimson knew almost nothing about Nicaragua. He used the week before departure to study and confer. He saw the President and Kellogg and went

[2] *El Diario Nicaragüense* (Granada), Apr. 23, 1927, p. 2.

over the issues. He believed, and Coolidge agreed, that he should not reopen the presidential issue: The United States had recognized Díaz, and to review that decision would show weakness. If the Liberals refused to lay down arms, both President and emissary agreed that force would follow; but Coolidge was anxious to avoid it. Stimson, in bringing up the idea of a supervised 1928 election as the best way to bring a settlement, asked if Coolidge were ready to take a chance on Liberal victory. The President replied that he saw no other way if the vote were to be fair.[3]

Meanwhile the department instructed the legation in Managua to keep all avenues of information open for Stimson. On arrival he put himself in touch with persons who might give advice. He conferred with Eberhardt, Latimer, and General Logan Feland, Díaz and other Conservatives, and many Liberals.

In conversation Stimson stressed a free election; to him it lay at the front of the whole problem. His visitors agreed, but Conservatives were usually hazy on details and Liberals not ready to give up claims to the presidency. The Liberals seemed more interested in the present than in what might happen. In counterarguments Stimson emphasized that if fair elections were assured then everyone could probably arrange present difficulties. He advised the Liberals that it was time to sacrifice pride, and if Liberal calculations on party strength were correct, he once told them, by accepting supervised elections Díaz would be sacrificing a Conservative victory.[4]

After a few days of observation Stimson notified the State Department of his impressions. He felt they were important, for

[3] Memorandum of a conference with the President, the Secretary of State, Assistant Secretary Robert E. Olds, and Mr. Stimson, Apr. 7, 1927, found in Henry L. Stimson diary; MS. in the Stimson Collection of the Yale University Library. Hereafter cited as Stimson diary.

[4] Memorandum of interview with Dr. Cuadra Pasos, minister of foreign affairs, Apr. 18, 1927, Stimson diary; memorandum of talk with some Granada Conservatives, Apr. 19, 1927, Stimson diary; memorandum of interview with group of Liberals, Apr. 20, 1927, Stimson diary.

they belied some recent department calculations concerning the military situation. According to reports arriving in the United States during early and mid-April, 1927, Conservative troops had achieved victories at Muy Muy and Tierra Azul. Dispatches indicated that Liberal forces were fleeing in disorder and that an end to the war was possible. Relying on these reports, the department had begun to feel it might have been precipitate in sending a special representative. If Díaz could win the war, that would be fine; the department did not want to interfere with a Conservative victory. It cautioned the legation not to characterize Stimson's mission as mediation, nor did it want pressure on Díaz to give up any advantage won by military operations. Washington did feel that the Nicaraguan government in its moment of victory should exhibit generosity toward the revolutionists. At the same time the department indicated it was reverting to pre-1925 diplomacy—willingness to have a legation guard in Managua for the sake of stability but unwillingness to guarantee fair elections.[5]

To counter this thinking, Stimson quickly notified Washington of his early findings. He had discovered that reports exaggerated Conservative military victories. After their supposedly disorganized flight, Moncada's troops reappeared at Boaco, forty miles from Managua. On May 1, four hundred revolutionists boldly attacked and held for a few hours a small town within twenty-five miles of Managua. One commentator dryly remarked that another crushing defeat would bring Moncada into the capital.[6] Far from being routed and demoralized, the Liberals were ready to continue the fight, if not as organized bodies then as guerrillas. The Díaz government, on the other hand, was almost bankrupt, and Stimson estimated its treasury could last only six weeks.

The department's new reluctance to supervise the 1928 elec-

[5] Department of State to Eberhardt, Apr. 15, 1927, 817.00/4706a.

[6] H. N. Denny, *Dollars for Bullets* (New York, 1929), p. 293; intelligence reports no. 15 and no. 17 of the force intelligence office, naval force on shore in western Nicaragua, Marine Corps files, box 178, folder 200.1. Marine Corps files refer to records in National Archives, Navy branch, concerning Marines in Nicaragua, 1928–32. Hereafter cited as Marine Corps files.

tion troubled Stimson. His feelings were so strong on this point that he indicated his mission would be of little value unless he could use at the bargaining table a promise of supervised elections.[7] This was especially important, since Stimson had been emphasizing to everyone he met that the United States would not reconsider recognition of Díaz. After receiving Stimson's information, the State Department assured the envoy that it was willing to reconsider its policy, adjusting it to allow for election supervision.[8]

After finishing a few days of general talks, Stimson felt it wise to get the Díaz government on record about a settlement, and sitting down with Foreign Minister Cuadra Pasos, he discussed terms. The two men reached agreement, but the Conservative foreign minister expressed doubt that the Liberals would accept the terms. When Cuadra Pasos tried to find out what the United States would do in the event of Liberal refusal, Stimson could not answer.

The following day—April 22, 1927—Díaz handed Stimson an outline of peace terms, essentially those Stimson and Cuadra Pasos had discussed:

1. immediate peace, in time for the new crop, and delivery of arms simultaneously by both parties to American custody;

2. general amnesty, and return of exiles and confiscated property;

3. participation of representative Liberals in Díaz's cabinet;

4. organization on a nonpartisan basis of a Nicaraguan constabulary commanded by American officers;

5. supervision of the election in 1928 and succeeding years by Americans, who would have ample police power;

6. continuance, temporarily, of a force of Marines sufficient to make the foregoing effective.[9]

Armed with proposals as much American as Conservative,

[7] Eberhardt to Department of State, Apr. 20, 1927, 817.00/4714.

[8] Department of State to Eberhardt, Apr. 22, 1927, 817.00/4714.

[9] Henry L. Stimson, American Policy in Nicaragua (New York, 1927), pp. 63–64. See also Eberhardt to Department of State, Apr. 23, 1927, 817.00/4720.

Stimson was ready for the second stage of his mission. Hoping to find out how the Liberals felt, he met with some prominent members of that faction, a few brave souls in Managua. The meeting was not entirely harmonious. Stimson told his visitors that Conservatives had shown a conciliatory spirit which he had not found among the Liberals. Having heard that Liberals were planning a military demonstration to influence his report, Stimson suggested a conciliatory attitude. But the Liberals were not convinced. General Gonzalo Ocón, a member of the directorate of the Liberal party, questioned whether, having recognized Díaz, the United States now intended to become his ally, since, in the face of Liberal successes, he could not maintain himself without United States assistance. Although Stimson expressed doubt about a Liberal victory, he refused to be drawn into a discussion of the military situation. Instead he bluntly queried whether Ocón believed Sacasa could win and establish a permanent regime (something in which Chamorro had failed) in spite of United States refusal to recognize him and the continued presence of Marines to protect American interests menaced by the struggle. Stimson emphasized that United States policy would not change. He suggested the only way out of the impasse was a supervised election.[10]

None too subtly, the American had stated Washington's views, purposely working to destroy any hope which Sacasa might have had for recognition. Understandably the Liberals, believing military victory was within their own grasp, were not happy with Stimson's suggestions, but they finally agreed to submit the proposals to Sacasa.

Although Stimson felt the Conservative terms were generous, he had small hope that Sacasa would accept them. What little hope there was lay in the offer of supervised elections and the idea that both sides should disarm. If Sacasa refused, Stimson feared the United States must either leave the country to anarchy

[10] Memorandum of interview with Liberal group, Apr. 22, 1927, Stimson diary.

or use Marines to disarm insurgents.[11] The American government
had considered neither alternative acceptable, but the State Department, in part because of Stimson's observations, was coming
to see that halfway measures were not enough.

After receiving Stimson's appraisal the department wanted
information about disarmament of rebels. Could American forces
in Nicaragua disarm the insurgents if that measure should be
necessary? How long would it take? Was there likelihood of
guerrilla war? What resistance could insurgents put up against
attempts to disarm them? Lastly, desiring to gain disarmament
without force, the State Department wanted to know whether
an intimation to Sacasa that refusal to accept the Díaz peace
terms would result in forcible disarming by the United States
might bring the rebel president to accept the Díaz offer.[12] Stimson replied that most responsible Liberal military leaders did not
want or intend to fight American forces. Probably there would
be some guerrilla action in remote areas, but on the west coast
he did not expect trouble. He felt that United States troops
already in Nicaragua could do the job, but that eight hundred
reinforcements would help. If he could suggest to Sacasa that
force would follow refusal to disarm, there would be more
chance for success in the talks, especially if at the same time
Admiral Latimer announced that insurgent forces could not cross
the Tipitapa River.[13] Stimson realized that while the threat

[11] Eberhardt to Department of State, Apr. 23, 1927, 817.00/4720.

[12] Department of State to Eberhardt, Apr. 25, 1927, 817.00/4720.

[13] Admiral Latimer received permission to stop insurgents at Tipitapa
River. Stimson diary, Apr. 27, 1927. By Apr. 26, 1927, General Logan
Feland was aware that Moncada's forces (about three thousand men)
had interposed between two parts of the Federal army which were occupying Teustepe and Boaco and that Moncada might defeat them sep-
arately at any time. Feland recommended that the line of the Tipitapa
River be occupied by a Marine regiment to halt the Liberals at the river
if they reached the government forces and attempted to march on Managua. Feland believed this maneuver essential, since it was his understanding that the United States recognized Díaz and did not want him
deposed by the revolutionists. Feland to major general commandant, July

would have an unpredictable effect on rebel politicians, it would convince military leaders. Since Stimson wanted to end the war, military acceptance of the Díaz offer was much more important to him than its acceptance or rejection by the Puerto Cabézas government.

Meanwhile Sacasa had sent his response. It troubled Stimson because of its technical nature, which he felt delayed talks. Although Liberals in Managua felt the latest proposition to Sacasa was not as favorable as that offered at Corinto, they were nevertheless optimistic about the reception it would get from Sacasa. Sacasa recognized the importance of a direct representative from Coolidge and by April 25 did agree to send delegates—Rodolfo Espinosa, his foreign minister; Leonardo Argüello, minister of gobernación; and Manuel Cordero Reyes, his private secretary— to confer with Stimson. The party boarded the destroyer *Preston* on April 27 and two days later was in Managua. Conferences began April 30.

Stimson went to the conference table armed with three important diplomatic-military weapons. He could intimate that Liberals might be disarmed if they refused to agree; he had authority to announce that insurgent troops could not cross the Tipitapa River; he knew reinforcements were available to back American policy.[14] For two days Stimson and Eberhardt talked with

31, 1927, records of Marine Corps units in Nicaragua, 1927–33, box 4, file 13, United States Naval Records Management Center, Historical Branch, G-3, Records and Research Section, Navy Annex, Arlington, Virginia; hereafter cited as Marine Corps in Nicaragua records, Navy Annex.

[14] Department of State to Eberhardt, Apr. 27, 1927, 817.00/4727. The discussions, as they opened, were to be between only the Sacasa delegates and Stimson. Stimson felt, however, that once the Liberals were here their presence would lead to negotiations between the two parties, Stimson aiding. Coolidge's emissary wanted the conference to be wholly a U.S.-Nicaraguan affair. He recorded in his diary, Apr. 30, 1927, that the new foreign minister of Salvador had been trying to get the four other Central American states "to butt into my conference with Sacasa delegates." He wired Secretary Kellogg to try to pull them off.

Sacasa's representatives. Relations were friendly. Argüello thought highly of Coolidge's emissary and told the press that Stimson's attitude would bring justice to the Nicaraguan people. Liberals showed cordial feeling toward the United States, and in their proclamations of friendship there was little to distinguish them from Díaz. They agreed that America should supervise the 1928 election; they recognized an American zone of influence extending to Panama; they believed the United States was the only country which could or should build a Nicaraguan canal and assist in development of the country; and they held that America's moral and technical guidance was in the best interest of Central America.

It was not surprising that Stimson broached the subject of Mexico's aid to the Liberals, approaching it obliquely. Yes, we were interested in the Caribbean region; no, we had no intention of exploitation or tyranny; yes, we did resent intrusion of any other country in the area. Only after these preliminaries did someone refer to Mexico by name. The three Liberal delegates denied any understanding with Mexico which would interfere with relations with the United States. Argüello, credited with a remark at the Corinto conference about an understanding with Mexico, repeated a denial.[15]

A major stumbling block still remained: Díaz in the presidency. Regarding this obstacle the Liberal delegates were "absolutely silent." Rightly or wrongly, Díaz was the personification of the Chamorro coup d'état. Liberals had been fighting him for months, refusing to recognize his claim to the presidency. How could they ignore everything that had happened since November, 1926? To Stimson it was clear that Díaz personally was not objectionable to the Liberals but it was Díaz the symbol they could not accept. One Liberal exclaimed that if "Díaz would only change his name the whole difficulty would be solved!"[16]

[15] New York Times, May 3, 1927, p. 23; Stimson, American Policy in Nicaragua, pp. 71–72; memorandum of second conference with Sacasa delegates, May 1, 1927, Stimson diary.
[16] Stimson, American Policy in Nicaragua, p. 70.

Although appreciating their dilemma, Stimson did not feel the United States or the Conservatives should give way.

While Stimson was taking a cordial but firm stand with the Liberals, the State Department was growing restive; it desired to end the Nicaraguan business, even with sacrifices. The Stimson mission and conferences with the protagonists brought hope of success. The press, generally hostile to Coolidge-Kellogg Nicaraguan diplomacy, supported Stimson, and Washington was not immune to the contagion. Indeed, as a last resort to prevent failure of Stimson's mission, Washington would even encourage Díaz to retire.[17]

However, Stimson would not rush into concessions. His investigation led him to believe Díaz should stay; from the American view he was an ideal president: He was cooperative; he was not eligible for reelection; he was willing to allow United States supervision of elections and, most important, to forgo many executive powers regarding constabulary and election officials, thus insuring fair voting. Stimson's preference for Díaz was further enhanced by his inability to find a suitable substitute president; the men who were suggested had behind them "ulterior expectations of partisanship." The rump Congress could not elect a replacement, nor was the country ready for congressional elections. It was clear that Díaz must retain the executive office until a new president took over according to the constitution, and the Conservative leader must have United States support. Stimson's brief for Díaz brought agreement from the State Department.[18]

After two days of exploratory talks the Liberals desired to reach General José María Moncada, Sacasa's secretary of war and field commander, whose opinions they needed before conversations continued. Stimson welcomed this opportunity to talk with the

---

[17] Department of State to Eberhardt, Apr. 30, 1927, 817.00/4736.

[18] Stimson, American Policy in Nicaragua, pp. 65–70; Eberhardt to Department of State, May 2, 1927, 817.00/4744; Department of State to Eberhardt, May 3, 1927, 817.00/4744.

man who was the most important Liberal in the revolution, excepting perhaps Sacasa. Three American naval officers went through the lines to Moncada's camp with an invitation for the general to meet the negotiators. Moncada viewed the invitation as tantamount to a military order. The tone seemed to reflect Stimson's desire to bring a cease-fire by force if necessary; and, piqued by the peremptory tone of the note, the Liberal leader reflected that one caught more flies with honey than with vinegar.[19] Nonetheless, Moncada called a council of Liberal chiefs to discuss the proposals. Since there were no guarantees for Moncada's safety, the chiefs objected to the trip, but after the American officers promised protection for the general and his party, Moncada agreed to a meeting on May 4, 1927, at Tipitapa, a small village on the river of the same name, not far from Managua.[20] Americans arranged a forty-eight-hour truce, to last until noon on May 5, and five hundred Marines moved between the opposing armies.

While awaiting Moncada the Liberal delegates maintained their anti-Díaz position. On the morning of May 3, Anastasio Somoza—whom Stimson described as a frank, friendly, likeable young Liberal whose attitude impressed him more favorably than almost any other—spent some time with Stimson, urging the North American to make concessions on Díaz.[21] Somoza suggested that Moncada would hold out against retention of Díaz and that most Liberals would support the general, thus preventing an agreement. At one point the future Nicaraguan dictator proposed the return of Solórzano to the presidency, even though the ex-President was weak and vacillating. Stimson remained unmoved; in fact, he became more firmly convinced that opposition to Díaz was only formal, for during the conversation Somoza

[19] José María Moncada, Estados Unidos en Nicaragua (Managua, 1942), pp. 4–5.

[20] Anastasio Somoza, El Verdadero Sandino o El Calvario de las Segovias (Managua, 1936), pp. 19–20.

[21] Somoza would become head of the Nicaraguan government in 1936, a position he held until 1956.

admitted that many Liberals felt Díaz was the best person at that time for the presidency and were opposing him mainly on moral grounds. Brushing aside the moral argument, Stimson pointed out that Coolidge had agreed to undertake the burden of electoral supervision even after the Liberal press had bitterly attacked him as being under the influence of moneyed interests for recognizing Díaz; the emissary thought it inappropriate to ask Coolidge to start his work of reform by an act which could be interpreted as admission of guilt. Besides, Díaz had served well and was the author of the peace plan. The United States might make some concessions but not on the Nicaraguan presidency.[22]

The Tipitapa conference began, as scheduled, on May 4. Moncada had come against the advice of his generals. Stimson believed he could deal with a man who had shared the sufferings of the revolution and who would compromise.[23] José María Moncada, in his middle fifties, was a politician and revolutionist of good education. He had fought against Zelaya in the revolution which had overthrown that dicator and had later been a newspaperman. After the Chamorro coup he joined the Sacasa supporters and rose to head the Liberal forces, although he had not been a professional military man; it was generally believed that the title "general" had been self-assumed. Moncada was not hostile toward the United States; he had already voiced support of Díaz's Platt-Amendment proposals, and even earlier, in 1925 when Congress had debated the constabulary plan with such opposition, Moncada spoke of the debt of gratitude which his country owed America for independence from European greed. Nicaragua needs, he said, to receive civilization as other nations have received it; we cannot civilize ourselves. "Greece received it from Egypt; Italy was aided by the progress of Greece; and for us this civilization will come from the United States" by the strength of our relations with that great nation.[24]

[22] Memorandum of interview with Anastasio Somoza and Gustavo Argüello Cervantes, May 3, 1927, Stimson diary.
[23] Stimson, American Policy in Nicaragua, pp. 75–76.
[24] La Noticia (Managua), Apr. 3, 1925, p. 1.

For about fifteen minutes the Liberal general and the Sacasa representatives conferred, after which Moncada and Stimson sat down alone in the shade of a large blackthorn tree in front of the hotel. Refeshed by the breezes from the lake not far away and watched from a distance by curious local citizenry, the two exchanged views.[25] In broken English, Moncada began. He told Stimson that neither he nor Díaz could pacify the country without United States help. He approved all the proposed peace terms, except retention of Díaz. This he did not feel he could accept. He said, however, that he would not oppose American troops if the United States insisted on Díaz.

Stimson was in a mood to be frank. He told Moncada that Coolidge had instructed him to insist on retention of Díaz as essential to a supervised election. He "was authorized to state that forcible disarmament would be made of those unwilling to lay down their arms." Hearing this, the Liberal commander agreed to recommend that his troops yield, but he wanted a letter giving the United States position. At Moncada's suggestion they called in the other delegates, along with Eberhardt and Latimer. Stimson related what had taken place and repeated his statement. Then the Americans withdrew, leaving the Liberals to deliberate.[26]

During the interval Stimson dictated a letter outlining plans for America's supervision of the 1928 election, retention of Díaz, and general disarmament. United States forces would accept the arms and "disarm forcibly those who will not do so."[27] He later

[25] *El Diario Nicaragüense*, May 5, 1927, p. 2, has a description of the meeting.

[26] Stimson diary, May 4, 1927.

[27] Stimson, *American Policy in Nicaragua*, pp. 76–77; Stimson diary, May 4, 1927; Eberhardt to Department of State, May 4, 1927, 817.00/ 4753. The text of Stimson's letter was: "Dear General Moncada: Confirming our conversation of this morning I have the honor to inform you that I am authorized to say that the President of the United States intends to accept the request of the Nicaraguan Government to supervise the election of 1928; that the retention of President Díaz during the

explained the last sentence was aimed at the bandit fringe, not Moncada's loyal troops. Liberal delegates refused to agree to the settlement, but since they were unwilling to fight the United States, they had no alternative but to recommend that Sacasa yield.

There remained prevention of accidents between the two armies. The conferees agreed to a two-day extension of the truce, during which government troops would pull south of the Tipitapa River. American Marines, ready to receive arms from both sides, took positions between the contenders.

Stimson knew that Moncada's job would not be easy, and he endeavored to keep silent about happenings at the conference table. When he and Eberhardt left for Managua he told the press that the conference was over and there was nothing for publication. The Liberals, too, had little to say, although one spokesman on Moncada's staff indicated that if the United States issued an order that Liberals must cease fighting, they would have to comply.[28]

The following day Stimson and Moncada met in Managua to arrange details of disarmament. The general was to convince his men to turn over their arms within eight days. Liberal soldiers would receive supplies, clothing, and ten dollars for each rifle or machine gun.[29] After this second round of talks Stimson believed the insurgent leaders would cooperate. Moncada prepared to face his troops, first telling an Associated Press correspondent that if fighting continued it seemed certain that the

remainder of his term is regarded as essential to that plan and will be insisted upon; that a general disarmament of the country is also regarded as necessary for the proper and successful conduct of such election; and that the forces of the United States will be authorized to accept the custody of the arms of those willing to lay them down, including the government, and to disarm forcibly those who will not do so."

[28] New York Times, May 5, 1927, p. 16.

[29] Memorandum of understanding as to matters discussed between Stimson, Eberhardt, Latimer, and Moncada as to arrangements for disarmaments, May 5, 1927, Stimson diary.

United States would take the field against the Liberals. The general was ready to lay down arms, for, as he told a group before he returned to his troops, he had no desire for immortality. He thought a fight with the American army would be disastrous for his men and for Nicaragua. Nonetheless, if after he explained the situation to his men they still chose to fight, he would direct them, even against the Americans.[30]

Díaz tried to make the settlement as easy as possible. On May 5 he amnestied all political prisoners and exiles, and announced that freedom of the press would be resumed as soon as disarmament began. He took the first steps toward bringing Liberals into national political life by stating that there would be reconstitution of the Supreme Court as it was prior to the Chamorro coup d'état and that he would appoint Liberal *jefes políticos* in six departments where that party was in the majority.[31]

Moncada now proceeded to Boaco, and there in the plaza he reported to his troops what had transpired. He told his men that continued fighting would mean destruction, that more United States troops would come as they had in 1912. The general recognized his obligation to consult his men, however, and he assured them that if the army desired to continue fighting, he would not abandon it—he would go with his troops to the sacrifice.[32]

Stimson remained in Managua. Perhaps as he waited he philosophized about his mission and his approach to the Nicaraguan problem. As a lawyer he may have considered that his training ideally suited him for stabilizing troubled political situations. Many years later, when summing up his public service, he noted that his legal background had helped him recognize that questions have two sides and that a fair hearing was important in

[30] *New York Times*, May 6, 1927, p. 1. Somoza, *El Verdadero Sandino*. p. 23. Even though Liberals could not resist continuation of Díaz, they would not sign an agreement with that provision.

[31] Eberhardt to Department of State, May 6, 1927, 817.00/4673; Stimson, *American Policy in Nicaragua*, p. 80.

[32] Moncada, *Estados Unidos en Nicaragua*, p. 25.

every controversy. He realized the importance of persuasion as opposed to force or threats, and he recognized the lawyer as a trained advocate of persuasion.[33] In Nicaragua he had negotiated from strength and convinced the important Liberal army leader that his conditions offered more than did fighting. A few days and his success would be complete. Yet waiting bred uncertainty; however confident he might be that logic and power of the United States would determine the affair, there could always be exceptions.

Stimson became edgy. He worried about public opinion, for he did not know how the home press was taking the situation but had received criticism from Central American sources. The Liberals exasperated him. In working out plans for an election law, he found them evasive. At one conference he "blew up" and accused them of not meeting him in a responsive spirit. Moncada's dispatches, too, worried Coolidge's representative. Finally Stimson called another meeting at Tipitapa.[34] On May 11 the two principals met once more under the blackthorn tree by the dry riverbed and clarified points raised by the army. It relieved Stimson to find his fears groundless; Moncada was loyal and apparently had the situation in hand. Stimson told Moncada of unrewarding talks with politicians but noted how different matters were in talking with soldiers; he proposed, he said, to settle the problem with the latter.[35] Before he and Moncada completed their meeting, the American diplomat dictated another letter reiterating United States pledges to train and command a nonpartisan constabulary, supervise a free election, and influence the Díaz government to restore in Nicaragua the prerevolutionary political situation. With regard to the last point he outlined many of the steps already taken. When Stimson revealed his recommendation for reinstatement of congressmen whom Chamorro had illegally ousted and whose terms had not expired, Moncada

---

[33] Stimson and Bundy, *On Active Service in Peace and War*, p. xxii.
[34] Stimson diary, May 7, 1927; May 9, 1927.
[35] *Ibid.*, May 11, 1927.

sensed inconsistency. Had not the admittedly illegal representatives completed the quorum for the election of Díaz, whom the United States then recognized as constitutional President?[36]

The next afternoon Stimson received the following telegram signed by Moncada and all his prominent chiefs except Augusto C. Sandino:

> The military chiefs of the Constitutional Army assembled in session today have agreed to accept the terms of the declaration made by General Henry L. Stimson, personal representative of President Coolidge of the United States, and consequently have resolved to lay down their arms. They hope that there will be immediately sent to receive these arms sufficient forces to guarantee order, liberty and property.[37]

Marines and trucks were dispatched to receive the arms. United States planes dropped thousands of leaflets telling isolated troops about the settlement and offering money for their arms if delivered to the nearest American detachment. By June 6 the armies had turned in more than 14,600 rifles, 339 machine guns, and almost 6,000,000 rounds of ammunition. Although most of this work proceeded smoothly, there were a few skirmishes involving scattered groups before disarmament was complete.[38]

The war was over—at least so Stimson thought and the United States and most Nicaraguans hoped. Accompanied by women and children and bearing their few household goods, troops of both armies crowded the roads toward Managua to turn in their weapons and go home. On Saturday, May 14, Moncada, as if victorious, entered the capital. Thousands greeted him with "Viva Moncada" and "Viva la Revolución!"[39] There was

[36] Moncada, Estados Unidos en Nicaragua, pp. 35–36.

[37] Eberhardt to Department of State, May 12, 1927, 817.00/4775.

[38] Captain Julian P. Brown to General Logan Feland, June 10, 1927, Marine Corps in Nicaragua records, Navy Annex, box 4, file 13.

[39] For an account of Moncada's entry see Arthur Ruhl, The Central Americans (New York, 1928), pp. 90–95. See also Moncada, Estados Unidos en Nicaragua, p. 38.

relief, happiness, some good will toward the United States. If everyone were not friendly, at least there was hope the new constabulary under Colonel Robert Rhea and the promise of free elections in 1928 would ensure a tranquil future.

Stimson, the peacemaker, left Nicaragua on May 16, completing what he considered one of the best months of his life. Although the special envoy received some recognition for his accomplishment, including Collidge's reference to "the eminent services of a peace-loving American to the general cause of humanity," Stimson always felt that Charles Lindbergh's flight to Paris the same month deprived the Nicaraguan venture of much publicity.[40]

How had he brought peace? Stimson later said that he had threatened forcible disarmament because of the bandit fringe, not Moncada's loyal troops. However, the State Department was, in fact, contemplating disarming the insurgents and Stimson told Moncada that Washington had authorized him to disarm those unwilling to do so. In light of this knowledge it appears that Stimson's statement had broader application. Admiral Latimer thought so, for when asked by the Senate Foreign Relations Committee if Stimson's statement had meant that the Liberals must either acquiesce or be disarmed, the admiral said he and Moncada had understood it that way. Some of the Nicaraguan press also accepted this interpretation. El Diario Nicaragüense editorialized, in support of Stimson, that it was no discredit to have imposed peace. The paper said that Stimson did what he could within Nicaragua's possibilities, its state of moral prostration.[41] A few months after his mission Stimson himself commented that "we made Moncada lay down his arms in reliance

[40] Stimson and Bundy, On Active Service in Peace and War, p. 111, 116; New York Times, June 14, 1927, p. 21.

[41] Hearings before the Committee on Foreign Relations, United States Senate, 70th Cong., 1st Sess., pursuant to Senate resolution 137, A Resolution Requesting Certain Information from the Secretary of the Navy Relative to the Use of the Navy in Nicaragua, Feb. 11 and 18, 1928, p. 39; El Diario Nicaragüense, May 18, 1927, p. 2.

upon this promise [supervised elections]." There was more to the Stimson mission than just stopping war; there was willingness to incur responsibilities for Nicaragua's future. Stimson went to Tipitapa with guarantees for the Liberals. Supervised election, nonpartisan constabulary, and complete disarmament were parts of a longer-range program. The American-backed settlement gave greater hope for a stable Nicaragua than did a victorious revolution. America's interest in Nicaragua was, of course, not entirely altruistic. Concern about the Caribbean long had influenced foreign policy. Trouble in Nicaragua threatened United States interests; to stop it Stimson went south. The mission sought to stop the war and keep it stopped.

To much of Latin America the Stimson intervention was the enforced will of a large nation, for it meant weakening the autonomy of a people. It is true that America's actions did not show the customary relations between equal nations. There was much of the paternalistic or white man's burden idea in United States policy, at least in the thinking of the agent of that policy. Stimson felt that nations like Nicaragua were not capable of independent existence; they could not sustain the responsibility that goes with independence. He objected to closing one's eyes to facts and believed the upright course for the United States was supervision or intervention, provided it were based on the welfare of the nation in question and not selfish interest. The United States, Stimson asserted, should use its giant strength together with the idealism exhibited in Cuba and the Philippines.[42]

After Moncada became a candidate in the 1928 election, many opponents of United States policy charged that the general had sold out for political preference. A representative of the All-America Anti-Imperialist League alleged, in early 1928, that Moncada was chosen as the next president in the peace pact he negotiated with Stimson and Díaz. And in more recent literature

[42] Letter from Stimson to Rev. John Franklin Carter, June 3, 1927, Stimson papers, box 161. Note Richard Current, *Secretary Stimson: A Study on Statecraft* (New Brunswick, N.J., 1954), p. 11.

with anti-American leanings one finds similar accusations. One author suggests that through force of logic everything indicated that Moncada agreed to the peace with tacit understanding that he would be the future president, and another declares that the general agreed to betray his own people in exchange for the good will of Washington in his presidential aspirations.[43] While Moncada did enjoy friendly relations with the United States and although he made political capital of his relationship vis-à-vis Washington, there is no evidence that any deal was made.

Probably most Nicaraguans who had suffered in the war did not care about the formalities of peacemaking. They could now go home to tend their farms and ponder why the United States had not acted sooner.

For a time the Sacasa government continued its refusal to accept Díaz and deplored the stand taken by the United States. Liberal delegates on their way home from conferring with Stimson asserted that true Liberals would refuse to participate in any way in the Díaz regime. In Puerto Cabézas, Sacasa reported that the Nicaraguan people would see the great deception of America and should distrust assurances of justice and neutrality.[44] But the Liberal army was turning toward peace, and it was time for the government to do likewise. When the Standard Fruit and Steamship Company informed the State Department of Sacasa's request for transportation out of Nicaragua and asked depart-

---

[43] New York Times, Mar. 23, 1928, p. 2; Gregorio Selser, Sandino, General de Hombres Libres (Buenos Aires, 1959), I, 206; Ramón Romero, Somoza, Asesino de Sandino (Mexico, 1959), p. 21; William Krehm, Democracia y Tiranías en el Caribe (Mexico, D.F., 1949), pp. 156–157.

[44] New York Times, May 13, 1927, p. 10; May 15, 1927, p. 5. The Sacasa delegates at Tipitapa were bitter about Stimson's intervention— intervention which came as the Liberal armies were at the gates of Managua. They felt Stimson's action hurt their honor and the republic's liberty. Moncada recorded that he shared these ideas; but in the face of forceful disarmament the general accepted the terms. He did not want to succumb to heroics or madness by exposing his nation to greater fighting. See Moncada, Estados Unidos en Nicaragua, pp. 36–37.

ment opinion, Washington quickly replied, "Be glad to have you transport Sacasa and party to any port he desires which is convenient for you."[45] On May 20 the not quite half-year-old regime of Sacasa ended. The former Nicaraguan Vice-president and twenty-six of his followers left for Costa Rica the same day.

By mid-May, 1927, the United States had begun preparations for Nicaragua's future. That future was not to be free from problems; although Stimson was right when he said civil war was ended, guerrilla warfare would soon begin.

[45] Standard Fruit and Steamship Co. to Department of State, May 18, 1927, 817.00/4798; Department of State to Standard Fruit and Steamship Co., May 19, 1927, 817.00/4798.

8: SANDINO AND THE MARINES—
MAY, 1927–NOVEMBER, 1928

The year and a half beginning in May, 1927—from the time
Stimson left Nicaragua until the Nicaraguan presidential election in November, 1928—was a trying period. These months
would tell how successful the Stimson mission had been. Would
the country turn to peace? Could Nicaragua have a free election? Could the country subordinate politics in the interest of
democratic, stable government? Unfortunately for Nicaragua
and, to a lesser extent, the Coolidge administration, the answers
were not entirely what Stimson had hoped. The election, topic
of the next chapter, was fair but only after Americans overcame
major troubles in supervising it. As for Nicaraguan politics, there
was continuing evidence of partisanship. The hand of Emiliano
Chamorro was everywhere. And when Chamorro was not stirring
up trouble, it was some other leader, Liberal or Conservative.

While a stable Nicaragua through a free election was the goal
of American policy, other problems had to be dealt with. Most
difficult was Augusto C. Sandino. This man, patriot or bandit,
for a time kept nearly five thousand American troops occupied,
and threatened the entire United States program. Problems of
the Sandino type were not unfamiliar to world powers which
at times intervened in other nations' affairs. The United States
had encountered a similar situation in the Philippines with
Aguinaldo. But Nicaragua was an independent country—a fact
much used by opponents of the Coolidge policy.

To be sure, the United States-Sandino clash came from interference in Nicaragua. The United States had long been inter-

ested in Nicaraguan affairs and had not disdained to send
Marines when it felt their presence necessary. Such measures
aimed at some exigency or, in the case of the extended stay
from 1912 to 1925, toward preventing emergencies. "Discourage
revolutions," then, was the State Department watchword. Washington disliked using troops; but while nonrecognition of any
revolutionary government was its first choice in deterring insurrection, it often resorted to establishment of neutral zones and
the stationing of a legation guard—a policy of adding weight to
the lid of the kettle to prevent steam from blowing it off. There
was no safety valve: The opposition in Nicaragua could not gain
office if the "in" party controlled the elections.

Washington was aware of criticism. Nicaragua needed free
elections. To the American way of thinking this would remove
the need for revolutions. Nonetheless, the United States government wanted to avoid interfering in anything so internal as a
nation's elections, and, of course, Nicaraguan politicians who
were in power wanted to keep their protector from being med-
dlesome. The result was a series of mishaps. There was the 1924
election, called by some the fairest election Nicaragua ever had—
faint praise indeed for our small Central American neighbor.
The succeeding events—the Chamorro coup d'état, Chamorro's
resignation, the Díaz government, the Liberal revolution, American neutral zones—have been noted.

The perennial Nicaraguan confusion was unsatisfactory to the
United States. When traditional United States policy toward
Nicaragua offered no solution, Stimson was sent down. In return
for a cessation of hostilities Stimson guaranteed a free 1928 election impartially supervised by the United States. In addition, the
American negotiator agreed to use his influence with the Díaz
regime to restore Liberals to posts from which they had been
ousted by Chamorro and offered American supervision for the
establishment of a nonpartisan Guardia Nacional. Under these
agreements the Coolidge administration accepted responsibilities
which it before had shunned. But then, in May, 1928, Sandino
came to the attention of the State Department. On May 12,

Stimson notified Washington that General Moncada and the other chiefs of the Liberal army had agreed to lay down arms. All the prominent chiefs save Sandino signed the agreement. The latter had agreed to disarm but not at the same place. In a letter reportedly from Sandino to Moncada, accepted as authentic by the State Department, the Liberal lieutenant told his commander that because of difficulty in collecting his men he had decided to go to Jinotega; there he would gather their arms. Sandino would stay in Jinotega and await Moncada's orders. Meanwhile he offered no objections to Moncada arranging things as suited the army commander.

Supporters of Sandino have related this episode differently. They report that Sandino found everything decided when he arrived at the meeting of Liberal chiefs and that Moncada told his lieutenant he would have to accept the terms. But Sandino held off. One author notes that Moncada offered him a position in Neuva Segovia with good pay and use of riding animals under his command. Sandino's continued reluctance to enter the agreement reportedly brought Moncada to ask him who had made him a general. To which Sandino replied, "My companions in the struggle. I do not owe my title to traitors or invaders." Sandino, then fearing detainment, declared he would have to consult his comrades before surrendering arms; thus he was able to leave Boaco without trouble in order to prepare for resistance.[1]

At first Sandino's failure to sign and his trip to Jinotega did not bother American officials. They had expected resistance to the cease-fire. In late April the State Department asked Stimson what size American forces could disarm the Liberal insurgents and whether insurgent bands would fight on. Stimson and Admi-

[1] Eberhardt to Department of State, May 12, 1927, 817.00/4775; *Foreign Relations: 1927*, III, 344; G. Aleman Bolaños, ¡Sandino! Estudio Completo del Heroe de las Segovias (Mexico and Buenos Aires, 1932), p. 16; Sofonias Salvatierra, *Sandino o la Tragedia de un Pueblo* (Madrid, 1934), p. 52–53; J. M. Moncada, *Estados Unidos en Nicaragua* (Managua, 1942), p. 25; Gregorio Selser, *Sandino, General de Hombres Libres* (Buenos Aires, 1959), I, 221–222.

ral Latimer believed guerrilla troops would make trouble in remote areas. While leaders of the Liberal revolution did not want to fight the United States, such men as Sandoval, Sandino, Escamilla, Mueller, and Cabulla, according to Stimson, were better off as insurgents and might cause trouble.[2]

Disarmament proceeded, and banditry lessened.[3] Even Cabulla agreed to turn over his arms. By the end of May, 1927, only one leader held out—Sandino. After leaving Moncada, Sandino was undecided what to do, but a few days of reflection brought him to a decision. He later wrote that he could not sell out his country; he would protest the treason to his nation and its ideals.[4] Marine action soon after Sandino's flight to Jinotega might have squelched him, but American authorities hoped to arrange peace without use of force and, besides, did not consider his actions important. Even before final agreement at Tipitapa the Marines had decided on tactics for operating against large bands of former Liberal army troops, but there was no desire "to make heroes out of a couple of cattle thieves by chasing them through the jungles with a squad of Marines."[5]

Also, the United States was eager to pull out its troops, for the Nicaraguan adventure had put a strain on the Marine Corps, which at that time had over 4,000 men in China plus those in Haiti.[6] Thus the Navy Department planned to reduce American forces as soon as possible, and the first seventy marines left in

[2] Eberhardt to Department of State, Apr. 26, 1927, 817.00/4728.

[3] According to Admiral Latimer's report to the Navy Department, between May 13 and June 6 the government forces turned over to the Americans 10,976 rifles, 308 machine guns, and 4,343,000 small arm cartridges; the Liberals turned over 3,391 rifles, 30 machine guns, and 1,519,000 cartridges. The United States Daily, June 10, 1927, p. 3.

[4] Selser, Sandino, I, 227–228.

[5] Colonel L. M. Gulick to Major H. G. Bartlett, May 8, 1927, Marine Corps in Nicaragua records, Navy Annex, box 8, personal file of Colonel Louis Mason Gulick.

[6] Clyde H. Metcalf, A History of the United States Marine Corps (New York, 1939), p. 422.

mid-June, 1927. A little more than a week later five hundred more left. Plans were to withdraw 1,000 more if conditions permitted, leaving approximately 1,700.[7]

Yet who was Sandino? There is no easy answer, for an emotional haze and a great deal of propaganda have beclouded this man. His supporters proclaimed him hero and savior of Nicaragua from the imperial yankee aggressor. Other people thought Sandino a thief, a pillager. They saw nothing heroic about his bandit ways. Most Americans engaged in carrying out the policies of the Coolidge administration felt his acts hampered their efforts to give Nicaragua a free election and that he was an opportunist in this awkward situation.

Sandino's birthdate is almost as uncertain as his character. He was probably born on May 18 or 19, 1893 or 1895, in the village of Niquinohomo, west of Granada. His brother described him as a man of not robust constitution, five feet eight inches tall, very white complexion, black hair and brown eyes. Sometimes he appeared in coffee-colored hat with sharp-pointed crown and broad brim, a red and black handkerchief around his neck, checked wool jacket, riding trousers and boots. At his hips were two pistols hanging from a belt with cartridge shells.

Sandino's father, a farmer, was an active Liberal who was at times imprisoned for political activity. The youth's early years were unexceptional. He received what education his village offered and some training at the Instituto de Oriente in Granada. While still in his teens he became a produce merchant. After some trouble with the political chief of his town he left Nicaragua for Honduras and eventually went to Guatemala and to Mexico, where he worked in the oil industry around Tampico. According to his testimony it was in Mexico that he began to think about American domination in Nicaragua and to form a social and political philosophy that Nicaragua's troubles lay in politicians and American imperialism. He was convinced that a

[7] *New York Times*, Jan. 4, 1928, pp. 1–2; *The United States Daily*, June 18, 1927, p. 3; June 21, 1927, p. 1; June 25, 1927, p. 1.

new movement, separate from the old parties, had to arise in his
native land. With this purpose he returned to Nicaragua in 1926,
went to work for the San Albino gold mine, and agitated reform.
Unsuccessful against the Díaz government, he turned to Liberal
leaders and joined the revolution with Sacasa and Moncada. By
his own account he gave valuable service to the Liberal cause,
at one time preventing the rout of Moncada's army. The end of
fighting and the Tipitapa conferences did not please him, so
he withdrew from those who would enforce the agreement. He
would try to organize an independent movement.[8]

As noted, at first Sandino did not alarm the American military.
The great body of revolutionists had disarmed and the few who
had not, so the thinking went, would offer no effective resistance
to plans of Díaz and the United States. Plans went forward for
reducing the Marine force. Washington hoped the new Guardia
Nacional, first under Colonel Robert Rhea and later Lieutenant
Colonel Elias R. Beadle, would handle any trouble.

At San Rafael del Norte in the Segovia Mountains, Sandino
again condemned the retention of Díaz. He suggested instead
that an American governor be appointed to Nicaragua to supervise the elections.[9] While the plan was unacceptable, his suggestion probably encouraged the Americans to try persuasion.
Accompanied by Sandino's father, Don Gregorio, and a detachment of Marines, Moncada went to Jinotega to call upon San-

---

[8] Sandino, quoted in Aleman Bolaños, ¡Sandino!, p. 3, n. 1, gives his
birthday as 18 May 1895. Another date is 19 May 1893, found in Carleton Beals, "With Sandino in Nicaragua," The Nation, vol. 126 (Mar. 14,
1928), 289; in an interview with Socrates Sandino reported in La Noticia
(Managua), Feb. 11, 1928, p. 3; and in Anastasio Somoza, El Verdadero
Sandino o El Calvario de las Segovias (Managua, 1936), p. 5. May 19,
1895, is suggested by Salvatierra, Sandino, p. 45. For other details of
Sandino's early life, I have relied on Aleman Bolaños, ¡Sandino!, p. 3, n.
1, and pp. 4–8, 12–13; Salvatierra, Sandino, pp. 45–47, 49; Joseph O.
Baylen, "Sandino: Patriot or Bandit?" HAHR, XXXI (Aug., 1951), 394–
395; Selser, Sandino, II, 114.

[9] El Diario Nicaragüense (Granada), May 29, 1927, p. 2.

dino to disarm. By that time the rebel had moved north in the mountainous area to a place called Yalí, partly to prevent disaffections from his small force, now composed of less than thirty men, not all of whom were dedicated to the project. The father followed his son but to no avail; rather, Sandino converted Don Gregorio to his cause.[10]

Even after Sandino's renewed refusal to accept terms, Washington was still not inclined to do anything. General Feland saw no need, for he felt sure Sandino's forces would disintegrate. Thus Marines and Guardia, ignoring Sandino, moved into Neuva Segovia to restore civil government. While Sandino made threats and extorted some money, he did not attempt to stop occupation of Jinotega, San Rafael, or Ocotal. No one thought he would make a stand.[11]

But at the end of June, 1927, the State Department heard that Sandino had plundered the mine of his former employer, Charles Butter, in Neuva Segovia. Some fifty armed men had carried off five hundred pounds of dynamite, with fuses and caps, with which, they said, they would kill yankees. Earlier he had seized some European property near Ocotal, demanding ransom for the managers; he left after taking money and goods worth $3,500.[12] These depredations brought recruits. At the same time they inspired criticism of American policy: There had been no Marine protection in Neuva Segovia.

Soon Sandino—hero of the Segovias—was carrying on a pen-and-ink campaign with Captain G. D. Hatfield, commander of a small detachment of Marines in Ocotal (about a hundred and ten miles north of Managua). Letters revealed a self-confident young man who knew the attraction of braggadocio for the brigands, adventurers, discontents, and yankee-hating patriots

[10] Aleman Bolaños, ¡Sandino!, p. 18; Selser, Sandino, I, 242.
[11] Copy of letter from General Logan Feland to General John A. Lejeune, July 8, 1927, Stimson papers, box 155.
[12] Eberhardt to Department of State, June 30, 1927, 317.115B98/2; H. N. Denny, Dollars for Bullets (New York, 1929), p. 314.

who made up the Sandinistas. In a communiqué to the Marine captain, Sandino pictured one of his followers hovering over a fallen Marine, about to decapitate him with a machete; Sandino asked, "What do you think of this?" In another communiqué Sandino advised the Americans to make wills before coming to his mountains. In a third he closed with "your obedient servant who wishes to put you in the tomb with handsome flowers." These semihumorous sallies continued through Sandino's guerrilla career. At least once he "paid" for supplies taken from mines with a promissory note: "The Honorable Calvin Coolidge, President of the United States, will pay the bearer $500."[13]

In mid-July, 1927, Captain Hatfield, following General Feland's lead in a tougher attitude toward Sandino, sent an ultimatum to the rebel to lay down arms or face attack. Hatfield pictured Sandino's future as very bleak if he did not surrender. While he might escape into Honduras, he could not return peacefully to his beloved country; he would be a criminal, outside the law, pursued and rejected. Hatfield urged him to turn in his arms, live a useful and honorable life.[14] Sandino refused, for, as he said, he wanted a free country or death. To gain this end he would rely on the patriotism and bravery of his men.[15]

Actually the American command still did not contemplate action. Feland announced that an expedition would restore government authority but not at the present. He did not take Sandino seriously, believing everything would work out.[16]

During these weeks of inactivity Sandino worked with his men on guerrilla tactics. He taught them to make best use of rough terrain, to prepare traps, to perfect primitive military strategy. Obviously the few Sandinistas, short on supplies and money, would have to pick their own places and times for battle. They

[13] New York Times, Jan. 8, 1928, p. 29; Mar. 18, 1928, p. 4; Denny, Dollars for Bullets, p. 313.
[14] El Diario Nicaragüense, July 13, 1927, p. 2.
[15] New York Times, July 17, 1927, sect. 2, p. 1.
[16] Ibid., July 16, 1927, p. 28.

would have to rely on harassment and hit-and-run battles, wearing down United States will to fight in the unpleasant jungles of Nicaragua. Their task was to be everywhere, yet nowhere.[17]

Sandino caused the first clash when on the morning of July 16 he moved against Hatfield and a group of eighty-seven Marines and Nicaraguan national guardsmen. Reportedly offering his men freedom to loot and agreeing to join them in drinking yankee blood, Sandino attacked at one o'clock in the morning. Firing on the city from all directions, Sandinistas estimated at as many as five hundred swept into the town attempting to gain vantage points for a final push against the city hall headquarters of the Marines. Serious fighting continued through the day and might have ended in a Sandino victory had not two Marine scouting planes noticed the battle and informed Managua. Five bombing and strafing planes set out, reaching the fighting around mid-afternoon. Two hours later Sandino was gone. Later accounts explaining the defeat noted that Sandino had only sixty men with adequate arms for sustaining combat and that the guerrilla chief both underestimated the "combative capacity of the invading forces" and lacked experience with aviation in battle.[18]

Newspapers reported tremendous losses—three hundred insurgents killed and a hundred wounded, one Marine killed. The American minister repeated these statistics to the State Department. The inhabitants of Ocotal, however, estimated that the attackers lost no more than forty men.[19] The clash disturbed the State Department: bombing operations and bandit forces of five hundred men!

Unfortunately the legation in Managua knew little about Sandino. Minister Eberhardt received a report that the troublemaker

[17] Selser, Sandino, I, 243.

[18] Ibid., p. 254.

[19] New York Times, July 19, 1927, p. 1; Eberhardt to Department of State, July 17, 1927, 817.00/4936; Department of State to Eberhardt, July 18, 1927, 817.00/4936; Eberhardt to Department of State, July 20, 1927, 817.00/4940; Aleman Bolaños ¡Sandino!, pp. 18–19; Denny, Dollars for Bullets, p. 316.

was "an erratic Nicaraguan about 30 years of age with wild Communist ideas acquired largely in Mexico." Sandino, he said, had every opportunity to surrender or leave the country, and General Feland had ordered no advances against the rebel. The minister felt that Sandino interpreted this policy as weakness. But Ocotal, he concluded, was a disaster for Sandino.[20]

Skirmishes continued, with a detachment of Marines and constabulary under Major Oliver O. Floyd pursuing Sandino toward Jícaro. There was fighting at San Fernando, and Marine planes uncovered an ambush just outside that town. The planes returned fire and dropped bombs.

The situation in Nicaragua was not conducive to information. American newspapers often carried accounts of engagements before the State Department had information. Such journalistic enterprise embarrassed the department, piqued because of assurance of peace in Nicaragua. To the American legation, Washington emphasized that it had to be informed. The department insisted on knowing whether it had to face the probability that Sandino would field sufficient forces to engage American Marines.[21] But fighting was in primitive areas, and reports of encounters were slow in coming to Managua. Marines later resorted to stringing messages on cords and having them picked up by planes with grappling hooks. Obviously Eberhardt had a difficult job; he explained the lateness of reports, as compared with newspaper stories, by saying that as soon as activity occurred or seemed likely local telegraph operators submitted guesses to correspondents in Managua, from whence reports went immediately to the United States. Although often the guesses were right, the minister and General Feland did not want rumors and frequently had to wait a day or two before confirmation of reports.[22]

With regard to Sandino the American minister could not send precise information. He had none. Sandino was a question mark,

---

[20] Eberhardt to Department of State, July 20, 1927, 817.00/4940.
[21] Department of State to Eberhardt, July 27, 1927, 817.00/4953b.
[22] Eberhardt to Department of State, July 31, 1927, 817.00/4959.

and everything reported had to have the preface "it is believed," "it seems," "I feel . . . but others believe," or "it is estimated." When Eberhardt reported at the end of July that Sandino's arms were diminishing and that he must soon face annihilation or leave the country, it was no more than a guess. Marine intelligence admitted they did not know Sandino's whereabouts and could not determine his actions "because of his demented condition." Then, in a suggestion more of hope than of fact, an intelligence officer recorded Sandino's broken power in the mountain district around the Honduran frontier, his bands decreasing, stability increasing. There should be no further trouble of any nature in the republic.[23]

Whether the department would have changed its policy if it had known more is a good question. Sandino had little to do with objectives of the Coolidge administration in Nicaragua. Washington had committed itself to a supervised election while Sandino was just another Liberal chief. Once parties reached a modus vivendi it would not have been easy to deter the United States. Its attitude toward Sandino is easy to understand. Knowing that both parties had agreed to a cease-fire, believing a free election the best solution to Nicaragua's problem, noting that leaders of both parties had renounced Sandino, noting looting by Sandino, the department came to think him a bandit.

Bandit or not, the "Segovia hero" was a source of agitation against American Marines in Nicaragua. After Ocotal, Sandino hurled defiance at the Stimson agreement and the men who had consented to it. He had attacked Ocotal, he said, to defend the constitutionality of the Sacasa presidency and disabuse those who believed he was a bandit. Death was preferable to slavery. The peace of Moncada was domination. "The only one responsible for what has happened here is the President of the United States, Calvin Coolidge, who has supported Adolfo Díaz."

Sandino was not the only one to speak out against American

---

[23] Intelligence report no. 85, headquarters, second brigade, Managua, Aug. 8, 1927, Marine Corps files, box 178, folder 200.1.

policy. William Green, president of the American Federation of Labor, deplored the use of arms by the United States in Latin America. His fellow labor leader Salomón de la Selva, of Nicaragua, continued in a more intemperate vein when he offered the opinion that the Marines, if they did not leave his country, would have to destroy the whole population. T. S. Vaca, former representative of Sacasa in the United States, pictured the fight at Ocotal as wholesale murder of men protecting their homeland against a foreign power.

General Moncada, on the other hand, supported the United States. His former lieutenant, he declared, had preferred bandits and assassins to order. Ocotal would not have occurred had not Sandino attacked the garrisons in that town.[24]

By the first of August, 1927, the situation in northern Nicaragua had quieted. People returned to villages and farms, and reports had Sandino fleeing down the Coco River along the Honduran border. Small groups committed some depredations, but trouble seemed over. General Feland told an interviewer that Sandino was either hiding with a few men or had left the country. Moncada believed that the Nicaraguan constabulary could subdue the roving bands, which were made up largely of criminals who would not turn in their arms. The Liberal leader felt the critical period of pacification was over.

The American government accepted these reports and allowed Marine withdrawals until, by the end of August, 1927, about 1,700 Marines remained in Nicaragua. Feland returned to Quantico, Colonel Louis M. Gulick taking his place. Passing through Panama on his way home, Feland said force was no longer necessary. Sandino was through.[25]

But October and November, 1927, saw the situation in northern Nicaragua grow difficult. Marines and constabulary occupied most of the larger towns, but outside these centers antigovern-

[24] These statements are in *New York Times*, July 20, 1927, p. 2; July 21, 1927, p. 5.
[25] *Ibid.*, Aug. 21, 1927, p. 9; Aug. 28, 1927, p. 14.

ment bands were active. The rainy season made roads and trails almost impassable. Lack of forces and reasons of policy also kept down American action. But the rains would end in about a month, and it was expected that the reluctance to act would then be over. Colonel Gulick asked for more men, and the Guardia Nacional had a large force for duty. Hopefully, these troops—especially the Guardia—would stop the Sandinistas, who reportedly were now holding the department of Nueva Segovia and large parts of Estelí and Jinotega.[26]

Meanwhile Marine planes continued reconnaissance flights, watching for insurgent groups here one day, gone the next. Eventually officials heard about a base called El Chipote. By November, planes located the mountain fortress—a hill wooded at the top, with several long thatched houses besides machine-gun nests and rifle pits. Here was the opportunity Americans had been awaiting. El Chipote was something to grasp, to attack, perhaps for the coup de grâce to the pest of the Segovias.

At the beginning of the year 1928 American troops engaged in their biggest battle since the World War. Sandinistas had ambushed Marines moving on Quilalí, the guerrillas' "capital," and a fierce struggle ensued, ending in rout of the rebels but at a cost of five Marines killed and twenty-three wounded. United States forces were now within fifteen miles of El Chipote. Reinforcements rushed to the scene through the Sandinista-infested jungles. By January 4, 1928, the Marines were entrenched at Quilalí and looking toward the towering summit, on whose slopes Sandino and his men were reportedly well armed and dug in.

Attack offered serious problems. To soften resistance four Corsairs dropped fragmentation and fifty-pound demolition bombs in addition to strafing and throwing grenades. Softening continued until, on January 18, reports came that El Chipote appeared abandoned. Sandino had avoided the Americans, and rumor had it that the leader was wounded or dead. The Marines

[26] Dana G. Munro, chargé in Nicaragua, to Department of State, Oct. 18, 1927, 817.00/5084.

cautiously advanced to the summit, reaching it near the end of January.

Sandino later explained that bombardment had done little damage to his men but had killed many horses and cattle. The stench from decaying animals, and activities of the buzzards thus attracted, made the position unpleasant. The Sandinistas made hay figures for decoys and departed.[27]

While Sandino crept southward to the vicinity of Jinotega, Nueva Segovia appeared to return to peaceful ways. Streams of natives, including women, moved homeward, and washing appeared along rivers and creeks. But before optimism could rise, Marine reinforcements were moving to Matagalpa in response to reports that Sandino was in this rich coffee area. Refugees crowded the road from Jinotega to Matagalpa, and some headed toward Managua. By mid-February danger had subsided, even though flare-ups on the southern border of Nueva Segovia during the next two weeks made nerves tense.

Increased activity against Sandino which began on New Year's Day, 1928, stirred Washington to take measures for ending the trouble. Major General John A. Lejeune, commandant of the Marine Corps, sailed to Nicaragua on an inspection trip. General Feland accompanied him, resuming command. An additional thousand Marines went to the troubled spot. Another thousand arrived in March, bringing the force to 3,700, supported by five cruisers and 1,500 sailors offshore.

At the same time Admiral Sellers, new commander of the special service squadron, sought once more to persuade Sandino to lay down his arms. The admiral explained American policy of protecting lives and property in Nicaragua and supervising the election. He pointed out the buildup of American forces and suggested that Sandino might consider the unnecessary sacrifice of human lives and stop his resistance. Two weeks later the rebel answered the "Representative of Imperialism in Nicara-

---

[27] Aleman Bolaños, ¡Sandino!, p. 30.

gua."[28] He refused. He was fighting foreign invasion and would not cease until Marines were out of Nicaragua and President Díaz replaced as head of the country.

With characteristic suddenness Sandino now moved eastward and in mid-April, 1928, was in the mining district of Prinzapolca department. He occupied several mines, including La Luz and Bonanza. After stripping the mines of what they could and destroying much of what remained, the raiders posed a threat to towns of the northeast coast. To the manager of La Luz, Sandino wrote an explanation of his act. The mine was destroyed to protest the invasion of American troops, and North Americans, he said, would have no guarantees until their soldiers departed. In the beginning Sandino felt Coolidge did not have the support of the American people, but now he thought differently and vowed to destroy everything North American that reached his hands. He said that intervention to protect foreign lives and property was a hypocrisy and charged that the present destruction was a result of that policy. "You the capitalists will be appreciated and respected by us, so long as you treat us as equals and not in the erroneous manner of today, believing yourselves lord and masters of our lives and interests."[29]

Two hundred Marines immediately went eastward via the Panama Canal, arriving at Puerto Cabézas on April 29, and within a few hours were on their way to the mining district. Information was scarce, and although the force made contacts with small groups of rebels throughout the spring and into the summer, Sandino again withdrew into an obscurity which lasted long enough to allow a peaceful election. Meanwhile Marines occupied the major centers of Nicaragua. By April they had garrisons or outposts at forty-eight different places and operated an average of twenty-five patrols daily. They built emergency land-

[28] Munro to Department of State, Jan. 27, 1928, 817.00/5451; Secretary of the Navy Wilbur to Department of State, Mar. 16, 1928, 817.00/5590.

[29] The Bluefields Weekly, May 26, 1928, p. 1.

ing fields throughout the region where Sandino had been active.[30]

At the same time Washington pressured Honduras to tighten security along the border to prevent guerrilla forays from Honduran bases. Dana G. Munro, first secretary of the American legation in Managua, stressed some of the problems with the Honduran capital, Tegucigalpa. He complained that George T. Summerlin, the American minister there, never seemed to grasp the situation in Nicaragua, never understood "that this was our war in Nicaragua and that getting Sandino was a matter of vital importance to the United States."[31] After repeated urging that Summerlin press the Honduran government, a coolness developed between the two legations—Summerlin accepting at face value the assurances of Tegucigalpa and not desiring to interfere in internal affairs, while Munro and Eberhardt considered American lives at stake. Their position is revealed in a letter from Munro:

> I realize how hard it is for the Government of Honduras to take really effective action, and how disagreeable it is for the Legation to have to press them to do things that are inconvenient and perhaps politically harmful and to have to question the good faith of their assurances. It seems to me however that when American lives are actually at stake every possible pressure should be exerted to obtain a maximum of co-operation, without being held back by sympathy for the President's troubles or by a desire to maintain pleasant and cordial relations.[32]

Not until Munro consulted the State Department did the matter improve.

While Sandino was giving hard knocks to the Coolidge administration, there were also assaults at home. Congress took an interest in Nicaragua. Members offered resolutions for information on

---

[30] New York Times, Apr. 13, 1928, p. 16.

[31] Munro to Assistant Secretary Francis White, June 28, 1928, Francis White papers in the National Archives, box 14. Hereafter cited as White papers.

[32] Ibid.

naval forces there. Some senators, many of them Democrats willing to embarrass a Republican president, questioned whether the executive had power to employ forces in such operations. When the naval appropriation bill came up for consideration, Senate opponents tried to tack on amendments to get the Marines out of Nicaragua or to force the President to ask Congress for consent to have them there. The administration defeated all amendments, in part because of the belief of the Senate majority, including even William E. Borah, that the United States was under moral obligation to supervise the elections and that the job needed Marines.[33]

Those who supported or opposed Coolidge's policy because they thought it right or wrong were not easily distinguishable from those who took advantage of it for political reasons. After all, it was a presidential year in the United States. Republicans met that summer in Kansas City. Convention keynoter Simeon D. Fess, Ohio senator, told his listeners that the one undeviating principle for which America stood was protection of American citizens in their rights of life and property, wherever they were as long as they had a right to be there. The government, he said, must not fail this duty. The Republican platform supported Coolidge policy in Nicaragua; America must protect lives and property and carry out the election agreement.[34]

Two weeks later Claude G. Bowers, the historian, told Democrats assembled in Houston that through the stupidity of dollar diplomacy the administration had stumbled into petty war with Nicaragua. Poking fun at guaranteeing a free election or preventing riots during election time, the speaker recalled that we could not even guarantee a free election in Philadelphia or stop bombings in Chicago. He praised the noble spirit of Woodrow Wilson's Mobile, Alabama, speech of 1913, forgetting, of course, the

[33] New York Times, Apr. 26, 1928, p. 1; Apr. 20, 1928, p. 24. The Congressional Record for the period contains the remarks of the members and the resolutions on Nicaragua.
[34] New York Times, June 13, 1928, p. 8; June 15, 1928, p. 8.

Wilson of Haiti, the Dominican Republic, or Veracruz. The Democratic platform hence abhorred conquest and imperialism, desired protection of American lives and rights, proclaimed non-interference with elections of other nations, wanted to abolish presidential agreements with a foreign government for protection of that government against revolution or foreign attack or supervision of internal affairs when the Senate had not given advice and consent to such agreements.[35]

The administration also faced criticism from others, for Sandino had a rather exalted reputation outside his own country. In the United States, *The Nation* ran articles by Carleton Beals which pictured the Nicaraguan hero struggling against foreign oppressors. The All-America Anti-Imperialist League was vocal. It held meetings featuring Sandino's half brother Socrates in which this Brooklyn mechanic spoke of his brother as a Nicaraguan George Washington, Simón Bolívar, San Martín. The league called for contributions, sold pro-Sandino stamps, picketed the White House with signs reading: "Wall Street and not Sandino is the real bandit," "Millions are unemployed, we squander the Treasury on conquest," "We demand immediate withdrawal of Marines from Nicaragua," "We are for Sandino and not against him."[36]

Opinion in the country was difficult to fathom. Newspapers followed party lines, and the public, if it cared at all, probably did the same. No one liked the deaths of United States Marines, but hostility to American intervention did not reach such proportions that Coolidge brought the Marines home. The administration had support of a majority of Congress in keeping the election agreement even if this meant troops in Nicaragua.

The Nicaraguan situation was a thankless task. The most

[35] *Ibid.*, June 27, 1928, p. 8; June 29, 1928, p. 5.
[36] C. Beals, "With Sandino in Nicaragua," *The Nation*, vol. 126 (Feb. 22, 1928), 204–205; (Feb. 29, 1928), 232–233; (Mar. 7, 1928), 260–261; (Mar. 14, 1928), 288–289; (Mar. 21, 1928), 214–217; (Mar. 28, 1928), 340–341; *New York Times*, Jan. 16, 1928, p. 44; Aug. 15, 1928, p. 21.

unpleasant job went to the Marines. They faced the rainy season —over two hundred inches in places—soaked khaki, rotting leather, rusting rifles, sulky mules, mosquitoes, horseflies, black stinging ants, malaria, bone fever, dysentery. Patrols were never easy. In a patrol up the Coco River, for example, Marines contended with rapid rises and falls in the water level; waterproof seabags sprang leaks; rains dampened the blankets and clothing, which seldom dried; kapok life jackets served well until they became water-soaked and thus a menace. Insect bites and infected sores made sleep impossible. Little wonder patrols usually returned worn out and nervous.[37] The jungle-covered mountains had no roads, and footpaths were almost indistinguishable. The enemy could be a sharpshooter in ambush or an innocent Nicaraguan walking unarmed under the Marines' noses. The terrain was perfect for ambush. It was not possible to advance a whole line, nor could flankers be provided for single-file columns moving through the forests. The Marines' toil and hardship were unrewarded with victories, since the guerrillas' tactics gave little opportunity. By the time American forces arrived at the scene of any disturbance, the Sandinistas had often disappeared.

Regardless of conditions, failure to end the trouble caused much dissatisfaction in Washington. Kellogg took advantage of the visit to Nicaragua of General Frank R. McCoy (head of the American electoral mission) in early 1928 to have him report on Marine operations. The Secretary noted much criticism of the fact that American lives were being sacrificed without result. "People cannot understand why the job cannot be done and frankly I do not understand myself." Kellogg wanted to know about the campaign and the leadership. He remarked that inquiries to the Navy Department invariably elicited the same reply: "The situation is satisfactory."[38]

[37] Note report of Coco River expedition to area commander, northern area, Oct. 12, 1928, Marine Corps files, box 151, folder 855.

[38] Kellogg to McCoy, Mar. 3, 1928, Library of Congress, Frank R. McCoy papers, general correspondence, box 20. Hereafter cited as McCoy papers.

McCoy, too, was concerned about the military situation, for it might handicap a free election. He recognized the hardships of guerrilla war in Nicaragua, but regardless of the extraordinary conditions, success depended on locating Sandino and attacking and pursuing his forces. McCoy believed information was too belated and there was failure to maintain contact with Sandino. He praised both Sellers and Feland but indicated the latter lacked "a certain vigorous and compelling quality needed under present conditions in order to energize operations everywhere." General McCoy confided to Feland his dissatisfaction with the military situation. He criticized the intelligence service and indicated that the Marine general did not go out enough to encourage his men. At one time in April, 1928, McCoy suggested that if the Marines did not have Sandino in a month he would consider that Feland had failed.[39]

Such opinions disturbed Feland and Sellers, for they thought McCoy was overstepping his task. Much of the friction undoubtedly was interservice jealousy. Sellers backed Feland in dispatches to the chief of naval operations and later talked the matter over with McCoy. The conversation glossed over the differences.[40] McCoy's presence in Nicaragua as head of the electoral commission rankled the Marine general and the admiral. When there were hints of Army aviators or officers coming to Nicaragua, Feland and Sellers and even Admiral C. F. Hughes, chief of naval operations, showed opposition. Near the beginning of December, 1928, Hughes sent an interesting letter to Sellers. He had noted that Dana Munro, who had served at the legation in Managua, was to relieve Stokeley Morgan in the State Department's Latin American division. Hughes thought Sellers might

[39] McCoy to secretary of state, Mar. 5, 1928, 817.00/5450; Feland to Admiral David Foote Sellers, Apr. 19, 1928, Library of Congress, Admiral David Foote Sellers papers (Naval Historical Foundation Collection), box 251. Hereafter cited as Sellers papers.

[40] Sellers to Feland, Apr. 20, 1928, Sellers papers, box 251; Sellers to Hughes, Apr. 29, 1928, Sellers papers, box 251; Sellers to Feland, May 11, 1928, Sellers papers, box 251.

"indoctrinate" Munro about having Navy and Marine officers in Nicaragua instead of Army officers. "We had Morgan agree to let us know if the subject came up but he was not . . . more than halfhearted about it."[41]

Other problems in Nicaragua concerned charges of Marine cruelty and destruction. Latin American publicists and such writers as Beals spoke of American depredations. But Harold Denny, a New York Times reporter in Nicaragua, found no evidence of the destruction the Marines supposedly had wrought. Nor did he find the cruelty which was so glibly spoken of. Nicaraguans often asked the leathernecks to settle problems—hardly an indication of hate for a cruel oppressor. Marine headquarters gave orders to harm no one but rebels; Americans were to avoid being hard on people. When in contact with the enemy, they were to destroy nothing except rebel possessions; if the enemy were in a house, Marines were to destroy the building only if the rebel owned it. In cases of the shooting of a Nicaraguan, there was an inquiry, unless it was apparent the victim was an insurgent.[42] Sometimes officers and men ignored orders and treated Nicaraguans unjustly. There were cases of Marines burning small villages, mistreating prisoners or civilians. But these were appar-

[41] Feland to Sellers, May 19, 1928, and Sept. 8, 1928, Sellers papers, box 247; Sellers to Hughes, Sept. 30, 1928, Sellers papers, box 247; Hughes to Sellers, Dec. 3, 1928, Sellers papers, box 247. At another time it was agreed that inclusion of Army personnel in the Guardia Nacional along with Navy and Marine personnel would make administration, discipline, and operation exceedingly difficult. The Navy also reasoned that support of diplomatic agents was clearly recognized as a function of the Navy—especially in Central America. Director, division of operations and training, L. McCarty Little, to the major general commandant, Oct. 19, 1928, National Archives, U. S. Marine Corps, adjutant and inspector's office, general correspondence, 1913–1932, record group 127, entry 29, box 83, folder 1375-40 Nicaragua. Hereafter cited as adjutant and inspector's office.

[42] Salvatierra, Sandino, pp. 62–64, tells of Marine brutality. For the other side see Denny, Dollars for Bullets, pp. 339–352, and New York Times, June 1, 1928, p. 27.

ently exceptions, and Marine headquarters kept a careful eye out for such activity.[43]

What may we conclude about the Sandino affair in its first months, May, 1927, to November, 1928?

This police action, which by mid-April, 1928, had cost the United States the lives of twenty-one marines and $1,530,170, was a difficult issue to define. Sandino was hardly the bandit of State Department press releases, but neither were the Marines tools of imperialists. Sandino's activities did attract many Nicaraguans who were thieves and plunderers, but the chief himself was complex. Whether, as some suggested, he had delusions of grandeur, no one is likely to know. He showed bravery and some military skill, at least for guerrilla warfare. It is probable that he had a sincere desire to expel the Americans. United States forces were on his country's territory and must have rankled even a man of moderate patriotism. Imbued with Latin pride, hurt by what he considered yankee domination, Sandino found the intervention intolerable.

Sandino's struggle aroused much enthusiasm in the Americas and the rest of the world. He had his agents abroad, of whom Honduran poet Froylán Turcios was perhaps the most important. Through his review, Ariel, Turcios broadcast praises and statements of Sandino until the two men parted ways in early 1929.[44] In Mexico, Pedro José Zepeda represented the Nicaraguan leader and helped in fund-raising. The Communists, too, were interested in Sandino. In Mexico they organized the Hands Off Nicaragua Committee (Manos Fuera de Nicaragua or "Mafuenic"),

[43] Major W. Dulty Smith, second brigade executive officer to Colonel R. H. Dunlap, commander, northern area, Jan. 30, 1928, Marine Corps files, box 185, folder 946; headquarters, second brigade, to Colonel R. R. Wallace, commander, southern area, May 16, 1928, Marine Corps files, box 185, folder 949; intelligence information memorandum for all officers and units, May 11, 1928, Marine Corps files, box 177, folder 616.

[44] Neill Macaulay, The Sandino Affair (Chicago, 1967), p. 146, suggests that the desire of Turcios for a government position as well as disagreement over policy brought the split.

and from its 1928 meeting in Moscow, the Sixth Congress of the Communist International sent greetings to the heroic strugglers in Nicaragua.[45]

Sandino's relationship with the Communists was not an easy one; one source of friction was the proper role of the middle class and intellectuals in the anti-imperialist movement. Troubles also arose between Zepeda and "Mafuenic" when the latter tried to claim credit for funds raised by the former. During the Sandino war, the Communists sent the rebel leader only a thousand dollars, most of which was used to pay expenses of the courier.[46] When Sandino decided to go to Mexico in 1929, the Communists argued against it, and after he went they accused the general of accepting sixty thousand dollars from the United States to leave Nicaragua. The charge caused Socrates Sandino, Augusto's half brother, to break with the Communists, who had been using him for propaganda purposes, while Augusto C. Sandino denied the charge and asserted that he had come to Mexico in large part because he had received so little help from the outside; the small amounts sent often reached no further than the pockets of the unscrupulous. After early 1930, Sandino had no more correspondence with the Communists.[47] The connection had been one of convenience—the Nicaraguan hoped for outside support and the party desired to use the popularity of the guerrilla leader to further its ends in Latin America. When Sandino finally made peace with his government (in 1933, after the Marines had withdrawn from Nicaragua), the Communists were bitterly critical because the act seemed to define the struggle as being only against the invading troops.[48]

The Sandino affair also brought gross misrepresentation of

[45] Víctor Alba, Historia del Comunismo en América Latina (Mexico, D.F., 1954), p. 85; Robert J. Alexander, Communism in Latin America (New Brunswick, N.J., 1957), p. 378.

[46] Alba, Historia del Comunismo en América Latina, pp. 85-86.

[47] Ibid., pp. 86–87; Alexander, Communism in Latin America, pp. 378–379; El Comercio (Managua), Dec. 27, 1929, p. 1; Jan. 1, 1930, p. 1.

[48] Alexander, Communism in Latin America, p. 379.

American aims. There was no intricate intrigue of Wall Street capitalists or power-hungry imperialists. In the past, New York bankers had been reluctant to lend money to Nicaragua and did so only at urging of the State Department. By March, 1928, estimates put Nicaragua's debt to Americans at only $1,200,000— hardly a sum which would cause the United States to move over five thousand troops into that small nation. American capital investment in business enterprises in Nicaragua in 1928 was lower than in any other Central American country.[49] It must be admitted that the United States was interested in Latin America and the Caribbean area; but it wanted influence, not Nicaraguan territory. America wanted stability and, if possible, democracy, because those factors in Nicaragua not only would favor the United States but also would aid Nicaragua. The United States had faith in free elections and agreed to supervise the vote in Nicaragua. To fail to do so would renege on the Stimson promise and leave the small nation to chaos or more intervention.

The Sandino business was awkward, unexpected, difficult to handle, and embarrassing because United States troops were on foreign soil. Sandino with a few friends was able to defy a world power. (Whose heart could refuse to be impressed by such odds?) He was imaginative and nationalistic; he galvanized anti-United States feeling in Latin America.

Amid the aura of glamour and adventure generated by the little fellow, one should not lose perspective. For Nicaragua a balance between independence and guidance seemed necessary. Whether the actions of United States were in total accord with this ideal balance is questionable, but undoubtedly the U.S. was seeking equilibrium. Sandino wanted to push away the intervening hand. The two sides raised many questions—some of power, some of morality. Certainly no one could claim victory from the affair. Sandino hurt the United States in Latin America. But he also did little for Nicaragua.

[49] *New York Times*, Mar. 18, 1928, p. 3; Jan. 15, 1928, pt. 9, p. 3.

9: THE ELECTION OF 1928

Up to 1928 no government in the entire history of Nicaragua had sponsored a free election. Every four years the people of this small Central American country went through the motions of electing their government. Each time foreign observers had little trouble determining the direction of the political tide; just one interview was necessary—a talk with the president of Nicaragua. Candidates backed by the chief executive never lost. Dishonesty, bribery, intimidation, force were hazards any Nicaraguan voter faced on election day, only to find out the next morning that it had happened again—the "in" party had won.

An "out" party in Nicaragua could get in only by revolution. Since the ballot box did not provide entrance to government, perhaps the rifle and machine gun would. There were revolutions in 1909 and 1925, and there would have been more if the United States had not had a thinly veiled "legation guard" in Managua.

Earlier chapters have related events leading to the overthrow of President Solórzano by Chamorro in 1925 and the withdrawal of this bold revolutionary in 1926 in favor of Adolfo Díaz. But Sacasa, Solórzano's vice-president, had never resigned although he was forced to flee the country; he claimed the presidency from exile and worked to that end from the United States and Mexico. Revolution began in 1925 and ended in 1927 only when Stimson of the United States came down from the north with a mandate from President Coolidge. He threatened complete intervention of American troops unless Nicaraguans accepted a cease-fire proposal, which included the disarming of all troops and the promise of an American-sponsored election in 1928.

The important point was the election. Without this, United States-Nicaraguan diplomacy might have fallen back to the pre-1925 policy, which was stability in Nicaragua by silent influence of the legation guard. Secretary Kellogg and his advisers in the State Department hoped it would not fall back. They knew well the pitfalls of the old policy. Nationalism was spreading by leaps and bounds in Nicaragua, and Kellogg wished to get the Marines out while at the same time giving the country stability. Stimson also had recognized the peculiarities of the situation. What Nicaragua needed, both men believed, was a truly free election—not one as in 1924 that could be called the freest in the history of the country but which did not say much for freedom. Stimson, in 1927 at Tipitapa—in his riverbed conversations with the rebel General Moncada—therefore opted for the election.

Shortly after arriving in Nicaragua, Stimson had found Díaz willing to have the United States supervise the election of 1928 and even elections of succeeding years. This offer he embodied in peace terms which the Díaz Conservatives accepted and which became the basis of agreement with the Sacasa Liberals. A fair election seemed the only promise by which Liberals would lay down their arms. For the next year and a half, from May, 1927, until November, 1928, this was the theme of United States diplomacy in Nicaragua. The Americans would allow neither Chamorro nor the enigmatic leader Sandino to interfere with bringing stability via democracy.

Stimson returned home confident that the free election would end Nicaragua's troubles. He brought a formal request from President Díaz to President Coolidge for the United States to help prepare an election law. The Nicaraguan President suggested that Coolidge choose an electoral expert to draft the law setting up a national electoral commission headed by an American whose concurrence would be necessary for any action of the body. Each department of the country was to have a similar commission, each polling place an election board. Americans would head the commissions and boards. There also would be an impartial, newly organized constabulary. Díaz, as well as most individuals with knowledge of Nicaragua, knew that the national army was a partisan force and could intimidate voters. He proposed to disband it and establish a constabulary under American officers. To reinforce the constabulary he requested that American Marines remain in the country during the election. Coolidge acceded to this request and discussions began on how best to assist Nicaragua in its election.[1]

The United States took the next move. Early in July, 1927, the summer White House at Rapid City, South Dakota, announced that the President had nominated Brigadier General Frank R. McCoy, veteran of San Juan Hill, campaigns against the Moros in the Philippines, the Rio Grande in 1915–16, and the World War, as chairman of the electoral commission. The general was to make a preliminary trip the following month, as personal representative of the President, to familiarize himself with Nicaragua. He was to study political and military matters and make recommendations.[2]

If the State Department or President thought that supervising an election was a simple matter of appointments and troops at each polling place, they were to learn differently. Conservatives remained Conservatives, Liberals still Liberals. Intervention had brought willingness to compromise and even to agree on a supervised election, a major concession for any "in" party. Even so, now that tranquillity seemed assured, the politicians pondered whether they had gone too far. The master of Nicaraguan politics, Chamorro, decided to return home from Europe by way of Washington. General Moncada likewise packed his bags for Washington. During the summer and autumn of 1927 the capital of the United States was a mecca for presidential aspirants. However much the State Department might proclaim nonintervention

[1] Díaz to Coolidge, May 15, 1927, 817.00/4902; Coolidge to Díaz, June 10, 1927, 817.00/5323a.
[2] New York Times, July 3, 1927, p. 6; Kellogg to McCoy, June 26, 1927, McCoy papers, box 18.

in Nicaragua, politically wise Nicaraguans knew this was true
only within limits. Acceptance in Washington was important.
Chamorro and Sacasa, losers in the recent revolution, could
attest to the troubles involved in lack of proper sponsorship.

Chamorro was an especially tricky factor. He headed probably
the largest faction of the Conservative party. His popularity was
high and his influence in the Congress of Nicaragua decisive.
But he was not popular with the State Department. Many party
leaders also feared him. What he would do between Tipitapa
and November, 1928, was not clear; perhaps even Chamorro
himself did not know.

Conservative leaders made the first move to clear the situation. In August, 1927, they urged that Díaz advise Chamorro to
renounce any intention of being a 1928 presidential candidate.
But knowing Chamorro's power in Nicaragua and perhaps desiring to avoid political retaliation as well as wishing to add more
weight to their appeal, they wanted the Department of State
and the legation to join, at least tacitly, in the disqualification.
Kellogg was willing, for, as he asserted in a telegram to Minister
Eberhardt in Managua, he did not believe Chamorro eligible
for the presidency under Article 104 of the Nicaraguan constitution. The department chose to believe that Chamorro, though
unrecognized, was president during part of the term prior to the
1928 election and thus not qualified for the subsequent term.
While believing this action would suffice, Kellogg confided in
Eberhardt that he would go farther if necessary; the Secretary
would tell Chamorro that even if he were elected the United
States would not recognize him.[3] Washington strongly felt that
a Chamorro election could cause all sorts of constitutional questions and animosities which might well negate the efforts put
forth for a free election. Still the department was reluctant to
intervene obviously in Nicaraguan issues and was content to let

[3] Eberhardt to secretary of state, Aug. 20, 1927, 817.00/4995; Kellogg
to Eberhardt, Aug. 22, 1927, 817.00/4995; Foreign Relations: 1927,
III, 358. For Article 104 see chapter 2, footnote 16.

Conservative party leaders handle Chamorro while the department itself remained in the background.

Messages from Díaz and leading Conservatives thereupon informed the troublesome general that he ought to eliminate himself. These messages, however, emphasized the United States role and tried to create the impression that the Conservative action had come after consultation and "presumably in accordance with an intimation from McCoy." The American minister guessed, probably correctly, that these machinations indicated regret on the leaders' part to have to support Chamorro but reluctance to oppose him, and a willingness to leave the work to the United States.

In search, then, of what an editorial in *La Prensa* of Buenos Aires called the mysterious word that was to consecrate him "*presidenciable*" in Nicaragua, Chamorro came to the United States. He first visited Stimson on Long Island. Stimson afterwards wrote the department that the hour-long interview was plainspoken but not bitter. He told Chamorro that the general was not constitutionally eligible for the presidency. He declared that the devastation in Nicaragua came largely from Chamorro's actions under very bad advice; for this reason, he continued, no one would wish to modify on the general's behalf what seemed the plain construction of the constitution. Chamorro argued, believing this view would hurt his party. He was the strongest, most popular man in the Conservative party; for the State Department to remove his candidacy would hamper Conservative success. Stimson would not budge and assured his visitor the United States would do its best to hold a fair election. He advised Chamorro to back his party's candidate, whoever that might be.[4]

A few days later the Nicaraguan minister in Washington, Dr. Alejandro César, asked the State Department for an inter-

[4] Stimson to Francis White, Sept. 26, 1927, Stimson papers, box 161. See also Stimson to White, Sept. 26, 1927, 817.00/5044½; *La Prensa*, Oct. 24, 1927.

view between Chamorro and the secretary. Stokeley Morgan of
the department's Latin American division wanted the requests
granted in order to clear up any misconceptions the Nicaraguan
might have. Morgan had learned from César that Chamorro
had been seeing Chandler Anderson, who had said there was no
reason the Conservative leader could not have the candidacy and
that no grounds existed for withholding recognition from him
if elected. Chamorro naturally preferred Anderson's advice to
that of Stimson. Giving this information to Morgan, the minister
added that Anderson carried weight with Chamorro because the
former allegedly knew how the department felt about these matters. Morgan suggested the department grant Chamorro an interview and that Anderson be present so he would have no illusions
about the department's attitude.[5]

Other persons in the department became concerned about
Chamorro. Assistant Secretary Francis White, former chief of
the Latin American division, thought the general should know
that the United States would not recognize him or permit him
to run. Chamorro, White thought, was responsible for the trouble in Nicaragua and the department should veto his candidacy
even in face of charges that the Secretary was picking presidential candidates.[6] The chargé in Managua, Dana Munro, came to
much the same conclusion: A Chamorro election would intensify
party arguments and make stable government impossible. Munro
advised the department to take advantage of Chamorro's presence in Washington to tell him off. It would be almost impossible to do so after Chamorro returned to Nicaragua. Munro felt
that most Conservative leaders in Nicaragua could not prevent
Chamorro's candidacy; therefore the United States must.[7]

Shortly before Secretary Kellogg was to see Chamorro, Anderson had a talk with the Secretary during which Kellogg said

[5] Memorandum of conversation between Morgan and Dr. Alejandro
César, Sept. 29, 1927, 817.00/5049.
[6] White to Robert E. Olds, undersecretary of state, Oct. 1, 1927,
817.00/5853.
[7] Munro to Department of State, Oct. 4, 1927, 817.00/5054.

the department was interpreting Article 104 of the Nicaraguan constitution against Chamorro. Anderson told Chamorro what Kellogg said and advised him not to raise the question of his candidacy in the forthcoming interview, "so as not to give him [Kellogg] a chance to state officially . . . what he had stated to me."[8] Anderson and Chamorro then kept their appointment. Francis White and Stokeley Morgan were present, anticipating, so Anderson thought, the question of Chamorro's candidacy. Chamorro skirted that topic, contenting himself with phrases about approval of a supervised election. This first interview ended without the Secretary stating point-blank the department's position.

Some time later Chamorro returned to see Francis White. The general wanted the department to be friendly to him and "restore his civil rights." He talked about the Conservative party's candidate for president, hoping that it would be someone acceptable to the United States. White replied that the department had to answer only one question—whether it would recognize the person elected. He handed Chamorro a statement that he was ineligible for the presidency under the constitution. Chamorro read the statement but made no comment except to ask for another conference. Four days later the department gave its position to the press.[9]

[8] Anderson diary, Oct. 9, 1927, box 7.
[9] Memorandum by White of conversation with Chamorro, Oct. 22, 1927, 817.00/5096. In answer to inquiries by press correspondents the Secretary, on Oct. 26, made the following statement: "As I have said before, the United States is not going to select any candidate for President of Nicaragua either Conservative or Liberal. Neither is the United States going to back or use its influence for the election of any particular person. The United States is going to do its best to see that there is a fair, open and free election where everybody who is entitled to vote has an opportunity to do so. This has been made perfectly plain. Of course following the Constitution of Nicaragua and the Treaty [of Peace and Amity, signed Feb. 7, 1923] the United States cannot recognize anybody who is not qualified under the Constitution to hold the office." *Foreign Relations: 1927*, III, 369–370.

Actually Washington's views had been known for some time, though Chamorro had tried hard to prolong the issue. The anti-Chamorrista press in Managua emphasized the general's discomfiture, giving it front-page coverage. One paper carried pictures of Kellogg and Chamorro along with statements that the Nicaraguan was prohibited from candidacy.[10] Such news undoubtedly caused rejoicing and sorrow according to one's political affiliation. Perhaps among some who had strong nationalistic feelings, there was resentment. Strange indeed it may have seemed to a Nicaraguan reader that this decision was made two thousand miles away in Washington.

Chamorro attempted to recruit for his cause American businessmen with interests in Nicaragua, but apparently he had little success.[11] On November 2, 1927, Chamorro capitulated; he told White he would not be a candidate for the presidency. The general had learned from his experience of the past year. He prepared to go home where, although not a candidate, he still was politically strong. He returned to Nicaragua, to fireworks, band concerts, and Te Deum at the Managua cathedral.

Meanwhile another would-be president arrived in the United States. Moncada, former head of the Sacasa army but now a supporter of free elections, came in October, 1927, ostensibly to work in support of this policy and a new election law.[12] Minister Eberhardt, somewhat of a Díaz-Conservative sympathizer, looked upon Moncada's visit as part of a dash for the presidency, an attempt to use the department to raise prestige at home. He believed Moncada "one of the shrewdest intriguers in Nicaragua." Eberhardt told the department he thought Moncada too successful in creating the impression that he was the United States' choice as Liberal candidate. Such a situation came, the minister guessed, because the Americans dealt with him as sole representative of the Liberal party and because he had corre-

[10] La Noticia (Managua), Oct. 8, 1927, p. 1.
[11] Ibid., Nov. 12, 1927, p. 1.
[12] New York Times, Oct. 9, 1927, p. 5.

sponded with Stimson.[13] Eberhardt thought Moncada should not visit the United States.

The department had instructed Eberhardt to do nothing to prevent Moncada's visit, for the minister's plan would undoubtedly have dealt a blow to Moncada.[14] Since the negotiations under the blackthorn tree at Tipitapa, Moncada had dominated the Liberal party. He had brought the insurgent armies to the United States point of view; he had received accolades of the people for ending the fighting. Some of the other radical Liberals castigated him for a sellout to the North Americans, but he nonetheless stood at the fore of the party.[15]

Stimson concurred in the State Department's attitude, regarding Moncada "as our strongest real friend in Nicaragua."[16] The first time the two men met, Stimson felt the Liberal general was a man he could deal with. After Tipitapa, Stimson had advised the department of Eberhardt's closeness to Díaz and the Conservatives and suggested it might be well to caution the minister against any Conservative attempt to undermine the May, 1927, settlement. Discussing Moncada with the department,

[13] Eberhardt to Stimson, Aug. 7, 1927, Stimson papers, box 156; Eberhardt to Department of State, Sept. 8, 1927, 817.00/5022. See also Munro to Department of State, Oct. 12, 1927, 711.17/207. Interestingly, the American minister to Nicaragua in 1916 had planned, if asked by the Liberals, to nominate Moncada. See Dana G. Munro, *Intervention and Dollar Diplomacy in the Caribbean, 1900–1921* (Princeton, N. J., 1964), p. 412.

[14] Department of State to Eberhardt, Sept. 10, 1927, 817.00/5022.

[15] The situation in the Liberal party was, from the American legation's view, somewhat cloudy until early October when Munro visited friends in León. He was then convinced that Moncada, at least for the time being, had most of the party behind him. He noted the bitterness of the old Sacasa people and thought they caused much of the agitation in the northern part of Nicaragua and in the rest of Central America. Munro believed that if Moncada's people thought the campaign to get rid of the Marines would succeed, many of them would go over to the Sacasa group.

[16] Stimson to Olds, June 24, 1927, Stimson papers, box 161.

Stimson later agreed to watch his step and cautioned the department to do likewise, so as not to give the impression that this Nicaraguan was the candidate of the United States. Moncada, Stimson said, had

> won his present advantage last spring by being brave enough to stand for friendship with the United States and an open acceptance of our help when the Sacasa people were stickling in technicalities and were afraid to pose as our friends. Now that he is reaping the reward of that we cannot turn around and throw him down even if he is not unnaturally doing his best to cash in his reward politically.[17]

Thus when Moncada made his trip to the United States, Stimson cordially received him, and Secretary Kellogg (at request of the Nicaraguan minister) had an appointment with him, just as with Chamorro. Nicaraguans followed the visit with interest. One headline blared, "General Moncada in Washington," followed by a boldface subheading, "General Moncada has been especially well received in the United States."[18] There was full coverage of the visit with Stimson, the lunch, and the complete text of Stimson's letter introducing Moncada to the State Department. These announcements were followed by others more emphatic: "The Department of State Opens Its Doors to General José María Moncada." The succeeding story stressed the general's acceptability—neither the Nicaraguan constitution nor the Central American treaties hindered him. And later there was the story of the "complete triumph of General Moncada."[19]

Chamorro naturally was unhappy about the attentions given his adversary, but apparently they did not have as much political effect in Nicaragua as the Conservatives or Eberhardt feared. There was disappointment that the State Department did not give the visitor more attention; Moncada had to go with the Conservative minister, César, to see the Secretary and the visit

---

[17] Stimson to White, Sept. 23, 1927, 817.00/5043½.
[18] La Noticia, Oct. 29, 1927, p. 1.
[19] Ibid., Nov. 13, 1927, p. 1; Nov. 20, 1927, p. 1.

lasted only five minutes.[20] During the brief visit the Secretary repeated a press announcement—that the United States was not selecting any candidate for president of Nicaragua and was going to do its best for a free election. However much the United States might dislike some other Liberal candidate, there is no evidence that it intentionally boosted Moncada. That the Liberal general made the most of his trip and his contacts—particularly with Stimson—is true. That the Nicaraguan people believed he was in special grace with Washington is true. That he was eventually nominated and elected is also true, but one cannot show that American design brought these attitudes and events.

After the trips of Nicaragua's leading politicians, Washington turned attention to supervising the election; the first concern was an election law which would grant General McCoy almost dictatorial power. The Sandino trouble, noted in the last chapter, was another consideration; fortunately it had quieted by autumn 1928, so as to allow voting in the northern departments. In Washington a third question arose: What should be Latin America's part? Stimson believed other countries should observe the election. Before going on his mission he discussed this point with Coolidge and Kellogg. They reached no decision. Future resolve would depend on whether observation would interfere with American responsibility for the election. After returning, Stimson again suggested the idea to Coolidge in mid-August, 1927. He wrote the President that it would forestall criticism and that the forthcoming Havana conference, the Sixth International Conference of American States, offered opportunity to approach other nations.[21] There was still no decision. Stimson took it up with the State Department. He wanted to "invite the sunlight of publicity as an antiseptic of all . . . backdoor gossip" circulating in Latin America about the election. McCoy and Munro did not like the idea. Who could tell what observers would come

[20] Munro to White, Nov. 26, 1927, White papers, box 14, Munro file.
[21] Memorandum of a conference with the President, the Secretary of State, Colonel Olds, and Mr. Stimson, Apr. 7, 1927, Stimson diary; Stimson to Coolidge, Aug. 20, 1927, Stimson papers, box 161.

and what stories might emanate? Nothing resulted from Stimson's suggestion.

A nonpartisan Guardia Nacional under American direction needed founding and financing. Communications had to be made available to all parties. Control of *aguardiente*, a native brandy, was necessary, since it could thoroughly confuse an election. There had to be a watch on internal taxation to make sure it did not influence voting. And, of course, the electoral apparatus had to be set up, including boards and committees and ballots. Provisions had to be made for registering voters, keeping repeaters to a minimum, counting votes, certifying results.

By mid-November, 1927, McCoy and the election expert and veteran of the 1924 affair in Nicaragua, Harold W. Dodds, had produced the special election law. It gave McCoy sweeping powers. The national board of elections, of which he would be chairman, could prescribe regulations having force of law for registration of voters, casting and counting of ballots, and any matters pertaining to the election. The chairman had to consent to acts of the board, and if necessary could declare emergency measures which would have the same force as an act by the board. The chairman would have command of the national guard, so as to prevent fraud.[22] Such a law, enforced by a citizen of the United States, could prevent another election like that of 1924. The State Department had learned in 1924 that in election matters Nicaraguan sovereignty would practically have to cease. To be sure, in both elections the department's goal was not just a free election but peace and stability. However, circumstances had changed. In 1928 United States honor—its pledge— was at stake, for the Díaz government and the Liberal army headed by Moncada agreed, at Stimson's insistence, to lay down arms.

But interest in the electoral law was two-edged. While the United States and the Liberals were striving for a free vote, there

[22] For the full text of these provisions see *Foreign Relations: 1927*, III, 379–380, 382.

was no great enthusiasm from the Conservatives, especially the Chamorro faction. Chamorro led the antisupervision movement. His attitude would have been the same whether a candidate or not; if running for the presidency he would have wanted all traditional means to win. Even though not in the race, he saw no reason to give up these advantages, particularly if a Chamorro candidate headed the ticket. One might say that Chamorro wanted revenge on the State Department, but this would be only surmise. A close reporter saw no revenge in Chamorro's attitude, only the wish to prevent defeat of his party.[23]

After Chamorro's return there were outspoken comments about the department's attempts to put Conservatives and Liberals on an equal basis. Conservatives questioned the constitutionality of appointing foreigners to government positions—Americans to head election boards and train the proposed Guardia. Newspapers carried statements by Chamorrista congressmen. Rumor circulated that President Díaz might resign, to be replaced by a *designado* chosen by a Chamorro-dominated Congress.

Near the end of December, 1927, the American legation in Managua received the opinion of two prominent lawyers who had studied the proposed election law. They questioned the heart of the proposed act—whether a citizen of the United States could be president of the electoral board and whether the board could make regulations with force of law.[24] Still the department convinced itself that its plans were in agreement with the supreme law of Nicaragua. Reviewing discussions leading to the Tipitapa settlement, Stimson recalled that Cuadra Pasos, the foreign minister and a lawyer, had no doubt about constitutionality of the proposed arrangement.[25] Stimson asserted he would not have entered an agreement and presented it to Coolidge if it had been illegal. The department recalled the request of President Díaz to Coolidge that the United States supervise the elec-

[23] H. N. Denny, *Dollars for Bullets*, (New York, 1929), p. 355.
[24] Munro to Department of State, Dec. 29, 1927, 817.00/5210.
[25] Department of State to Munro, Jan. 10, 1928, 817.00/5240a.

tion and noted that the McCoy proposal followed the Díaz memorandum. Coolidge had made a solemn engagement.

The Nicaraguan Congress proved uncooperative when the McCoy proposal went to the Nicaraguan Senate on December 28, 1927. The upper house approved it, but the lower chamber balked. The committee studying the proposition filed a report charging that it would be a derogation of sovereignty. The chamber suggested that the United States have representatives on election boards and power to make recommendations and propose changes in laws, but that everything then must go to the Nicaraguan Congress for approval.[26]

The conflict now was coming into the open. A free vote was just not compatible with partisan control of election machinery. The Chamorristas first pressed the constitutional issue, claiming a constituent assembly should deal with the matter. Chamorro complained the United States was showing favoritism and had chosen Moncada for the presidency. Predicting Conservative defeat, he intimated there was no need to take part in the election. In mid-February, 1928, when Sandino's bands were near Matagalpa threatening to attack that coffee center, the Conservatives argued against the electoral law because of the condition of the country. As an alternative Chamorristas advocated a coalition ticket with one presidential candidate, in hope of preventing a purely Liberal government. In Washington, the department distrusted the Nicaraguan minister, who encouraged the dissidents in Managua and assured the United States that Nicaragua wanted a supervised election but was against the McCoy measure. The minister endeavored to explain supervision as observation. Stimson, visiting in the capital, told him "to disabuse his mind of that idea."[27] Munro believed that failure of the depart-

---

[26] Munro to Department of State, Jan. 15, 1928, 817.00/5274.

[27] Memorandum of conversation between Kellogg and César, Jan. 10, 1928, 817.00/5260; memorandum of conversation among Stimson, César, and Olds, Jan. 10, 1928, 817.00/5261. Munro reported to the Department of State that the Nicaraguan minister had failed to make clear the department's interest in the passage of the election law and had given

ment to demand César's recall (which Munro had urged) strengthened the opposition.

It looked like deadlock. In Managua the lower house showed no relenting. Efforts by the legation and Cuadra Pasos to press the deputies came to nought, and the Chamber of Deputies approved a substitute unacceptable to the United States. The department hurried McCoy and Eberhardt, who had been in the United States, on their way to Nicaragua. Stimson urged frank discussion. Kellogg should say that officially or unofficially our representatives would be in every polling place and tabulate the vote, and further, we would not recognize any president whose election was not legal by tally of our representatives. Through authority over the constabulary, Stimson felt, we could prevent fraud. If we had to use strong methods to carry out a righteous purpose, we would be safer than by breaking our promise to the Liberals.[28] The department showed a willingness to allow a few amendments to the proposed law, as long as they did not diminish supervision. After consideration of the Chamber of Deputies' substitute, there appeared little chance for agreement, as it was not the constitution but the supervised election

the impression that the department could be convinced of the unconstitutionality of the law. This encouraged the deputies in their opposition. Munro to Department of State, Jan. 16, 1928, 817.00/5276. The department replied that for some time it had felt César was playing a double game. "We have already been thinking seriously of suggesting his recall. It has recently become more and more plain that he virtually represents Chamorro here rather than the Government of Nicaragua and that he is using his position as a base for the conduct of propaganda both with the Department and with the American public, in direct interest of Chamorro faction. César knows Department's deep interest in law as a *sine qua non* for a free election. He was called in twice on January 10 and told this. Seldom has a diplomatic representative in Washington been spoken to with more earnestness and emphasis than on this occasion when Col. Stimson was present. We do not want to complicate situation by asking for recall but inform Díaz what César is doing here." Department of State to Munro, Jan. 17, 1928, 817.00/5276.

[28] Stimson to Olds, Jan. 19, 1928, 817.00/5274½.

which bothered the Chamorristas. Washington turned to the Stimson line and instructed Munro to tell Díaz to fulfill the Tipitapa agreement, as the United States intended to do.[29] The department, like Stimson, hoped firmness would make the Nicaraguans agree.

Through January, 1928, through February and almost half of March, the department dickered with the Conservatives. Each side held out, convinced the other would give in. The department emphasized the gravity of the situation, referred to the Tipitapa agreement. Chamorro threatened to withdraw from politics, even if he destroyed his party by doing so. His followers talked about the constitution and the illegal demands of the United States. Department officers attending the Havana conference in February cooperated with Foreign Minister Cuadra Pasos, also at Havana, to find some solution. They drew up a new draft—merely a rewording—of the McCoy-Dodds election provisions. Then, facilitating Cuadra Pasos' return to Nicaragua on an American man-of-war—in hopes he could bring his supporters into line—they submitted the new proposals to the Nicaraguan Congress. The bill moved through the Senate, but the Chamber of Deputies again balked.[30]

The showdown in Nicaragua came early in the evening of March 13, 1928, at the congressional palace. Protected by the Guardia Nacional, the deputies voted along factional lines— Liberals and moderate Conservatives for, Chamorristas against. The Chamber turned thumbs down on the "McCoy Law." Three days later, after a futile attempt to pass an election law and a bill for the Guardia Nacional, Congress adjourned sine die. Emiliano Chamorro and his followers had defied Uncle Sam.

One could explain Chamorro's act by his interest in Conservative victory—especially through a Chamorro candidate. What-

---

[29] Department of State to Munro, Jan. 21, 1928, 817.00/5294.

[30] Admiral Sellers to chief of naval operations, Mar. 18, 1928, general records of the Navy Department, general correspondence, 1926–1940, record group 80, record identification EF 49, box 2009. Hereafter cited as general records, Navy Department.

ever the motive, to the United States Chamorro was a trouble-maker. A few weeks later McCoy met the general, and the American remarked diplomatically that Chamorro had never before been so concerned about the constitution. The Nicaraguan replied, with a smile, that he had become an apostle of the constitution since his return from the United States.[31]

Díaz seemed partly responsible for the Nicaraguan confusion in the spring of 1928. Eberhardt reported a month after the election law's failure that the President had admitted he could have dominated the situation. Chamorro was still drawing his salary as minister plenipotentiary to France, Spain, and Italy, and out of the January treasury surplus Díaz paid a large sum to the deputies for back salaries. He could have applied pressure. As President and as an adherent to the Tipitapa agreement he had obligations both to the Conservatives and the United States. As party leader he had to hold the Conservatives together, avoiding a split which might injure chances for victory in the autumn election.[32]

The situation was made even more unsatisfactory by the President's illness during part of the debate, and by January, Chamorro was practically running the government, sending orders

[31] McCoy to Department of State, Apr. 3, 1928, 817.00/5611.

[32] Munro to White, Feb. 18, 1928, White papers, box 14, Munro file. Eberhardt did not have kind words about the Nicaraguan Congress. In his dispatch to the Department of State, Apr. 13, 1928, 817.00/5609, he asserted that "the whole history of the consideration of the election law by Congress had illustrated in a striking manner the venality and the incompetence of the majority of the individuals who compose the Nicaraguan Congress. Overwhelming consideration in their minds appears to be the question of personal pecuniary profit and one of the factors which led to the defeat of the law was the belief that this action would compel the President to call a special session which would mean additional pay. The Minister of Finance repeatedly suggested that the Legation recommend to Mr. [Roscoe R.] Hill [resident American member of the high commission] the use of a part of the High Commission's funds to purchase votes for the measure. In default of such persuasion deputies followed Chamorro."

in his own name to local police and dictating policy of several government departments. This development, added to César's reports from Washington that the department was not really insisting on the law's adoption, encouraged Chamorro's resistance and Díaz' passive refusal to stand firm.[33]

Another factor in the election law was Cuadra Pasos, the foreign minister. Outwardly, he too was supporting the measure, but the American legation considered his support less than wholehearted. Munro felt that the President and Cuadra Pasos did not want to repudiate their earlier promises of support but were willing to give Chamorro a free hand. Friends of the foreign minister opposed the law until Americans pressured him at the Havana conference. Munro also reasoned that Cuadra Pasos hoped Chamorro might so discredit himself in American eyes as to boost the foreign minister's own presidential chances.[34]

What did the Conservative politicians have to lose by opposing electoral reform? To be sure, Americans threatened, but as Chamorro told McCoy, "no one is ever ruined in Central America."[35]

Whatever the explanations in Nicaragua, the United States wanted an immediate decision—the electoral mission needed to get started. Nothing had happened since December, 1927, and while the State Department desired congressional approval of the measure and was willing to negotiate for some time for it, Washington now felt other steps were needed. Eberhardt and McCoy closeted themselves with Conservative and Liberal leaders. When Díaz agreed to promulgate an electoral law, the Americans saw no need to keep the Nicaraguan Congress in session any longer.

Supporters of supervision now moved rapidly. The Nicaraguan Supreme Court was willing to elect McCoy president of the

[33] Munro to White, Feb. 18, 1928, White papers, box 14, Munro file.
[34] Ibid.
[35] Ibid.

national board of elections.[36] Cuadra Pasos sent a telegram asking Joaquin Gomez, president of the board and then in Washington, to resign. Gomez did so by return wire, and on March 17 the court elected McCoy. Arrangements proceeded for the presidential decree. There was some doubt about its legality, but McCoy felt the Nicaraguan constitution had provision for executive decrees. There was ample custom in Latin America to cover them. These points, however, were all secondary to McCoy's thinking. Stimson had arranged a cease-fire largely on promise of free elections; the President of Nicaragua had agreed, and President Coolidge had consented. The President's representative felt the Nicaraguan government should do its duty.[37] The decree became law on March 2, 1928, and was proclaimed, in the old Spanish custom, on the streets of Managua that afternoon.

Political questions continued, with a split Conservative party. Conservatives struggled over the choice of a party standard-bearer. Cuadra Pasos wanted the nomination, but Chamorro, already ruled out, supported individuals more friendly to himself. Eberhardt, McCoy, and the department feared that the Conservatives —or a large portion of them—would abstain from voting, thus casting doubt on the election. Or both factions might enter candidates and create a three-sided contest. This could make necessary a decision of the Nicaraguan Congress, which already

[36] In agreement with the election law of Mar. 20, 1923, which was still in effect, the Supreme Court chose the president of the national board of elections. Cuadro Pasos, Moncada, McCoy, and Eberhardt approved this action because it would help avoid criticism that the executive, if he issued a decree for the same purpose, was depriving a coordinate branch of a lawful duty. It also had the advantage of allowing the Supreme Court to participate in the arrangements leading to a presidential decree for the election provisions and committing that body to the legality of such procedure. Eberhardt to Department of State, Mar. 16, 1928, 817.00/5471.

[37] Draft of statement, "Legality versus Necessity," by General McCoy, records of the United States electoral mission to Nicaragua, 1928, record group 43, entry 366. These records are in the National Archives, foreign affairs branch.

had mangled United States plans. Handling it as a strictly party matter seemed the least perilous approach. The department interpreted the Tipitapa understanding as contemplating that intraparty controversies would be settled within the party and that the presidential elections would be conducted with only two candidates, each representing a major party.

The Conservative factions continued bickering. Each attempted to control delegates to the national convention. Two separate Conservative conventions met on May 20 and nominated two tickets. Each asked recognition from the national board of elections, but after hearing arguments, the board under McCoy refused to recognize either as the historic Conservative party. Two more weeks passed, during which McCoy "struggled Solomon like" for a compromise.[38] Then Cuadra Pasos and Vicente Rappaccioli, the Chamorro candidate, withdrew in favor of Adolfo Bénard, a wealthy sugar grower from Granada who was sympathetic to United States policies. Meanwhile the Liberals had nominated Moncada on February 14.

Another problem was the attempt of an autonomist party, under Toribio Tijerino, to get on the ballot. The autonomistas opposed American interference in Nicaraguan affairs and planned to run a candidate on such a platform. Eberhardt noted that it would be difficult to defend a policy of third-party exclusion.[39] Fortunately for the United States the Tijerino movement failed to marshal much support.

Two other parties asked recognition, Conservative Republicans and Liberal Republicans. Luis Felipe Corea headed the latter group. He was a former United States citizen who had run in the 1924 Nicaraguan election, polling about seven thousand votes, less than 10 percent of the total. Since that time his party had practically ceased operating, and it appeared that attempts to resuscitate the old organization were for trading purposes.

[38] McCoy to family, July 19, 1928, McCoy papers, family correspondence, box 6.
[39] Eberhardt to Department of State, May 30, 1928, 817.00/5709.

Some Liberal leaders saw an attempt to split their party and throw selection of the president into the Nicaraguan Congress. Conservatives reportedly were financing the Liberal Republicans. As one east coast Liberal newspaper observed, it seemed strange that a man who had lived in Washington almost continuously since 1899 and had renounced his citizenship should now return during a presidential campaign.[40] Near the end of July, 1928, the national electoral board considered requests of these two parties and turned both down. The board, headed by McCoy, was unanimous, asserting that neither group had standing as a party.

Another group, calling itself the Partido Laborista (organized in 1924), made a brief appearance but caused no problems for election officials, since its purpose was not participation but protest against American supervision. Its argument was that electoral participation would sanction the farce of electoral freedom, freedom which did not exist, since the supervisors had sustained an unconstitutional situation in Nicaragua. The supervisors had deprived Sacasa of his rights and ceded them to a citizen of their own sympathies.[41]

The election law, the split in the Conservative party, and the third-party issue were major questions. There were other problems involved in the mechanics of voting and the attempt to provide an atmosphere of freedom and fairness. Most of these things were minor, but their satisfactory solution was essential. The problem of repeat voting, for example, required that some simple method be devised for identifying those who had already voted. McCoy decided on a chemical marking which was non-injurious, cheap, available, transportable, and so effective it would not come off for a day or so. The resulting search involved the State Department, the chemical warfare service of the War Department, the Bureau of Engraving and Printing in the Department of Commerce, and the Treasury. The answer was

[40] The Bluefields Weekly, Sept. 29, 1928, p. 2.
[41] La Tribuna (Managua), Oct. 10, 1928, p. 1.

mercurochrome! Every voter had to dip two fingers of the left hand so that the solution spread under the nail and around the cuticle. Election officials kept the entire method of marking a secret. By chance someone might find out how to dissolve mercurochrome. They also feared the red color might cause objections from Conservatives (red meant Liberal). During the election no one—not even President Díaz or the candidates—was excepted from the marking. Later, anti-Americans emphasized the indignity of the procedure and felt it was a good example of the results of intervention.[42] One irate Nicaraguan editorialist believed it was the same as saying to a voter, "You are a degenerate citizen and capable of fraud; thus you must be marked." And regardless of election board claims that the mark was inoffensive and noninjurious to health, the writer scoffingly asked, "What are the psychological or sociological effects?" "What will it do to the national soul?"[43]

The campaign was a strenuous and bitter one with some lives lost. The party leaders worked hard under heavy strain. Cuadra Pasos, who fell ill, attributed it to too many swallows of bad liquor on the campaign trail, and Moncada and Chamorro, too, felt the effects of long tours. Because the elderly Bénard wisely remained out of the country until the final stages of the campaign, Chamorro was the Conservative mainstay. He combined his organizing talents and popularity with "energy in shaking down the wealthy but stingy Granada crowd for money for the campaign." As a member of the American legation remarked, "I never realized until recently how unfairly we should have treated

[42] Editorial in La Presna of Buenos Aires, quoted in Gregorio Selser, Sandino, General de Hombres Libres (Buenos Aires, 1959), II, 40.

[43] Editorial from El Diario Nicaragüense (Granada), quoted in La Tribuna, Sept 30, 1928, p. 1. In 1920 when the American military attaché in Nicaragua made a similar suggestion to prevent repeat voting, the Department of State rejected it because it would result in personal indignity. See Munro, Intervention and Dollar Diplomacy in the Caribbean, 1900–1921, p. 421.

the Conservatives if we had listened to the suggestion that he be not allowed to return."[44]

Other electoral problems involved alcohol and communications, police, taxes, registration, and in the background always hovered Sandino. Periodic reports had Sandino preparing a major offensive just before election day, and some rumors suggested the Conservatives, anticipating defeat, were collaborating with him to obstruct the election.[45] But, as noted in the last chapter, Sandinistas were fairly quiet around election time. Alcohol, potential cause of innumerable problems, was strictly regulated by election officials. Aguardiente, a government monopoly in Nicaragua, had frequently been used to buy votes, leading sometimes to disorder and death. By a decree of August 30, all government distillers and liquor warehouses were padlocked on September 1 and the keys entrusted to officers of the national guard. Possession of aguardiente was forbidden from September 17 until November 16, and other distilled liquors could not be purchased on the registration days or election day.[46] Prior to the registrations national guard troops replaced all local police, and from November 3 to November 6 the national council of elections took control of the main telegraph lines from Managua to most towns and cities.[47]

The United States supervisors did the jobs required and set up 432 polling places so that, as McCoy said, "no blooming native will have far to go to vote, like Charlie Armstrong's lordly cow, not one has to carry himself more than a mile to drink."[48] Record numbers of voters registered beginning Sunday, Septem-

[44] Munro to White, Sept. 17, 1928, White papers, box 14, Munro folder.
[45] The Bluefields Weekly, July 14, 1928, p. 1; La Tribuna, Oct. 10, 1928, p. 1.
[46] The Bluefields Weekly, Sept. 22, 1928, p. 6.
[47] McCoy to Feland, Oct. 11, 1928, Marine Corps in Nicaragua records, Navy Annex, box 6, file 1.
[48] McCoy to family, Sept. 15, 1928, McCoy papers, family correspondence, box 6.

ber 23, and then for the next two Wednesdays and Sundays, ending October 7. On November 4, 1928, they voted—a majority picking Moncada. The Liberals increased their seats in Congress, although they did not gain control of the lower house.[49]

Unquestionably most of the Nicaraguan voters wanted Moncada as president. United States policy makers had hoped for such a clear-cut win. Yet Eberhardt feared that the Conservative Congress might mar the victory. Hoping to force the United States to additional military control, the legislature could refuse to proclaim the presidential election. The minister felt that Chamorro would prefer this to government by Moncada. But on December 28, 1928, the Nicaraguan Congress approved the report of the national board of elections and on the first day of the new year Moncada took office.

Some Latin Americans greeted Moncada's victory with a sneer, calling the President-elect a "Liberal Chamorro" or "mediocre opportunist." One newspaper insisted that those who desired to maintain the tradition of a great nation, which was more than sanitary well-being or financial comfort, should view the election with hostility; but, the editorial continued, the people of Nicaragua have the government they deserve. "A proud people would have abandoned the ballot boxes; would not have submitted to the humiliation of exercising under foreign control the maximum function of democracy."[50] Even in Nicaragua a very few had harsh words; one commentator believed that the world observing Nicaraguan events would not know where to attribute greater evil—to the great power which with a mask of justice hides its inequity, or to those who knowingly accept the farce of aiding the enslavement of their country.[51]

[49] The total registration was 148,831; total vote was 133,633. Moncada had a majority of 19,689. The make-up of the Senate after the election was twelve Liberals and twelve conservatives, and of the Chamber of Deputies, nineteen Liberals and twenty-four Conservatives.

[50] El Tiempo of Bogota as quoted in Selser, Sandino, II, 40, 41.

[51] Editorial from Actualidad (León), quoted in La Tribuna, Dec. 15, 1928, p. 1.

The free election of 1928 was a major move in United States diplomacy for a stable Nicaragua. Ending the revolution in 1927 had been first; disarmament of combatants followed; the Marine action against Sandino went on during the entire era with organization of the nonpartisan Guardia Nacional. Now the election was over. On January 1, 1929, Nicaraguan affairs were where the State Department had wished them four years earlier, when the small force of Marines had prepared to withdraw during the summer of 1925 after Solórzano's inauguration.

Although the 1928 vote culminated almost a year and a half of planning which began with the Stimson agreements, Washington was not now inclined to retire precipitately. One fair election did not change a century of Nicaraguan political history. To accomplish that would take more time than the North American nation was willing to spend in Nicaragua. The United States wanted the Guardia built to power and efficiency, wanted to pacify the Sandinista-infested areas as much as possible, and was considering supervising the next presidential election in 1932. Then the Americans would withdraw and hope for the best.

10: RETRENCHMENT: 1929–1930

In the four years after Moncada's inauguration the United States continued to intervene in Nicaragua. If the Tipitapa agreement of 1927 was meant only to end the revolution and ensure a fairly chosen president, the United States had fulfilled its goals by January 1, 1929. If, however, Stimson had intended to bring peace to Nicaragua, that condition had not appeared. Frank B. Kellogg, nearing the end of his tenure as secretary of state, recognized the lack of stability in early 1929.[1] Nor would it be present when the Marines withdrew four years later. An unfortunate (for the United States and Nicaragua) combination of patriotism, megalomania, banditry, and jungle terrain made pacification impossible.

With hindsight one can make such an assertion. At the time, the task of the United States in Nicaragua did not seem insurmountable. In 1929–30 and thereafter, resolving the Sandino problem was not essentially different from the pacification of 1927. The United States followed the pattern of Stimson, not wholly unexpected since Stimson was Kellogg's successor in the Department of State. Yet there was room for variation. While Washington pushed for an efficient Guardia Nacional and fair elections, aided by Marines, there was a desire to retreat from intervention, more importunate under Hoover because of lack of success against Sandino, the crescendo of criticism against intervention, and economic distress at home and abroad.

[1] Kellogg to Eberhardt, Feb. 14, 1929, 817.1051/256.

President-elect Hoover had shown an early interest in Latin American relations. Prior to his inauguration he toured South and Central America. At times he spoke against intervention, and reports from his ship, the U.S.S. *Maryland*, seemed critical of Kellogg's Latin American diplomacy. In Buenos Aires he declared opposition to intervention, just as Coolidge opposed it, and said he would do his utmost to avoid it in the future. This was no clear rebuttal of interference, and viewed along with Hoover's expression that he did not disagree with protecting lives and property of United States citizens when local conditions necessitated it, it revealed little change.[2] Yet during Hoover's four years the United States would withdraw. What influence Hoover's stop in Corinto had on later policies is not clear. Undoubtedly he received mixed evaluations of American policies in Nicaragua. From officials such as Díaz and Moncada there was probably little criticism; however, a group of *autonomistas* including former President Bartolomé Martínez and Salomón de la Selva sent Hoover a letter (whether he read it is not known) asking for retirement of Marines.[3]

Thus, early in 1929 when Moncada was replacing Díaz, Hoover was accepting the disturbing Nicaraguan question from Coolidge. The new administration thought withdrawal simply a matter of time—time to establish the national guard and pacify the northern departments. There had been no question that troops would remain until after the 1928 referendum, but with the election over, a reexamination was in order.

Since America's ultimate goal was withdrawal, in retrospect one may regret that possibly some opportunities were missed for ending the Nicaraguan affair in the immediate postelection period. Aside from a few loose ends, the essential promises of Tipitapa were accomplished. A conference of Nicaraguan fac-

---

[2] Department of State to American legation in Managua, Nov. 23, 1928, 003.1110 Hoover, Herbert/149; Robert W. Bliss to Department of State, Dec. 22, 1928, 003.1110 Hoover, Herbert/280.

[3] *La Tribuna*, (Managua), Nov. 30, 1928, p. 1.

tions—at least the incoming administration and Sandino—might have been able to settle Nicaraguan problems stemming from intervention and the guerrilla insurgency if Americans had assented to immediate withdrawal upon agreement. Even in 1928, Nicaraguan Salomón de la Selva proposed a similar solution. In letters sent to President Díaz, President-elect Moncada, and Sandino, he suggested that a conference be held to effect immediate United States withdrawal, the surrender of arms and recognition of the Moncada administration by Sandinistas, and the granting of amnesty for Sandino and his men.[4] Despite the many difficulties attendant to any solution, it is lamentable that there was no reponse at this seemingly opportune time when new administrations were aborning in Washington and Managua.

But Washington felt one could not expect too much from the election. It was no panacea but only one detail in a complex issue. The specter of 1925 haunted the thinking of the State Department. Too rapid withdrawal could be awkward. Had not the Navy Department withdrawn men too quickly after Tipitapa, thus helping create the Sandino trouble? To Francis White of the department the answer was yes, and when Admiral Charles F. Hughes spoke of taking out 1,600 men, White was concerned. He knew the fears of the Managua legation that a crisis might develop over canvassing the vote in December. Dana Munro foresaw that radical measures might be needed. At least the United States should indicate that it was ready for them. Troop retirement, showing weakness or unconcern, could bring what Washington wanted to avoid. White urged that United States intentions be guarded until both the election and congressional canvass were over. He recommended the matter be taken up with the Navy secretary or, if need be, Coolidge. Kellogg brought the matter up in a cabinet meeting of October 9, 1928, at which the President directed that nothing be done.[5]

[4] Ibid., Nov. 15, 1928, p. 3.
[5] White to secretary of state, Oct. 5, 1928, 817.00/6026; note from W.H.B. to White, Oct. 9, 1928, 817.00/6026.

The decision settled the question until January 1, 1929. There was little doubt that a reduction of troops would come then, although even on this date there was disagreement. In November, 1928, Kellogg contemplated a great reduction after the inauguration, and Admiral David F. Sellers and General Logan Feland favored lowering the force to around four thousand. Sellers believed Sandino's prestige was almost nil. General McCoy disagreed; he felt the Nicaraguan's prestige had risen simply because he had been able to defy United States troops, and McCoy advised remaining in strength to fight Sandino.[6] The department bided its time until the turn of the year, when Moncada's attitude would become apparent and McCoy would go home.

When Moncada wished to have Nicaraguans combat the trouble in the northern departments, the State Department was willing. However, it thought this should be done through the Guardia Nacional. If the national guard would take over the job of policing, then the Marines could confine their activities to protecting foreign lives and property. The switch would be gradual, and as United States troops were taken from combat patrols, the excess numbers could be pulled out of Nicaragua. Hopefully this could be done without trouble, especially if the insurgents continued to show no more life than they had since the election.

Growth of the Guardia was important to department plans. As outlined by the Stimson agreement, it would prevent anti-administration uprisings and preserve order at elections. Nonpartisan soldiers were to be perpetuators of constitutionality in Nicaragua. The guaranteed free election of 1928 would be a futile example of democratic process if it were not the forerunner of nonpartisan law enforcement. Thus the national guard became the focus of United States-Nicaraguan relations in the first

[6] Kellogg to Curtis D. Wilbur, secretary of the Navy, Nov. 15, 1928, 817.1051/234; Sellers to chief of naval operations, Nov. 17, 1928, Sellers papers, box 250.

year of Moncada's presidency, for establishment of the Guardia meant a reduction in the Marine force. Early in 1929, the Marines in Nicaragua were reduced to 3,500, and by the end of the year there were 1,800.[7]

Steady reduction in the number of Marines did not indicate smooth development of the Guardia. In 1925 the Nicaraguan government had formed a similar body, just before the first Marine withdrawal. Chamorro's coup had shaken it; and although it survived in name, support of an extralegal government blemished its nonpartisan character. The Liberal revolution made the surviving shell untenable, and the retired United States Army officer who had acted as director left for home. The United States took much more interest in the new Guardia, detailing officers and enlisted men to train it.[8] A bill for the national guard met the same fate in the Nicaraguan Congress as had the 1928 "McCoy" election law, but President Díaz issued an executive decree establishing the constabulary. After Moncada's inauguration, the Guardia agreement (signed by the United States and Nicaragua on December 22, 1927) was resubmitted to the legislature. That body made several amendments, some unacceptable to the United States. Extended discussion of amendments caused Eberhardt to consider that there was truth in the rumor that Moncada, not wanting to oppose it openly, was against the bill. The United States minister later came to feel that the Nicaraguan Congress was primarily responsible for the trouble.[9]

[7] New York Times, Jan. 8, 1929, p. 30; undated statement prepared by Department of State in answer to Senate resolution 386 of Jan. 5, 1931, 817.00/6922.

[8] An act of Congress of May 19, 1926, authorized the president of the United States to detail personnel of the Army, Navy, and Marine Corps to assist the governments of the republics of North America, Central America, and South America, and Cuba, Haiti, and Santo Domingo in military and naval matters whenever the president felt it was in the public interest to do so.

[9] Eberhardt to Department of State, Jan. 23, 1929, 817.1051/239; Eberhardt to Department of State, Jan. 31, 1929, 817.1051/245.

Meanwhile a split in United States ranks in Nicaragua resulted in divided representations to Moncada. Problems arose between the American legation and ranking military officers, as well as between the Marine brigade officers and the American commanding the national guard. Stemming from many sources—ambition, jealousy, Nicaraguan politics, and probably misunderstanding—the conflict encouraged Nicaraguan recalcitrance. On the one side were the minister, Eberhardt, and the chief of the Guardia, Elias R. Beadle. On the other was General Feland, supported by Admiral Sellers. Beadle and Eberhardt, opposing anything that would weaken the guard, wanted the constabulary agreement passed as drawn. This organization should be the only military and police force in Nicaragua. While the president of the republic would be commander of the Guardia, they felt the chief should control recruiting, appointment, promotion, discipline, and operation, for these things in the hands of politicians could end any nonpartisan character. Eberhardt and Beadle wanted orders to come only from the president and not from lesser Nicaraguan officials. The minister and chief of the constabulary were supporting State Department policy, outlined by Stimson at Tipitapa and expressed in the Guardia agreement of December, 1927. In many respects this was an idealistic policy, time-consuming, and probably destined to fall short of the goal, but even approximate success was impossible if the department gave way on fundamentals.[10]

Many of Feland's actions led Eberhardt to conclude that the Marine general was giving Moncada advice contrary to what the department desired. At one time the minister reported that the Nicaraguan President looked upon Feland as his virtual minister of war and adviser on military and other matters, and that the general had agreed with Moncada in decreasing the national guard's importance. At another time Eberhardt noted that Feland did not agree with Beadle and himself in opposing reestab-

[10] Department of State to Matthew E. Hanna, United States chargé in Managua, May 29, 1929, 817.1051/280.

lishment of an armed corps of treasury guards (*resguardos de hacienda*). This force's task, until disbanded by Díaz, had been to prevent smuggling and contraband traffic in liquor and tobacco, but the president could use it in all sorts of jobs.[11]

Such differences, embittering relations between the ranking United States civilian and military leaders in Nicaragua, stemmed, so Eberhardt thought, from Feland's desire to have the Marines play a greater role in Nicaragua at the very time the State Department wanted to de-emphasize the military. The minister did not like the fact that a Marine, Lieutenant A. D. Challacombe, was acting as Moncada's personal aide. Nor did Eberhardt like the reported statements of the President that while he was glad to have State Department views explained by the minister, if he wanted real results he need only consult Feland, who seemed to be able to get results through his own organization and influence in Managua and Washington.[12]

Early in February, 1929, Eberhardt told the department that Sellers had said he and Feland could not see why Washington should not accept amendments to the Guardia agreement which were satisfactory to the Nicaraguan government.[13] This attitude, Eberhardt thought, encouraged Moncada in his disregard of legation advice against modification, and the minister did not conceal his belief from Sellers. The admiral denied he favored the amended bill, denied even having seen the changes. He supported the law as drafted by the State Department but felt "trivial matters" should not stand in the way. That he considered amendments to the final bill—not wholly acceptable to the department—such trivial matters is clear from a statement made by Sellers the month after the bill had passed. To his mind the changes

---

[11] Eberhardt to Department of State, Jan. 22, 1929, 817.1051/238; Eberhardt to Department of State, Feb. 1, 1929, 817.1051/262.

[12] Eberhardt to White, Jan. 24, 1929, and Feb. 9, 1929, White papers, box 11, Eberhardt file.

[13] Eberhardt to Department of State, Feb. 9, 1929, 817.1051/256.

did not interfere with a nonpartisan military organization.[14]

Complicating the constabulary issue even further was the open friction between Guardia chief Beadle and brigade commander Feland. The nature of these two organizations in Nicaragua was conducive to conflict, and even the Navy Department had difficulty defining their exact relationship. In November, 1927, the director of operations and training for the Marine Corps described the status in a memorandum. All officers and men of the United States Marine Corps and Navy assigned to the Nicaraguan constabulary detachment were also part of the second brigade and as such the commanding officer of the constabulary detachment (Beadle) was an immediate subordinate of the brigade commander (Feland). Thus Americans serving in the Guardia and having responsibilities to the Nicaraguan president also occupied a niche in the Marine Corps chain of command. At the same time Beadle was a lietuenant colonel in the Marines and subordinate to General Feland, he was also a general in the Nicaraguan national guard, directly under the Nicaraguan president, and in charge of Nicaraguan personnel in the Guardia. Neither special service squadron commander Sellers nor second brigade commander Feland could issue orders affecting Nicaraguan enlisted men in the constabulary. Complications could arise if the dual roles of American officers ever conflicted. Hopefully the Guardia Nacional and the brigade would cooperate to accomplish their mission.[15]

The following month Secretary of the Navy Curtis D. Wilbur emphasized that the two forces should operate independently, except in an emergency, and noted their separate chains of command. If Navy personnel serving with the Guardia were involved in any case which required trial by general court martial,

[14] Sellers to Eberhardt, Feb. 9, 1929, Sellers papers, box 251; Sellers to chief of naval operations, Mar. 11, 1929, Sellers papers, box 251.

[15] Memorandum from director of operations and training, L. McCarty Little, to major general commandant, Nov. 16, 1927, U. S. Marine Corps, adjutant and inspector's office, general correspondence, box 83, folder 1375-40 Nicaragua.

there would be transfer to the brigade.[16] General Feland, however, opposed a clear delineation of the two organizations, and he apparently used his relationship with Moncada to weaken the program for a strong, independent national guard, which Beadle aimed at creating. Feland, supported by Sellers, desired unity of command, with the Nicaraguan national guard a part of the second brigade so that he could control Navy men serving with the Guardia.[17] This policy Beadle opposed and, as later became apparent, so did the major general commandant of the Marine Corps.[18]

Assuredly, Beadle was unpopular with the new Nicaraguan President. During a conversation with Eberhardt, Moncada charged that Beadle had worked so long with the former Conservative administration that he had become a Conservative partisan. The President noted that any successor to Beadle who demonstrated fairness could have a free hand with the national guard, although he must cooperate with the Marine commander.

[16] Wilbur to commander special service squadron, Dec. 9, 1927, adjutant and inspector's office correspondence, box 83, folder 1375–40 Nicaragua.

[17] Feland to Sellers, Feb. 7, 1929, Marine Corps files, box 186, folder 55. Apparently this letter was not sent. See also memorandum by Feland for Sellers, Feb. 9, 1929, Sellers papers, box 251.

[18] Commander special service squadron to chief of naval operations, Feb. 14, 1929, adjutant and inspector's office correspondence, box 83, folder 1375-40 Nicaragua; major general commandant to chief of naval operations, Mar. 9, 1929, adjutant and inspector's office correspondence, box 83, folder 1375–40–20 officers-detail. Eberhardt commented on the Marine officers' feud in these terms: It is a story "in which the brilliance, energy, success and popularity of the younger officer have run afoul of the ambition and sensitiveness of a superior officer, with the odds, as always, in favor of the older officer." "In this whole affair, the fact that Beadle cooperated so well with McCoy (who had given Feland and Beadle some straight talk about virtual failures of the respective organizations) seems to have been largely the reason for Feland's attitude toward a subordinate officer whom he had in the first place recommended most highly for the important work with the Guardia Nacional." Eberhardt to White, Jan. 31, 1929, White papers, box 11, Eberhardt file.

Eberhardt was convinced that Beadle had been nonpartisan; his sin had been cooperation with the Díaz government. The department agreed that the constabulary chief had been highly successful under difficult conditions.[19]

Not long after Washington learned of trouble between Beadle and Feland, and apparently because of it and actions of the brigade commander, the Navy Department considered replacing the two officers. The State Department doubted whether the Marines could find an equally competent replacement for Beadle and favored retaining him. But Eberhardt counseled that both should go, although he shared the high esteem for the Guardia commander. In talking with Moncada, the minister found indications that Feland had prejudiced the President's mind against Beadle. Therefore, both men received new assignments and left Nicaragua in March, 1929.[20]

Early in April, Feland visited the State Department, where he talked with Francis White. White explained the department's feelings about a nonpartisan national guard. The Marine officer asserted such a thing was impossible in Nicaragua; there could be only a partisan Guardia.[21] He told White he felt Eberhardt

[19] Eberhardt to Department of State, Feb. 18, 1929, 817.1051/261; Eberhardt to Department of State, Jan. 22, 1929, 817.1051/238; Department of State to Eberhardt, Jan. 30, 1929, 817.1051/238.

[20] Eberhardt to Department of State, Jan. 31, 1929, 817.1051/244. One should note that Sellers felt Beadle had no legitimate cause for complaint against Feland. He believed that Beadle had shown a "lamentable lack of tact in dealing with both the President of Nicaragua and with the Brigade Commander." Sellers to chief of naval operations, Feb. 14, 1929, Sellers papers, box 251. Colonel Douglas C. McDougal of the Marine Corps took command of the Guardia on Mar. 11, 1929. Feland left on Mar. 26, but his replacement, Brigadier General Dion Williams, did not take command until Apr. 18, 1929.

[21] Memorandum of conversation between Feland and White, Apr. 9, 1929, 817.1051/283. Willard Beaulac, second secretary, American legation in Managua, sent White his view on the Feland affair with the slight intimation that it was not a black and white situation. "Since the Feland episode has been brought to the President's attention it occurred

had misinterpreted or misinformed the department about Moncada for Moncada was a friend of the United States and wanted to cooperate.

There was at least one other conflict which confused American relations with Moncada. This trouble involved the ranks of Feland and Sellers at official functions. Feland insisted on having a place ahead of the chargés d'affaires of other countries, and the Nicaraguan Congress granted the admiral and brigadier general the rank of minister plenipotentiary on special mission. The decision irked foreign representatives in Managua and embarrassed the State Department, which wanted to soft-pedal the United States military role in Nicaragua.[22] The legation suggested to Feland that he back down, but Feland refused. To settle the ridiculous matter the parties agreed that the honor would not pass on to replacements of the two men. Shortly before leaving office Secretary of the Navy Wilbur requested that the State Department make suitable acknowledgment of the courtesy. The letter reached the desk of Henry L. Stimson, the incoming secretary of state, who recorded some of the diplomats' pique. He did not think it appropriate to express appreciation of the Nicaraguan congressional act, since no one but the president of the

to me that the latter might force a showdown, in which case I should suggest that the Department be very cautious. While I absolutely agree with the Minister that Feland intrigued and generally acted the spoiled child I feel that in anticipation of a possible showdown the latter may have worked up a possible case against the Legation, and I am not sure that the Legation has always been frank and forceful with him as far as putting him in his place is concerned, and he might be able to give the impression that many things that he did were done with the Legation's knowledge and apparent consent, and that in certain cases the Legation even encouraged him." Apr. 8, 1929, White papers, box 8, Beaulac file.

[22] Note for example, the telegram from the Department of State to Eberhardt, Jan. 10, 1929, 817.452/3, which in part reads: "The department notes that you (Eberhardt) have endeavored on such occasions as Mr. Hoover's visit and the inauguration to avoid any display which might give an impression of American military domination and feels very strongly that this same policy should be followed at all times."

United States could confer the rank of minister plenipotentiary and envoy extraordinary of the United States. Secretary Stimson also noted that Eberhardt would soon depart Managua on leave and that the American chargé d'affaires, as representative of this country, would take precedence over both the special service squadron commander and the brigade commander.[23]

Meanwhile the Guardia agreement was having difficulties. No doubt, divided American opinion in Nicaragua aggravated the problem.[24] The extent to which this division caused trouble was not measurable. However, it was not the only factor hindering agreement. Much opposition came from Chamorro followers who had prevented the passage of the 1928 election law, and many Liberals spoke against the bill. A majority of newspapers clamored against it, emphasizing legal roadblocks as well as the heavy financial burden which the national guard would cause.[25] In view of the good work of the guard, Eberhardt concluded that party leaders who opposed any constabulary with broad powers had inspired the criticism.[26]

In late January, 1929, the Chamber of Deputies passed the amended Guardia bill. The personnel and monetary requirements as listed in the bill were the only ones authorized for the force except by special congressional approval. In the original bill these listings had been minimum requirements. The new version no longer referred to the constabulary as the sole military and police force, and it opened the door for officials other than

[23] Stimson to secretary of the Navy, probable date, Apr. 15, 1929, diplomatic post records, Nicaragua, Hanna, vol. I.

[24] One of the State Department complaints against Feland was that he had "usurped the prerogatives of the American minister by making direct representations to the President of Nicaragua regarding matters with which he had no proper concern and which should have been dealt with exclusively by the Minister." Memorandum by Dana G. Munro, Mar. 8, 1929, 817.00/6283.

[25] La Prensa (Managua), Jan. 8, 1929, found in Marine Corps in Nicaragua records, Navy Annex, box 13, file 11.

[26] Eberhardt to Department of State, Jan. 30, 1929, 817.1051/257.

the president to direct the Guardia. There were also changes dealing with punishment of members of the force and other regulations.

The amendments disappointed the State Department, but it was willing to accept many of them if this would bring Senate passage. On two points the department insisted upon no change —that the listed requirements be minimum and the Guardia be the only military and police force in Nicaragua. Washington later added a third point: The Guardia was to be subject only to direction of the Nicaraguan president. If the constabulary were to have any semblance of nonpartisanship, these points were essential. But Moncada told Eberhardt, just as Feland would tell Francis White, that such a group could not be established.[27] The minister believed that Moncada was thwarting plans to keep politics out of the Guardia, and this was probably true; since he believed it impossible to have a nonpartisan force, the President preferred Liberal to Conservative control.

Nonetheless, the United States continued its efforts along these lines. It was the only thing the department could do without admitting its policies might be wrong. The alternatives were to acknowledge that the Marines would have to stay, or to pull out the troops and wait for revolution. Making Nicaragua a permanent protectorate was impossible. Thus the United States, reminding Moncada of commitments under the Tipitapa agreement, insisted on a nonpartisan Guardia. Months before the 1928 election the Liberal leader had insisted on Stimson's program, and now the department felt Moncada must remember Nicaraguan obligations.

The new government, however, had other ideas. A spokesman for the Managua foreign office explained to the Chamber of Deputies that to end the revolution the Tipitapa understanding had created extraconstitutional law in Nicaragua but that this law had ended with the election. Congress could now decide if

[27] Department of State to Eberhardt, Feb. 14, 1929, 817.1051/256; Eberhardt to Department of State, Feb. 14, 1929, 817.1051/260.

Tipitapa conformed to the constitution.[28] Eberhardt felt this expression of opinion encouraged modification by Congress. Reluctance of the Nicaraguan legislature or executive to do the department's bidding was nothing new. The balky Chamorro faction of the previous year was evidence that Nicaraguans did not always follow Washington's suggestion. In 1928 the Díaz administration had to resort to a presidential decree after American diplomatic representations had failed. But Moncada was not Díaz, nor was the Guardia law the same as an election law. The Guardia agreement was a long-term project, and a constabulary would require yearly appropriations and approval of successive presidents.

The department decided that firmness toward Moncada might move him. Eberhardt was to tell the President that any attempt to make the national guard a partisan organization would violate the Stimson agreement. If Moncada persisted, Washington would consider withdrawing not only the Marine officers with the Guardia but all Marines; for this the Nicaraguan government would have to shoulder responsibility.[29]

A constabulary agreement finally passed the Nicaraguan Congress on February 19, 1929. Two days later the President signed it. The new law was not like the original agreement, but it deleted some changes made earlier by the Chamber of Deputies. It provided—as the department wished—that the Guardia be the sole military and police force. Still, other changes made the act unacceptable. The department felt the law did not provide sufficient strength for the Guardia; a provision might require subordinate officers of the guard to take orders from local Nicaraguan officials; the Guardia chief needed more authority over recruiting, training, and discipline; local judicial authorities might prosecute Nicaraguan members of the force who were acting in the line of duty. After Washington suggested an exchange of notes on interpretation of the amendments, talks among

---

[28] Eberhardt to Department of State, Jan. 30, 1929, 817.1051/257.
[29] Department of State to Eberhardt, Feb. 16, 1929, 817.1051/256.

Guardia chief Colonel Douglas C. McDougal, Chargé Matthew Hanna, and Moncada brought some agreement. While the United States recognized the large financial burden of the national guard to Nicaragua and consented to reductions, Moncada agreed to disband such armed groups as the *hacienda* guards and *voluntarios*.

These discussions did not settle the question, and 1929 ended with neither United States acceptance of the revisions nor agreement on interpretation. In spring and early summer 1930, the governments again explored the idea of exchanging notes. Drafting proceeded until the Nicaraguan foreign minister consulted the Supreme Court. When the court objected to some provisions, the diplomats revised the drafts, but revisions did not satisfy the court's contention that Nicaraguan civil officials had authority to give orders to the Guardia in their respective localities. This power the State Department was not willing to allow. There was little progress on the matter, and the Nicaraguan government lost interest.

Much of Moncada's reluctance to discuss the agreement and his growing disinterest stemmed from financial straits of the worldwide Great Depression. The main problem concerning the national guard came to be its cost. In line with supporting a strong Guardia, the United States wanted a minimum of 2,000 men and a yearly appropriation of at least a million dollars. Moncada believed these figures were too high, for such appropriation would absorb about 25 percent of total national revenue. Consequently money came to the Guardia on a month-to-month basis, and even then amounts were not as large as McDougal felt he needed. The Nicaraguan President initiated studies in which he proposed to lower the appropriation to $720,000, perhaps even $689,132 (the amount specified in the original agreement passed by the Nicaraguan Congress). McDougal believed such figures would force a reduction to 1,400 men, a number which was insufficient to pacify the northern areas and might even allow banditry in unaffected sections. He recommended that Marines reinforce the reduced Guardia or, if this course were contrary to United States policy, that American forces withdraw.[30]

Some United States officials thought the financial issue endangered United States policy toward Nicaragua. The American minister, now Matthew E. Hanna—a former Army officer and assistant to General Leonard Wood in Cuba—counseled that unreasonable concessions could bring difficulties, and because the constabulary was the foundation of United States efforts he wanted to hold firm on it. At first Washington was willing to make concessions. The department cabled the legation to accept a reduction to 1,500 men at a cost of $825,000. A letter from Stimson to Moncada was to convey this information. But American officials in Nicaragua thought such a cut would make law and order impossible, and wanted at least 2,000 men and no further cut until the Guardia could enlist and train an auxiliary local police force.[31] These officials also wanted the department to insist that Moncada rescind his order for the reduction by November 15. Washington agreed, and Stimson's letter went to the Nicaraguan President, who strongly defended his position and questioned the efficiency of the Guardia. Stimson sent a second letter protesting the President's ideas, yet indicating readiness to make some concessions; the department was willing to abandon certain Guardia posts outside the bandit area but insisted the force in the Sandinista-infested section remain the same.[32] Stimson's suggestion now pleased Moncada.

The department devoted so much time to formation of a nonpartisan constabulary because, as noted, there had to be a guarantee that the nation's police force would treat Liberals and

[30] Hanna to Department of State, Oct. 7, 1930, 817.1051/428; copy of letter from McDougal to commandant, Marine Corps, Oct. 17, 1930, 817.1051/452½.

[31] Hanna to White, Oct. 16, 1930, 817.1051/453½; Oct. 18, 1930, 817.1051/486; Department of State to Hanna, Oct. 31, 1930, 817.1051/439A; Hanna to Department of State, Nov. 1, 1930, 817.1051/442.

[32] Department of State to Hanna, Nov. 24, 1930, 817.1051/459. According to the department's figures an appropriation of a little less than $800,000 would suffice and the Guardia personnel would be 1,810.

Conservatives alike and not perpetuate one political faction. The
Guardia had other chores, especially Sandino. This hero-bandit
still roamed in the wilds of Segovia. For a time Marines could
protect the government, as they had done in 1927 and 1928, but
that situation could not last indefinitely. Nicaraguans would have
to handle Sandino.

Before November, 1928, the insurgents had been quiet and
their morale hit a low point after the election, but Sandino
remained an enigma. General Feland, in early 1929, asserted
that conditions in Nicaragua were the best in years but believed
an American force of around 3,500 men would have to stay for
a while to keep them that way. Fired with the usual vigor of
new executives, Moncada wanted to assume responsibility for
ending the northern trouble. He declared martial law in four
departments, and three Nicaraguan generals formed a volunteer
force of about three hundred men to stamp out banditry. The
State Department was uneasy about this group because of its
similarity to the old government-controlled army, but Feland
found it efficient, aggressive, and valuable.[33] After some weeks of
operations the department received a copy of a report from the
American military attaché in Costa Rica. The report alleged the
Sandino situation had ceased to exist, largely because of the volunteer group commanders. The attaché noted, however, that
Sandino hated Moncada and would continue to rally anti-
government elements to fight the President.[34]

In February a rumor circulated that Sandino had left the
country. The report was premature, but on February 21 the
Mexican government requested Ambassador Dwight Morrow's
advice on Sandino's plea for asylum. The State Department
thought Mexico should grant asylum if such would curtail the
Nicaraguan's revolutionary activities. The United States was even

[33] Feland to Sellers, Jan. 2, 1929, Sellers papers, box 249; Eberhardt to
Department of State, Mar. 16, 1929, 817.00/6244.
[34] Copy of report by Major Fred T. Cruse to War Department, Apr.
12, 1929, 817.00/6305; *Foreign Relations: 1929*, III, 562–563

willing to do what it could to have Sandino leave Nicaragua safely; it agreed to instruct its forces not to interfere with his departure.[35] In mid-June, 1929, Sandino left for Merida, Yucatan; he visited Mexico City in January, 1930, returning to Nicaragua the following May.

Throughout 1929 and 1930 banditry continued. Incidents were worrisome but of no major importance. The situation did not warrant a large Marine force. In January, 1929, there were over 5,000 men in Nicaragua; by July the number was halved, and by December it was 1,800. By January 31, 1931, the total force was 1,412.[36] The legation did not always concur in these cuts; nor was diplomatic evaluation of the bandit situation necessarily the same as that of military officers. The diplomat was often more pessimistic. In early May, 1929, the second brigade commander, General Dion Williams, told Eberhardt the military situation was excellent; the country had never been so peaceful. Later the legation, then headed by Hanna, reported disorder in bandit areas and very slow improvement. When the special service squadron commander and brigade commander recommended large reductions in the Marine force, Hanna opposed. The chargé pointed out disturbances around Matagalpa and noted frequent consultations with his British counterpart concerning protection of British nationals. According to Hanna, Sandino's prestige was higher than when he had left the country, and his propaganda continued in Nicaragua. Nonetheless, in August the Marine reduction began.[37] Differences in views again appeared when Colonel Robert H. Dunlap, who had taken part in operations

[35] Department of State to Morrow, Feb. 25, 1929, 312.1722 Sandino/2½; May 8, 1929, 312.1722 Sandino/28; memorandum of conversation between J. Reuben Clark, undersecretary of state, and the Mexican ambassador, Manuel C. Téllez, May 17, 1929, 312.1722 Sandino/30.

[36] Undated statement prepared by the Department of State in answer to Senate resolution 386 of Jan. 5, 1931, 817.00/6922.

[37] Williams to Eberhardt, May 6, 1929, 817.00/6320; Hanna to Department of State, May 24, 1929, 817.00/6325; July 17, 1929, 817.00/6372; July 23, 1929, 817.00/6376.

in northern Nicaragua, visited Dana Munro at the State Department in September. The Marine officer minimized the threat.
He estimated the guerrillas under arms at hardly more than one
hundred and fifty, and these were doing little damage.[38]

If reports of bandit raids continued, activity was minor. Sandino's earlier actions had conditioned most foreigners and Nicaraguans in the northern departments to be apprehensive at every
sign of bandit vigor. There had always been banditry, but the
Sandino movement had put an edge on it.

Although there was no immediate increase in attacks after
mid-May, 1930, when Sandino returned to Nicaragua, the Guardia made new plans for eliminating banditry. Officers had
observed the easy transition from peaceful farmer to bandit and
back to peaceful farmer. It was difficult to distinguish the two,
almost impossible to prove bandit affiliation unless a farmer-
bandit was caught in a raid or with weapon in hand. The Guardia commander of the northern area, Robert L. Denig, suggested
a concentration plan which would require inhabitants to move
to specified places. Such would keep people under surveillance
and deprive bandits of food and manpower. President Moncada
agreed. The plan went into effect—Nicaraguans were to move
to town. After the deadline Marines and Guardia would treat
all persons and property in restricted areas as circumstances war-
ranted. But confusion surrounded the project. There was no
money for refugees. An estimated 6,000 to 10,000 people entered
the department of Matagalpa in a "distressful stampede," many
blaming Americans for their plight. The United States minister
had not taken part in the planning, and on June 4 he pointed
out to Moncada the dangers of the project.[39] Moncada stopped

[38] Memorandum of conversation between Dunlap and Munro, Sept.
4, 1929, 817.00/6404.
[39] Denig to McDougal, May 10, 1930, Marine Corps files, box 144,
folder 815; McDougal to Denig, May 15, 1930, Marine Corps files, box
144, folder 815; Hanna to Department of State, June 6, 1930, 817.00/
6673.

the plan until the government investigated arrangements; after investigation he canceled all orders.

Throughout 1930 the usual mode of combating insurgents continued. Patrols crossed and recrossed infested areas. But the yankees or Guardia were always at a disadvantage, since bandits knew of almost every movement through a well-developed grapevine. It was deadly to be a friend of government forces, and people understandably tried to avoid aiding them.

Hanna failed to see progress in the fight against bandits. He felt that construction of three or four roads would make communication easier and move the Guardia into areas rather than just patrolling and withdrawing. Stimson showed interest and included the idea in letters to Moncada in November, 1930. He urged it in conversation with the Nicaraguan minister in Washington (and former claimant to the presidency), Juan Sacasa. Road building, in addition to aiding communication, would offer jobs to men who might otherwise turn to banditry. Moncada, however, hesitated to give up public projects in more populous areas.

In addition to establishing the national guard and combating banditry, Washington observed the congressional election of 1930. The election of 1928 had begun what the State Department hoped would become a tradition. Changing old habits is never easy, and one election could not transform the political history of Nicaragua. The 1928 vote was a good start but came only by heavy United States supervision.

During the 1928 campaign the two presidential candidates exchanged letters suggesting that the United States oversee future voting and in February, 1929, Moncada asked the Department of State to appoint an American citizen to head the national board of elections. He viewed this as a first step toward future free elections. Kellogg, nearing the end of his secretaryship, avoided any commitment. The Moncada government then appointed a Nicaraguan who would vacate the post if the Department desired it. Washington saw no hurry and not until more than a year did it act.

In March, 1930, the State Department turned to the War Department for an officer to head the national election board. At the same time the State Department informally approached the Navy about Marines, especially those with facility in Spanish. Such actions were in line with the supervision under McCoy. The Navy, willing to cooperate, desired to vary the pattern. It believed the election would run more smoothly if naval and Marine personnel conducted it. Admiral Sellers spoke of the never-ending irritation which Army officers caused the Marine Corps in Nicaragua. The State Department had acted with the idea of avoiding connection between the director of the election board and the forces of occupation, but the Marines did not appreciate this distinction. They saw an Army officer as going too far; indeed, they looked upon the idea as a reflection on their ability to complete the job.[40] The State Department notified the legation in Managua early in May that Captain Alfred Wilkinson Johnson of the Navy would be president of the electoral board. Captain Johnson, an Annapolis graduate of 1899, had had some experience in Latin America (naval attaché in Chile, 1911–12) and had served in the Philippines during the insurrection.

Election preparations during the next six months were similar to those under McCoy. A law was necessary for voting, and Washington submitted one which Moncada promulgated; the Americans found a substitute for mercurochrome for marking voters; the Navy sent extra help for the election.[41] One officer

[40] Navy Department to Department of State, Apr. 1, 1930, 817.00/ 6570; copy of dispatch from Sellers to secretary of Navy, Apr. 2, 1930, 817.00/6570; memorandum by Brigidier General B. H. Fuller, acting commandant, Marine Corps, to Ernest Lee Jahncke, acting secretary of the Navy, Apr. 18, 1930, 817.00 Johnson Electoral Mission/16.

[41] The law in some respects resembled the Dodds law of 1923 more than the McCoy act of 1928. The principal change from 1928 was the right of petition for the formation of new political parties. Moncada was not pleased with the change, but Johnson thought it an advance in electoral freedom. Johnson desired that the required number of signatures on a petition be 5 percent of the total votes cast in the last election. Because

who served in both operations reported to McCoy that "we are using the 1928 organization, the 1928 blank forms, the 1928 methods of dealing with problems and individuals so far as we can, and the 1928 solutions wherever possible."[42]

There were the usual conflicts between politicians and the electoral mission. Johnson worried about Guardia protection for his men and the voters. He wanted assurance of funds to support the guard. He did not think Moncada had gone far enough. Hanna reassured Johnson, who asserted the United States was being trifled with, and at one time he talked of withdrawing his mission. At another time Johnson said he felt like a man alone, that he was not receiving support from either the United States or Nicaragua. He also indicated that if he had known the situation in Nicaragua he would not have come. He complained that Moncada had not amnestied all political prisoners and expatriates, and had not restored municipal officials removed under martial law. He was also troubled by the niggardliness of Moncada's financial support. The department tried to calm the officer; it diplomatically told him he was expecting too much and should follow Hanna's judgment. Hanna was patient and optimistic. The department sensed that part of the trouble was competition between Navy and Army—Johnson versus McCoy. Johnson wanted to do as well as his predecessor; he was almost insisting that Moncada "crawl down from positions he has assumed and it is more than human nature to expect that Moncada will to it."[43]

Moncada wanted greater restriction, the figure was raised to 10 per cent, and a literacy test was required. Report of the chairman, American electoral mission in Nicaragua, 1930, 817.00 Johnson Electoral Mission/171.

[42] Matthew B. Ridgway to McCoy, Sept. 23, 1930, McCoy papers, box 20.

[43] Memorandum of conference at American legation in Managua, Aug. 21, 1930, 817.1051/417; J. P. Cotton, acting secretary of state, to Stimson, Sept. 11, 1930, 817.00 Johnson Electoral Mission/269; Hanna to Department of State, Sept. 19, 1930, 817.00 Johnson Electoral Mission/105.

Nicaraguans went to the polls on November 2, 1930. Fewer voters cast ballots than in 1928, a result to be expected in off-year elections. Liberals gained control of both houses of Congress. By mid-November most of the electoral personnel had left.

Johnson remained unhappy. At a luncheon attended by Moncada, who gave the American officer a medal, he refrained from any expression of appreciation for the Nicaraguan government's assistance. In his final report he asserted that Moncada had a stubborn personality which made cooperation difficult. The captain advised the State Department that if the United States were going to support only constitutional or legitimate governments it should guarantee constitutional rights. Otherwise it should abandon its recognition policy and interpose armed forces only to protect United States citizens during temporary disorders. As for reduction of Marines, he would either take them all out or leave them at strength. Any Marines in Nicaragua made the United States an intervening nation, yet the 1930 numbers were too small to fight banditry or supervise elections.[44]

Thus ended the first half of the Moncada presidency. The Guardia was more than two years old, yet on unsure footing. There had been another free election. Sandino was back home. Banditry still was going on. Some Marines were withdrawing. For two more years Marines would occupy Nicaragua; for two more years American policy would seek stability.

[44] Report of the chairman, American electoral mission in Nacaragua, 1930, 817.00 Johnson Electoral Mission/171.

11: RETRENCHMENT: 1931–1932

United States relations with Nicaragua were no less troublesome as the time for evacuation grew closer. The last two years of the Moncada administration probably offered more serious problems than the first two. There was increased activity by Sandino, the debilitating effect of the Great Depression, the tragic Managua earthquake of 1931, and inadequacy of the Guardia for completing a job which a much larger force of Marines had failed to do. In spite of poverty, unemployment, banditry, the undeveloped nature of most of Nicaragua, the United States continued to seek stability through democracy. Still, by early 1931 it did not matter so much whether the goal were possible, so long as the United States could plan a graceful exit shortly after Nicaraguan elections in 1932.

To land a few Marines to protect nationals had offered a clear goal—so temporary, so easy. It became a complicated, distasteful, expensive business. A general plan for withdrawal was evolved in 1929, and the United States followed this plan in 1930–31 and through Moncada's presidency. By the end of Moncada's term loose ends could be tied up, the first freely elected president would finish his administration, the country would elect another president, the Guardia would have more than four years' experience, and North American forces could gradually withdraw. Such was the ideal.

When Captain Alfred Johnson of the United States Navy returned from his electoral mission to Nicaragua, he visited Secretary of State Stimson in the latter's Washington house,

"Woodley." What Johnson had to tell, particularly about sup-
pression of banditry, was not encouraging. He felt the guard was
doing good work and, using the experience of 1930 as his pattern, thought Sandino a shadow of his former self, but Johnson
felt the bandit situation was more difficult than before. Bandits
seldom came together for attack, thus making it difficult for
government forces and Marines to round them up.[1] Johnson
doubted the success of a military approach and confirmed Stimson's own feelings that economic changes were needed.

Shortly after this interview, the Nicaraguan insurgents broke
their inactivity, on December 31, 1930, with tragic results for
ten United States Marines. Rebels ambushed a patrol of Marines
repairing telephone wires—eight Americans dead, two wounded.
Resolutions appeared in Congress, and the press again printed
editorials on Nicaragua. Intervention and withdrawal once more
were lively questions in the United States.

In Nicaragua the ambuscade had its effects, for the Marine
deaths marked a general renewal of banditry. Sandino resumed
propaganda against the North Americans. He said he would
destroy Nicaragua to save it. In characteristic vein he reasoned
that if invading assassins subverted Nicaragua's sovereignty and
robbed the people of their homeland, the intruders should have
to rebuild the country over the ashes of Nicaraguan bodies. A
Mexican representative of Sandino sent telegrams to United
States Senators calling for justice for Nicaragua. Another Sandino representative wrote later to Ambassador J. Reuben Clark
in Mexico City that Sandinistas would stop fighting as soon as
all the Marines left Nicaragua and that gradual withdrawal therefore would not bring peace.[2]

For the State Department the most troublesome result of
renewed banditry was its effect on Moncada-Guardia-Marine

[1] Stimson diary, Dec. 17, 1930.
[2] New York Times, Jan. 7, 1931, p. 2; Feb. 15, 1931, p. 14; Gregorio
Selser, Sandino, General de Hombres Libres (Buenos Aires, 1959), II,
111.

affairs. Killing American troops had aroused some sympathy and stirred demands for a national army. In Nicaragua, Liberal newspapers supported this idea while Conservatives saw danger in such a plan, feeling that this sort of force was too much like the army of pre-Stimson days.

Moncada had continually advocated forces in addition to the Guardia to combat banditry. During his first months he recruited some volunteer groups, but pressure from the State Department and lessening of bandit activity caused him to give up these measures and allow the constabulary to be the single police force in Nicaragua. As noted in a previous chapter, because of economic distress the President was reluctant to supply the guard with funds or keep it at the strength the United States wanted. But Moncada now had to meet the outlaw groups in the northern departments. Since he felt the Guardia was too expensive and knew Washington would frown on cheaper volunteer groups, he suggested an auxiliary force of five hundred men to cooperate with the guard, which would enlist, equip, and train recruits. The president would also support the road construction program in bandit areas (suggested by Hanna earlier) if he could arrange a million-dollar loan. Washington liked both plans.

The new force raised many problems. Guardia chief McDougal estimated cost of the auxiliary group at $110,000 for six months. Moncada had no desire to spend that much money, but had in mind an irregular force for a lesser amount. Hanna felt Moncada's idea meant troops without uniforms and inadequately officered, armed, and trained. The President suggested dropping the increase, but after conversations with the American minister he agreed to a smaller group of one hundred twenty-five men. The trouble was that the Guardia was not getting results and Moncada felt it was not only expensive but that its methods were ineffective.[3] Since Moncada had been a successful general against the Díaz regime, he naturally had suggestions on han-

[3] Hanna to Department of State, Jan. 14, 1931, 817.1051/484; Jan. 15, 1931, 817.1051/485.

dling Sandinistas, whose fighting methods were similar to those he had used. Central American warfare emphasized extreme mobility and freedom. It made use of mountainous jungle terrain; it was cheap, suitable for Nicaragua; but it was undisciplined and lent itself to coups d'état and oppression of political enemies.

Near the end of January, 1931, Stimson decided to clarify United States policies. The Tipitapa and national guard agreements had shown the way for three and a half years, but by early 1931, after outbreaks against the Moncada government and renewed criticism of the State Department, there was need for a statement on what Washington was going to do next. Stimson had told the Nicaraguan President in November, 1930, that he did not see how Marines could stay beyond the next presidential election. The Secretary now believed it was time to go beyond this intimation and make sure the United States could leave in 1932, should it seem wise. Stimson asked Secretary of the Navy Charles Francis Adams to instruct the Guardia commander to train Nicaraguan officers who could take command if Washington decided to pull out after the 1932 referendum.[4] Adams hesitated because he thought Nicaraguans would interpret the order as a statement of withdrawal. This interpretation did not bother Stimson; it was abnormal for Marines to be in Nicaragua and it could not be a permanent situation. He had told Moncada as much, because public opinion in the United States would not support indefinite retention of Marines. Stimson remarked that after the 1932 elections, our intervention would be five years old. By then the northern provinces would simply have to be stabilized. Thus instructions went out to have Nicaraguan officers ready to take command on January 1, 1933. Such action allowed the State Department to present to the Senate a date for withdrawal—to quiet the watchdogs of American foreign policy. Sena-

---

[4] Stimson to Moncada, Nov. 24, 1930, 817.1051/459; Stimson to Adams, Jan. 22, 1931, 817.00/6959a; Stimson to Adams, Jan. 28, 1931, 817.00/6962; memorandum of conversation between Stimson and Borah, Jan. 26, 1931, 817.00/6964.

tor William E. Borah, perhaps the chief vigilante, was one of the first to know.

The department also requested Hanna and McDougal to come to Washington for talks covering the status of Marines and national guard and also the Nicaraguan finances. The conversations, which included General McCoy, got under way near the end of January, 1931. Concerned lest Marine forces become involved in the new outbreaks of banditry, making it impossible to withdraw after the election or causing more demands for withdrawal, the department looked for a way out. The talks explored how to relieve Marine units of combat duties, taking them from Nicaragua and leaving only an instructional battalion for the Guardia. Stimson was interested, and perhaps a little surprised, to find the guard commander willing to try such a plan.[5] But if Marines were to come out, the department knew Nicaragua would need more constabulary, which required money. The conferees met again and worked out a financial plan calling for more money for the Guardia, railroad construction, and road building. To assure money for these Nicaraguan projects Hanna went to New York to talk with directors of the national bank of Nicaragua. At the same time Stimson called Paul Warburg of the International Acceptance Bank (fiscal agent for the Nicaraguan bank) and in explaining the situation noted it was important that the directors act intelligently on what the department wanted.[6] The board of the national bank consented to the loan.

[5] Stimson diary, Jan. 29, 1931.

[6] *Ibid.*, Feb. 2, 1931. The Nicaraguan government regained complete ownership of the bank in 1924, but for fear of what effect this might have on Nicaraguan finances, the Nicaraguan government engaged the Guaranty Trust Company and J. & W. Seligman and Company as fiscal agents of the government. These New York firms had members on the board of directors of the national bank. Moncada expressed dissatisfaction with these financial houses when he became president and at the end of 1929 they withdrew from their Nicaraguan connection. The following year the International Acceptance Bank, Inc., of New York became the American depository and fiscal agent of the national bank of Nicaragua and the Pacific railroad and had officials on the bank's board of directors.

By February 5, 1931, Washington had formed a Nicaraguan policy, approved by Moncada, for the last two years of its intervention. A new loan would allow a five-hundred-man increase in the Guardia and continuation of public works projects on roads and railroads. Additions to the constabulary would bring that force to over two thousand men, most of whom would replace Marines. According to the department's timetable, the change would take place by June 1 and the only Marines left in Nicaragua would be an instruction battalion and aviation force.[7] By these steps—taken in early 1931 because of Sandino's new activity and the growing congressional and public feeling about intervention—the Department of State was announcing what it had aimed at since the 1928 elections. The announcement had the desired effect on Congress, for shortly afterward the House of Representatives voted down a proposal to withdraw all but one company of Marines from Nicaragua by May 13, 1932; the Senate also viewed the news favorably.[8]

The Hoover administration also tried mending fences in Latin America, where the Nicaraguan policy had been so damaging. Background for this attempt at reconciliation lay in a memorandum on the Monroe Doctrine prepared in 1928 by J. Reuben Clark, then undersecretary of state. This work, published by the department in 1930, found the Monroe Doctrine a case of the United States versus Europe, not of the United States versus

[7] Memorandum by Secretary Stimson, Feb. 5, 1931, 817.1051/501. The department believed that the reductions would leave around five hundred Marines and Navy personnel in Nicaragua by June, 1931; in September, however, there were still a few over a thousand. Walter C. Thurston, chief of Latin American division, to Francis White, assistant secretary of state, Sept. 12, 1931, 817.00/7215. *El Centroamericano* (León), Feb. 21, 1931, p. 1.

[8] Sandino tried to encourage congressional dissidence when his aides in Mexico City announced that the Sandinistas would cease their struggle immediately if a Senate resolution for withdrawal from Nicaragua was favorable to Nicaraguan sovereignty. *El Centroamericano*, Jan. 27, 1931, p. 3.

Latin America, and that the terms of the doctrine did not justify the Roosevelt Corollary, the Rooseveltian idea which placed responsibility on the United States for seeing that Latin American nations behaved correctly toward European countries. Clark, of course, had not abolished the right of intervention, which he justified on the principle of self-preservation.

In November, 1930, with the analysis in mind, Stimson and Francis White considered a new policy statement on Latin America but discarded it as unnecessary and perhaps even dangerous. Differing slightly from Clark—who saw the Monroe Doctrine as a unilateral arrangement, with the United States deciding where and when to apply it—Stimson considered having Latin American nations join the United States in any intervention, if not in assertion of the doctrine.[9] Yet even the Secretary believed cooperative action should deal only with South America, since Central America more closely affected United States interests.

Two days before Christmas of 1930, Stimson raised with President Hoover the question of a speech on Latin American affairs in which he again would distinguish between South America and other southern neighbors. The President cautioned Stimson to soft-pedal the idea of an area of special interest around the Panama Canal. The Secretary wanted to show this interest as in keeping with independence of those countries. While believing the Roosevelt Corollary did not belong with the Monroe Doctrine, Stimson did agree with the idea of the corollary. He observed that our interest in Central America was to help those republics maintain their independence toward the outside world.[10]

Hoover approved the speech, and in New York City on February 6, 1931, Stimson spoke to the Council on Foreign Relations. He said much that Clark had outlined. He explained the

[9] J. Reuben Clark, *Memorandum on the Monroe Doctrine* (Washington, D.C., 1930), pp. XIX, XX, XXIII; Stimson diary, Nov. 11, 1930.

[10] Stimson diary, Dec. 23, 1930.

effect of Central America and the Caribbean on United States diplomacy: "That locality has been the one spot external to our shores which nature has decided to be most vital to our national safety, not to say our prosperity."[11] He agreed that the Monroe Doctrine involved the United States versus Europe, not the United States versus Latin America, but felt intervention necessary if conditions imperiled the national interest. The Hoover administration was working for withdrawal from intervention but not giving it up as a contingent policy—as is apparently true of later administrations. In Nicaragua, Hoover and Stimson felt no need for Marines and were withdrawing them.

But could the Marines leave easily? So long as armed bands roamed northern Nicaragua there was possibility that Washington might send Marines back. What would the administration do if bands endangered United States or foreign lives and property or if the Guardia were unable to stem a Sandinista offensive? The Hoover government urgently wanted out of Central America and would not increase its force there except in an extreme case. In late Janaury, 1931, an American-owned lumber company at Puerto Cabézas became alarmed by reports of a large force of Sandinistas attacking its property near the Honduran border. The commander of the special service squadron sent a gunboat to Puerto Cabézas. Report of this action reached Stimson in a cabinet meeting. The Secretary of the Navy disclaimed knowledge of the act, which disturbed Stimson very much, and at the Secretary of State's request the Navy Department recalled the ship.[12] The feared band of two hundred turned out to be about thirty—a number the local Guardia felt able to handle.

Calls for help from United States citizens typified one of Washington's problems in leaving Nicaragua to the Nicaraguans. After talks at the State Department, Hanna advised Francis White that Marines destined for home should not go from their posts to Managua until it was time to embark, in order not to

[11] New York Times, Feb. 7, 1931, p. 8.
[12] Stimson diary, Jan. 27, 1931.

give encouragement to the bandits by a hasty withdrawal. He predicted a clamor from foreigners when the Marines pulled out, even suggesting that some foreigners might create situations to try to prevent withdrawal: "One has to live in Nicaragua to understand the lengths to which foreigners might go to keep the protection of the marines."[13] Several prominent Nicaraguans expressed apprehension about the retirement, yet Hanna felt most Nicaraguans had national pride and, while welcoming the peace Marines brought, they desired their country to stand on its own feet.

Perhaps the greatest threat to United States plans in Nicaragua came on April 11, 1931, shortly before the rainy season and after the Managua earthquake, when Sandinista bands invaded the Nicaraguan east coast. The Guardia unit at Puerto Cabézas went to investigate. When the outlaws ambushed it and killed a Marine officer, the Navy sent protection.

It perturbed Stimson that the commander of the special service squadron sent ships without consulting Washington. The Secretary interrupted his Sunday afternoon to inquire of Secretary Adams what it was all about, but again the head of the Navy Department knew nothing. Later Stimson allowed the U.S.S. *Asheville* to continue to Puerto Cabézas but opposed landing more sailors or Marines.[14] The ship was to remain there only until the Guardia unit returned from the interior. As reports came that the town was in danger of attack, with no government troops present, the Secretary of State with great reluctance allowed Marines to land. Two days later when Stimson had opportunity to explain the Nicaraguan happenings in a cabinet meeting, he emphasized his opposition to new naval forces and Hoover agreed. The President recalled that these same people on the east coast had gotten the Coolidge administration to land troops, and he did not want to be caught the same way. But the Navy Department worried about Marines serving as officers with

[13] Memorandum by Hanna for White, Feb. 4, 1931, 817.51/2232–3/5.
[14] Stimson diary, Apr. 12, 1931.

the constabulary. One had died in ambush near Puerto Cabézas, and Adams felt a situation might arise in which the United States would have to help the Marines. Stimson demurred. The Guardia officers had volunteered, knowing well the dangers, and should not expect intervention. If they did not realize this, Stimson advised the Navy to tell them. The Secretary of State pondered whether the Navy understood the policy he was trying to follow, whether it believed instead that United States troops could stay in Nicaragua indefinitely.[15]

This imbroglio continued, for although the Marines from the *Asheville* reembarked, the chief of naval operations, Admiral William V. Pratt, wanted advance authority to land them again. Stimson agreed he might do so to save American and foreign lives but not to protect property. Americans on the east coast were a pampered lot, he felt, and he contrived to have United States citizens who felt their lives endangered board the warship in harbor. The Secretary of State believed the people of Bragman's Bluff Lumber Company, which had nearly stampeded the Navy to action, exaggerated the bandit threat.[16] Yet neither Stimson nor Hoover was ready to accept responsibility for keeping the original plan. The President was afraid to protect only lives and not property, if the bandits should attack while the ship was at Puerto Cabézas. Stimson fretted about an upset to withdrawal plans but with Admiral Pratt permitted the commander of the *Asheville* to resist an attack on the town but not to go inland. He later allowed another ship to go to Puerto Cabézas because he considered it unwise to accept responsibility for blocking the move.

This condition could prove embarrassing, Stimson pointed out to Hoover. The Secretary warned that if Marines protected property on the coast there would be pressure to do the same for property in the interior. On April 16, 1931, the department advised the legation in Managua and consul at Bluefields not to

[15] *Ibid.*, Apr. 14, 1931.
[16] *Ibid.*, Apr. 15, 1931.

undertake protection of its citizens throughout Nicaragua with American forces. If people did not feel safe under the local government, they should leave the country, or at least go to the coast towns where United States forces could protect or evacuate them.[17]

The frenzy continued. At Bluefields the consulate reported rumors of well-armed bandit groups entering the area, and there were only one hundred fifty Guardia troops to oppose them. Vice-consul Alvin Rowe recommended warships for Cape Gracias, Puerto Cabézas, and Bluefields and wanted Marines at each of these places.

Stimson was downcast, blamed the military for a great share of the trouble, and was amazed that groups sufficiently large to cause loss of life and property and threaten detachments of the Guardia moved eastward without warning. This indicated lack of leadership, no efficient intelligence group, no organized espionage. To his diary the former Army officer confided doubts about the Marines. He recognized their bravery and hard work, but when he compared their job in Nicaragua to that of the Army in the Philippines he saw that there "simply hasn't been a good job well done."[18]

It was difficult for Hoover and Stimson not to send more troops to Nicaragua. Strong forces bore down on the administration. What would happen if Americans, thinking protection insufficient, left Nicaragua? It could mean shut-down plants, unemployment, uprisings, looting, even killings—all beyond control of the Guardia! Retention of the naval vessel meant return to normal conditions. At least one banana company doing business around Puerto Cabézas subjected the administration to political threats. Stimson noted stories about department policy and attempts to make a campaign issue of not going into the

[17] Department of State to Hanna, Apr. 16, 1931, 817.00 Bandit Activities, 1931/31.

[18] Stimson to Hanna, Apr. 16, 1931, 817.00 Bandit Activities, 1931/33; Stimson diary, Apr. 16, 1931.

interior and protecting the company's workers upstream.[19] One New Orleans newspaper printed an emotional account of American survivors—nerve-shattered remnants of a once-happy colony —reaching home waters after the attack. These refugees expressed bitterness over the delay in landing additional American Marines. An official of the Standard Fruit Company believed "the Sandino banditry might have been put down definitely and for all time . . . had there been adequate forces landed to cope with the marauding forces. . . ."[20]

Then, too, there was the question of the Monroe Doctrine. In the 1928 revolt Great Britain and Italy had appealed to the United States. In 1931 the British consul at Puerto Cabézas applied to his minister in Managua for protection of 1,500 British subjects who he believed were in danger.[21] The Navy wanted to send two cruisers and an aircraft carrier. Nonetheless, at Stimson's direction and with Hoover's approval only the gunboat *Asheville* went, although three other ships later joined it. The Secretary of the Navy continued to worry about Marine officers with the Guardia, but Stimson maintained his position that these men had volunteered for hazardous duty and would leave when the United States withdrew the commander of the constabulary.

Reluctance to get entangled in Nicaragua and a statement released to the press on April 17, 1931, concerning impossibility of United States forces giving protection to its citizens throughout Nicaragua thus brought the above reactions. Fortunately, support came from the Senate—Borah and La Follette rejoiced that the American government was on the way out of Nicaragua. In Mexico City, Sandino's representative Pedro Zepeda also greeted the announcement and hoped it meant complete with-

---

[19] Stimson diary, Apr. 16, 1931.

[20] Story from *New Orleans Times Picayune*, Apr. 17, 1931, printed in *The American* (Bluefields), Apr. 29, 1931, p. 1.

[21] Hanna to Department of State, Apr. 17, 1931, 817.00 Bandit Activities, 1931/40.

drawal of Marines. Zepeda commented that the Americans recently killed died because they requested Marine protection instead of paying taxes to the Sandinistas.[22]

The State Department wanted to lessen talk that it had made any change in policy; Stimson seemed disturbed at the broad interpretations of his original statement. On April 18, therefore, the Secretary released an explanation showing how circumstances of 1931 differed from those of earlier years in Nicaragua and that he was not disavowing protection of nationals abroad.[23] The two contending forces in 1926 had professed to carry out the rules of warfare and protect neutrals and their property, but in 1931 small outlaw groups murdered and pillaged in thick jungle—"a region where it would be almost impossible for regular troops to operate efficiently even if it were attempted." Stimson continued: There was now a constabulary to take over police duties. As for protection of foreigners, the best way was to warn of dangers and give opportunity to escape to coast towns. Naval vessels were at threatened coast ports and would stay until danger passed.

There was indication that the Secretary was dissatisfied with the past but timid about breaking with it. The *New York Times* editorialized that the department had not considered its steps before taking them. The government was not doing what it wanted in Nicaragua but only what it could do. If this were so, it was hardly necessary to fire off a diplomatic gun about it. "Moreover, it was a gun which seemed to be doing more execution at the breech than at the muzzle."[24]

Even Stimson had doubts about the announcement. With regard to keeping Marines out of the interior of Nicaragua he thought he was right, but he wrote in his diary that the tone, form, and perhaps sending the note of April 16 was a mistake. Dispatching ships to coast towns was all right, but he did not

[22] The American, May 2, 1931, p. 1.
[23] Department of State, Press Releases, Jan. 3 to June 27, 1931, pp. 284–286.
[24] New York Times, Apr. 18, 1931, p. 18; Apr. 20, 1931, p. 18.

want people there to think the United States was going to make some permanent occupation of the interior. Such would require reinforcements, inconsistent with the policy formed in February, 1931, which called for gradual reduction and withdrawal shortly after Nicaragua's presidential election.

In late April, 1931, Stimson attempted to explain the situation to former-President Coolidge. Calling attention to warships along the Nicaraguan coast, he assured his old chief of no change in the policy of protecting American lives and property.[25] As for continuance or reinforcement of Marine forces inland, the purpose he claimed was to train a Nicaraguan national guard, not protect American citizens. Stimson asserted that the Sandino affair had unexpectedly drawn in these forces and it seemed dishonorable to quit until they had finished the constabulary training. The following month Stimson again explained. The United States had no intention of denying citizens protection: "All the counsel and assistance to which Americans were entitled under the law of nations would be given where their investments and claims abroad were imperiled, but . . . armed forces would not be employed for debt collection purposes."[26] And Francis White said sometime later, "Protection is not on a geographical basis in so far as supporting claims for damages . . . suffered by Ameri-

[25] Stimson diary, Apr. 20, 1931; Stimson to Coolidge, Apr. 29, 1931, Stimson papers, file no. 3F-0782.

[26] New York Times, May 10, 1931, p. 1; in a letter from Stimson to Stanley R. Yarnell, chairman, Peace Committee of the Society of Friends, June 9, 1931, 817.00 Bandit Activities, 1931/139-¾, the Secretary noted that international law allowed the United States to interpose and afford protection to an American and his property whenever that citizen residing in a foreign country did not receive protection which that law recognizes as adequate. Stimson said we did not intend to depart from this principle but intended to stress protection of life rather than property. "Where it unfortunately becomes necessary for us to interpose on behalf of either, we intend to do so in such a way as to avoid, if possible, giving rise to any apprehension that we are there for any other purpose than such necessary and temporary protection."

cans in the interior." If American property were destroyed in the interior, the United States would still support claims for damages and call on the Nicaraguan government to pay.[27]

If Washington could maintain its stand against going into the interior there was good chance the Sandino attacks would not affect withdrawal. On the important point of throwing American forces against the Sandinistas or placing them so they would get hopelessly into the affray, the Hoover administration shakily held its ground. The longer it could do so, the better chance of success. One thing might weaken the administration on this issue—appeal to the Monroe Doctrine and the Roosevelt Corollary. Invoking the argument of national interest against European intervention would have brought some support to the pro-intervention faction in the United States. Stimson some years before had described the principle of national self-preservation in relation to our interest in stability of Caribbean and eastern Pacific governments: If nations did not fulfill responsibilities, European or Asiatic intervention might follow, which could imperil the Panama Canal. "This vital policy has underlain the successive efforts of our government to protect the Caribbean Sea from such encroachment, both by securing our own naval protection of it and by forestalling causes for foreign intervention."[28]

A member of the British House of Commons brought up the matter on April 20, 1931, by asking Arthur Henderson, Britain's secretary of state for foreign affairs, about the situation in Nicaragua. Henderson reported deaths of two British West Indian subjects, but believed the national guard had checked the bandits. His stand pleased Stimson, who instructed Ambassador Charles G. Dawes to express appreciation. "It has taken the wind out of the sails of our jingoes here and has made it much

[27] White to W. W. Cumberland, Apr. 20, 1932, White papers, box 4, Cumberland file.
[28] H. L. Stimson, *American Policy in Nicaragua*, (New York, 1927), pp. 108–110.

easier to carry out a decent policy toward Central America."[29]

By the first of May the United States Navy and the Guardia had eased rebel pressure on the eastern coast. Sandinista activity continued until Marines withdrew, but never again was it much of a threat to department plans. Throughout 1931 there were contacts with outlaw groups—lootings, fears for the Managua-Corinto rail line, alarms of another sweep toward Puerto Cabézas which again brought cries for ships and men even from the American chargé in Managua, but this time moderated by the commander of the special service squadron who found the situation satisfactory.[30] Bandits captured and looted the town of Chichigalpa in November, 1931, and American Chargé William Beaulac saw the bandit situation as grave.

Unemployment helped much outlaw activity. Fruit companies had cut their purchases and were buying from their own farms or private owners with whom they had contracts. Many independent growers could not sell fruit, leaving hundreds of laborers without livelihood. A similar situation developed for workers on the Managua-Rama road. When the government, economically pinched, fired many laborers without pay, a mutinous spirit erupted, bringing attack on the Guardia post at Rama.[31] The situation improved when money came to pay them, but what would happen when that pay was gone and men remained unable to work? Still, by the end of 1931 the organized rebel bands had returned to the northern part of the country. At times they sallied forth, reminding the nation of danger, convincing some individuals of the foolhardiness of Marine withdrawal, but

[29] *Parliamentary Debates*, Apr. 20, 1931, vol. 251, columns 594–595; *New York Times*, Apr. 21, 1931, p. 1; Stimson to Dawes, Apr. 21, 1931, 817.00 Bandit Activities, 1931/63.

[30] A. St. Clair Smith, commander special service squadron, to chief of naval operations, Nov. 18, 1931, Marine Corps in Nicaragua records, Navy Annex, box 5, file 4.

[31] C. A. Wynn, eastern area commander, to director, Guardia, July 22, 1931, box 102, folder 44.0, Marine Corps files.

the year 1932 was not to be primarily a bandit-chasing year. It was an election time, a breathing space for completing Guardia arrangements.

United States Marines had officered the Guardia since its inception. Their task was to train the new group and launch its nonpartisan career. American leadership was temporary, and by early 1931 the plan was that not long after the 1932 presidential election the constabulary would be entirely in Nicaraguan hands. Marine officers had established a military academy whose graduates plus those commissioned from the ranks numbered about 100 by April, 1932, and more than 180 by mid-December. These men were young and inexperienced: Calvin B. Matthews, successor in 1931 to McDougal as Guardia director, felt they were too young and inexperienced to command higher ranks of the Guardia. Before the Marines withdrew, then, the Nicaraguan government would have to appoint men of age and military experience to the upper ranks. These arrangements became part of the plan to keep the guard nonpartisan and to complete the turnover to the Nicaraguans. The presidential candidate of each major party was to list an equal number of persons from each party who would be acceptable to him for replacing Marine officers. Both presidential aspirants were to sign a pledge, in presence of the United States minister, to preserve the nonpartisan character of the constabulary. After the election Moncada would appoint the winning candidate's nominees to the highest posts. American officers would work with the new appointees until withdrawal at the beginning of the new year.[32]

By mid-December, 1932, Nicaragua had taken the first steps. Nicaraguan officers by that time filled all Guardia posts, both parties sharing the positions, as provided by the preelection agreement. General Anastasio Somoza, former undersecretary for foreign relations, was to be chief of the national guard. Although from a family of modest means, Somoza had been educated in

[32] *Foreign Relations: 1932*, V, 857–858, 874–875, 887.

the United States. Returning to Nicaragua he married well and held, none too successfully, a series of jobs. The revolution of 1926 marked a turning point for him after he came to the attention of Moncada. Somoza acted as interpreter during the Tipitapa conferences and later was recompensed by a government position. American officials in Nicaragua often found the young Liberal very likeable; he impressed Stimson; and his personality attracted Minister Hanna and his wife, the latter apparently charmed by Somoza's dancing. Moncada appointed Somoza as constabulary chief in part at least to please Hanna.[33] A few weeks prior to Somoza's appointment, Hanna said of him: "I look upon him as the best man in the country for the position. I know no one who will labor as intelligently and conscientiously to maintain the non-partisan character of the Guardia, or will be as efficient in all matters connected with the administration and command of the Force."[34]

Before Marines withdrew Matthews felt it essential to clear one other point about the national guard. While United States troops were connected with the Guardia, the agreement of December, 1927, (never formally ratified by the Nicaraguan Congress) governed its conduct, but afterward that agreement would no longer operate and old laws governing military forces would take effect. Before departure the constabulary chief wanted a new law to put the organization on a sound basis. Matthews, Hanna, and the State Department drew up legislation similar to the 1927 agreement and presented it to Moncada, who submitted it to Congress. By the time the proposed basic law for the military force came to the legislature that body had adjourned for Christmas. The legislators did not act before the Marines left.

The major United States effort in Nicaragua in 1932 was, however, supervision of the November election. This was the last

[33] William Krehm, Democracia y Tiranías en el Caribe, (Mexico, D.F., 1949), pp. 160–161; Foreign Relations: 1932, V, 899–900.
[34] Hanna to White, Oct. 28, 1932, 817.1051/701½.

important act of the second intervention, a final attempt to illustrate democracy in action for the Nicaraguans.

The supervision of the 1932 election was the third such conducted by the United States in Nicaragua. The election of 1928 had been overwhelmingly supervised, the one in 1930 less so, the last one least of all. The pattern of decreasing control was not entirely planned, nor necessarily the logic of Nicaragua's growth toward democratic maturity. It reflected the State Department policy of determined withdrawal, enunciated in February, 1931, coupled with the world depression so severely felt in the United States. Fortunately for Rear Admiral Clark H. Woodward, head of the electoral mission, there was no insurmountable resistance to the referendum, and although he had problems the result generally was what the State Department hoped.

Woodward's mission took its origin from the 1927 conferences when Adolfo Díaz proposed that the United States supervise the 1928 and subsequent elections. The two candidates of 1928, Moncada and Adolfo Bénard, exchanged letters agreeing that the victor would request supervision for the next presidential election. Although these acts did not constitute a specific invitation for the 1932 referendum, Hoover, at the end of 1931, designated Woodward as head of the American electoral mission and his nominee for chairmanship of the national board of elections.

The first issue was how much supervision the State Department wanted or could provide. After consulting with Chargé Beaulac, the brigade commander, and the director of the Guardia, Woodward felt that protection during the electoral period required 1,800 more Marines plus a few men from the special service squadron. Reluctant to increase American forces in Nicaragua, the State Department disapproved these ideas. Maintenance of order during elections was the responsibility of Nicaragua and its national guard. Such increase in United States troops would appear inconsistent with the policy of getting out of Nicaragua. Even so, if the Guardia had to assume responsibility for the safety of scattered small groups of election workers,

60 percent of the military force would have to stop patrolling against Sandinistas.[35]

Secretary Adams approached Stimson about the matter at a cabinet meeting on March 1. The Navy Secretary talked in terms of suggestions from his Marine and naval officers. Estimated cost of supervision was three quarters of a million dollars, which the Navy budget did not provide. When the cabinet discussed the plan there was much criticism because it meant sending so many Marines back into Nicaragua and because Congress was demanding economy.

After extensive discussion between the State and Navy Departments, three alternatives evolved. Plan A called for complete supervision, as in 1928, requiring 1,115 electoral personnel and 1,800 additional Marines. In plan B, Nicaraguans, with some American inspection, would be chairmen of election boards in bandit areas (178 of the 432 polling stations). Under this latter plan about 1,350 election personnel and Marines would go to Nicaragua. It would cost about $500,000, or two-thirds the cost of plan A. The third proposal let Nicaraguans have complete control of all voting places in bandit areas. The United States would send 643 electoral personnel for the peaceful regions, but no special protective forces. It would cost approximately $200,000. Woodward favored the original plan—complete supervision—but if that were not possible he thought plan B would give a satisfactory election. He did not feel the third proposal would give results which the United States would want to approve.[36] The State Department, of course, wanted satisfactory results but wanted to keep down the cost and size of the mission.

Near the end of May, 1932, after Hoover and Stimson dis-

[35] Beaulac to Department of State, Jan. 12, 1932, 817.00 Woodward Electoral Mission/22; Department of State to Beaulac, Jan. 23, 1932, 817.00 Woodward Electoral Mission/22; C. B. Matthews to Beaulac, Jan. 27, 1932, 817.00 Woodward Electoral Mission/35.

[36] Memorandum by Laurence Duggan, division of Latin American affairs, May 3, 1932, 817.00 Woodward Electoral Mission/61.

cussed the matter, they decided to send no additional protective
troops to Nicaragua and to keep the extraordinary expense at not
more than $200,000. The decision disappointed Woodward, but
although there was some consideration that he might want to
withdraw, he continued under the straitened conditions.[37] In
mid-June 1932 the Senate made supervision more difficult by
attaching a rider to the Navy appropriation bill providing that
none of the money should go to send Marines to Nicaragua for
election supervision. But Hoover instructed Stimson to move
ahead with the project if the money could come from other
sources. The President did not choose to take the amendment
as prohibiting supervision of the election, and, although it was
not publicized, some Marines were drawn from the Canal Zone.[38]

All of Woodward's problems did not come from Washington.
As in the past, Nicaraguan leaders added their share of annoy-
ance, but no one blocked the mission. Moncada had financial
troubles and was usually late in monthly allotments for the election; the Liberal party split between factions in Managua and
León. Moncada suggested a constituent assembly to rewrite the
constitution, causing fears that he wanted to stay in office; General Chamorro, that hardy perennial, stimulated dissensions
among the Liberals by having quiet talks with the President (fox
met fox, as Hanna said) and later the old Conservative complained of the apathy of his party and suggested it might abstain
from the elections. Sandino, in the north, uttered threats and
urged the people not to participate.[39] But everything turned out
all right. Moncada did find money somewhere (about $150,000,
of which over $36,000 was returned) and, under pressure from
the United States, forgot about changing the constitution. The

[37] Memorandum of Edwin C. Wilson for Stimson, May 12, 1932,
817.00 Woodward Electoral Mission/72½.

[38] Stimson diary, June 18, 1932, Department of State to Hanna, June
21, 1932, 817.00 Woodward Electoral Mission/92A; New York Times,
July 7, 1932, p. 12; memorandum by Laurence Duggan to E. C. Wilson,
May 9, 1933, 817.00/7811.

[39] Selser, Sandino, II, 162, 176, 177.

Liberal split ended. The Conservatives participated. Adolfo Díaz was their presidential candidate, with Chamorro his running mate. Juan B. Sacasa and Rodolfo Espinosa opposed them. Chandler P. Anderson earlier had assured Chamorro that if the State Department had prejudice against him it was gone; Chamorro could have run if he had desired, but he chose to back Díaz.

The Conservatives were short of money during the campaign. In early February, 1932, they sent a representative to the United States to obtain financial support. Chamorro wrote Anderson introducing the agent and asking aid. He wanted funds "with the obligation of making payment for them in the manner which will be agreed upon as expedient, once the triumph of the Party has been realized." He assured Anderson that the contributors would be rewarded in proportion to their valuable services.[40] Anderson thought the only source might be voluntary contributions from American interests doing business in Nicaragua, who might want to give help toward a Conservative victory. Cautioning that such aid would have to be secret, he promised to do what he could.[41] There was little success.

Díaz, too, spent a great amount of time in the United States trying to raise money through a loan; as security he offered 5 percent of the salaries of Nicaraguan officials should he be elected. Díaz, failing to find takers, blamed the State Department. Upon hearing the charge, Francis White commented privately that "one would have to have been an Alice in Wonderland to expect to get a loan on any such terms even prior to 1929. . . ."[42] The disappointed Díaz returned to Nicaragua only on the morning of election day.

During the electoral period there were the usual Nicaraguan attempts to appear as having Washington's blessing. Díaz hoped to receive more than money in the United States. A year before the election he discussed with the American minister a trip north

[40] Chamorro to Anderson, Feb. 5, 1932, Anderson papers, box 44.
[41] Anderson to Chamorro, Mar. 9, 1932, Anderson papers, box 44.
[42] White to Hanna, Nov. 16, 1932, White papers, box 5, Hanna file.

to renew his contacts in the State Department. The department discouraged the trip but to no avail. After his arrival in New York, Díaz met cool formality and decided not to journey to the capital. The former President's later-expressed resentment disturbed White, who explained to Hanna:

> I do not want a man who has been friendly to the United States and has cooperated with us in the past to feel that he has been let down. We have not let him down; we have not changed our opinion regarding him, and if we seemed unresponsive it was merely on account of circumstances in which we were placed and the necessity that the Department, like Caesar's wife, should be above suspicion.[43]

Sacasa supporters, too, stressed the high standing of their candidate in the United States, while his opponents emphasized the old connections with Mexico.[44] The Liberal vice-presidential candidate, Rodolfo Espinosa, had been in Washington before his nomination and allowed his friends to spread the impression that he had had conferences with important persons.[45]

There were also proposals for United States aid in making preelection agreements which would ensure party cooperation after the voting. While Washington was not opposed to such agreements, it wanted to avoid assuming, even tacitly, any commitments under them. And again Francis White expressed the department's attitude:

> What I want to avoid is the continuance of the feeling in Nicaragua that they can turn to us to settle all their problems. I think they ought to be made to feel that the country is now being turned back to them and that it will be their responsibility, and solely their responsibility, to get together in some way which will insure stability and peace. I want above all to avoid a situation in which one party could in the future claim

[43] Ibid.

[44] El Centroamericano, Dec. 16, 1931, p. 2; La Prensa (Managua), June 5, 1932, p. 2; June 11, 1932, p. 1.

[45] Beaulac to White, Dec. 12, 1931, White papers, box 8, Beaulac file.

that we had assumed the responsibility of enforcing an agreement between the parties.[46]

Elections came off on November 6, 1932. The Liberals retained the presidency by close to a 23,000-vote majority. They
kept control of Congress as well.[47]

Woodward's work was done. But experience brought him to
make two suggestions:

> 1. That the Government of the United States seek, by
> every means possible, to avoid becoming involved in a com-
> mitment of the nature of the three recent Supervisions of
> Elections in Nicaragua.
> 2. That if it proves desirable or expedient for the Govern-
> ment of the United States to again assume such a responsibil-
> ity the most absolute powers for its "Electoral Mission" be
> ensured from the start.[48]

Although Sandino was still loose, the second intervention was
almost at an end.[49] Washington considered its job nearly done—
three elections, a national guard, and relative peace.

---

[46] White to Hanna, Sept. 23, 1932, found in a bound volume, "American Foreign Service Legation, 1909–1933, Hanna Papers," in the National Archives, record group 84.

[47] Conservatives polled 53,478 votes; Liberals polled 76,030. The new
Senate had fifteen Liberals, eight Conservatives, and the Chamber of
Deputies had twenty-nine Liberals, fourteen Conservatives. *Foreign Rela-
tions: 1932*, V, 827.

[48] *Foreign Relations: 1932*, V, 832.

[49] In early Feb., 1933, Sandino and President Sacasa signed a peace
agreement. Distrust developed between the Sandinistas who kept their
arms and the Somoza-led Guardia. About a year later Sandino came down
to Managua from his northern retreat to discuss political problems with
Sacasa; and on the night of Feb. 21, 1934, a detachment of the Guardia,
under orders from Somoza, abducted Sandino, who, along with his brother
and two military associates, was killed.

12: WITHDRAWAL

On New Year's Day, 1933, Juan B. Sacasa became president of Nicaragua and General Calvin B. Matthews, chief of the Guardia, turned over command to Nicaraguan officers. The following day—January 2—the last 910 Marines and sailors boarded ship at Corinto. The intervening units—second Marine brigade, first battalion of the fifth Marines, and the Nicaraguan national guard detachment—disbanded as organizations of the Marine Corps.[1] Withdrawal ended the second intervention.

At the time of evacuation the State Department released to the press a brief statement outlining the course of the second intervention. It noted that "withdrawal of the American forces . . . follows upon the fulfillment of . . . obligations and marks the termination of the special relationship which has existed between the United States and Nicaragua." And the announcement concluded, "the United States desires for Nicaragua, as for her sister republics in Central America, peace, tranquillity, well-being, and the just pride that comes from unimpaired integrity."[2]

Statistically the intervention meant 136 American troops dead from various causes: Thirty-two were killed in action; sixty-six were wounded in action, of whom fifteen died. Such diseases as malaria, pneumonia, typhoid and paratyphoid, appendicitis, dysentery, and myocarditis accounted for twenty-four deaths. Acci-

[1] Major general commandant to commanding general, second Marine brigade, Nov. 2, 1932, Marine Corps in Nicaragua records, Navy Annex, box 12, file 26.
[2] *Foreign Relations: 1933*, V, 849.

dental deaths (forty-one) ranged from drowning, plane crashes, earthquake, to fall from a horse and fall in a shower. There were twelve suicides and eleven homicides.[3] Untallied Nicaraguan casualties were undoubtedly much higher than the American.

Evacuation brought no demonstrations, few signs of regret, few of rejoicing. The mood of relief was mixed with apprehension, for only an unrestrained optimist could ponder without misgiving the future of this Central American nation. But the United States was glad to be through with the unrewarding business. And full sovereignty satisfied the Nicaraguans. If a few Nicaraguan newspapers denounced intervention, these were the exception.

Officials of the new Nicaraguan government could hardly realize that all power was in their hands. More than once in the next few years when Sacasa faced problems he turned for advice to the American minister in Managua or to the State Department; but it was true that American intervention had ended. Sacasa had to find solutions unaided by decisions made in the American legation or the presence of United States Marines. A few weeks before withdrawal, Francis White emphasized to Minister Hanna that the department had to make a clean-cut break between the period prior to January, 1933, and the subsequent era. "Nicaragua must deal henceforth with her problems in her own way and by her own efforts."[4] Thus it has been, at least outwardly, to the present day.

But what about the second intervention? What questions can

[3] Marine Corps casualties in Nicaragua, Jan. 1, 1927, to Jan 2, 1933, Marine Corps in Nicaragua records, Navy Annex, box 5, file 17.

[4] White to Hanna, Dec. 16, 1932, 817.1051/736. The Sacasa administration proved to be a weak one and, confronted with strong pressures from Somoza, the President and Vice-president resigned in early June, 1936, and left Nicaragua. Congress then elected Dr. Carlos Brenes Jarquin, a member of the House of Deputies, to accede to the presidency. In the regular Nicaraguan election (Dec., 1936) Somoza was elected to the presidency and was inaugurated on Jan. 1, 1937. He governed until his assassination in 1956.

be asked, what conclusions can be reached? A Managua city official once told Logan Feland that when the historian wrote of this period he would find that Washington's policy contributed to liberty and democracy. Another time the Nicaraguan minister to Washington, Alejandro César, thanked the United States for putting Nicaragua on the road to peace and stability, and concluded that American policy had safeguarded his country's autonomy.[5] There were also opinions that the United States brought a peace of death, trampling Nicaraguans and their freedom. Opponents of American policy saw Washington as a tool of Wall Street imperialism, whose design was Marine-protected investment and huge profit—at expense of the people.

Thus while the rest of Latin America was almost unanimous in condemnation of the United States, within Nicaragua itself sentiment was divided. General Dion Williams once discerned three groups in the populace. The great mass of Nicaraguans, he felt, had friendly tolerance of Marines. In this group were property owners who saw in the Americans some security for their holdings. Looking at Nicaraguan politicians, the general had difficulty ascertaining their feelings, for they were habitual turncoats on the subject of intervention and could be found on the side where their interests lay for the moment. And finally Williams found a considerable native element which hated Americans for their assumed and vaunted superiority, for economic supremacy, and for a deep-seated suspicion of United States policy in Latin America.[6]

Today, reviewing documents and newspapers of that period, one finds that these groupings are not far wrong, although it is impossible to know the strength of each. Editorials and letters in

[5] Address delivered at the centennial anniversary celebration of the American Peace Society at Cleveland by Dr. Alejandro César, May 9, 1938. Found in Anderson papers, correspondence, box 44. Letter from José M. Zelaya to Feland, Apr. 16, 1928, Marine Corps files, box 142, folder 801(1).

[6] Williams to commander, special service squadron, Dec. 9, 1925, Marine Corps in Nicaragua records, Navy Annex, box 5, file 18.

La Tribuna of Managua are good examples of the anti-American-ism in Nicaragua. At the height of intervention, during the months leading up to the 1928 election, most issues of the paper had caustic comments on United States policy, at one time con-demning shameful acts of the two parties fighting for American favor, at another yearning for a man of more understanding in the White House and for fewer admirals and generals moving troops "to place the interests of an incipient nation at the dis-cretion of an implacable usurer. . . ."[7] And answering the argu-ment that American intervention stopped bloody civil war, a Nicaraguan writer reminded his readers of Britain's stay in India to prevent bloodshed between Moslems and Hindus, to which Gandhi replied, "It would not be too great a price to pay for Indian liberty."[8]

On the other side of the debate were those who found the good services of the Marines outweighing their faults, and there were opinions that Nicaragua could never be independent, in the true sense of the word. Nicaragua needed to link with a major power, and of these the United States was best.[9]

One of the most often heard charges about American diplo-macy in Latin America was that it aimed to protect American investment. How did Nicaragua fit into this premise? Previous chapters have made little mention of economic or fiscal interven-tion. Throughout the period 1925 to 1933 the United States took close interest in Nicaraguan financial affairs—but for the same reason that it landed Marines: to promote stability. The United States determined that foreign bondholders should have no reason to complain about Nicaraguan credit; the American-sponsored national guard would have funds; the Nicaraguan government would refrain from using the national bank and Fer-

[7] See for example *La Tribuna* (Managua), Sept 5, 1928, p. 1; Sept. 6, 1928, p. 1; Sept. 9, 1928, p. 1; Sept. 12, 1928, p. 1; Sept. 18, 1928, p. 1; Oct. 17, 1928, p. 1; Oct. 18, 1928, p. 1.

[8] *El Centroamericano* (León), Nov. 17, 1931, p. 1.

[9] *The Bluefields Weekly*, May 25, 1929, p. 2; *El Diario Nicaragüense* (Granada), Sept. 13, 1927, p. 1.

rocarril del Pacífico de Nicaragua for political reasons; the Central American government would use internal taxes for national purposes only. Anything affecting this United States program brought State Department interest. Assistant Secretary of State Francis White displayed this attitude in 1927 in a letter to W. W. Cumberland, who was going to Nicaragua to make a financial survey. White believed the crux of the Nicaraguan situation was peace and order, if anything were to be accomplished. "To have peace and order we must have a proper constabulary; to have a proper constabulary we must have money, and to have money we must have an agreement with the bankers. The bankers, not unnaturally, are a pretty hard-boiled lot and want to see profits." White was disappointed because the bankers who had made an earlier loan of one million dollars, secured in part by 50 percent of surplus revenues, would not temporarily give up their share of the surplus so that it might be used for the constabulary. Reiterating Washington's desire for political and economic stability in Nicaragua, he stressed importance of the Guardia, the upcoming elections, and whatever else Cumberland might feel necessary. White cautioned that the State Department did not want to overburden Nicaragua, for "the department of state's solicitude in this matter is for Nicaragua; the bankers can take care of themselves."[10]

The chief American financial interest in Nicaragua consisted of controlling the customs. With the 1911 loan of one and a half million dollars by Brown Brothers and Company and J. & W. Seligman, anticipating Senate ratification of the Knox-Castrillo Treaty, an American (first Clifford D. Ham, then Irving A. Lindberg) held office as collector-general of customs. The secretary of state approved this appointment. Collections were fair and profitable. European and American bondholders received their due and the Nicaraguan government could count on increasing

[10] White to Cumberland, Nov. 19, 1927, White papers, box 4, Cumberland file.

return. Through the second intervention and even after, the arrangement continued.[11]

There were other financial concerns. Under the loan arrangement of 1911 the bankers acquired 51 percent of the stock of the national bank, and for additional credits in 1912 they obtained an option on 51 percent of the Pacific railway of Nicaragua, which they purchased in 1913 for a million dollars. There was further American involvement in that little nation's finances in 1917 with the creation of a high commission (the high commissioner was American, selected by the secretary of state) whose duties included supervision of certain monthly expenditures plus acting as fiscal agent for an issue of guaranteed customs bonds (1918) to be used in paying awards of the mixed claims commission.[12] By 1924 the Nicaraguan government had repurchased both railroad and bank, although Americans constituted a majority on the boards of both until 1929. Nonetheless, from 1925 until 1933, and especially after late 1926 when large Marine

[11] Note Roscoe R. Hill, *Fiscal Intervention in Nicaragua* (New York, 1933), p. 110. The arrangements for an American collector-general lasted until 1949. See Joseph O. Baylen, "American Intervention in Nicaragua, 1909–33," *The Southwestern Social Science Quarterly*, XXXV (Sept., 1954), 149, n. 113.

[12] Memorandum from Thurston to Munro, Sept 25, 1929, 817.51/2113½; Dana G. Munro, *Intervention and Dollar Diplomacy in the Caribbean, 1900–1921*, pp. 196–204, 392–397, 413–417; Isaac Joslin Cox, *Nicaragua and the United States, 1909–1927* (Boston: World Peace Foundation Pamphlet, 1927), pp. 713–716, 732–738. Charles Evans Hughes bluntly explained the status of high commissioner and collector-general vis-à-vis the Nicaraguan government. When the Nicaraguans desired the removal of Commissioner Roscoe R. Hill in 1923, Secretary Hughes told the Nicaraguan minister that President Chamorro could not give orders to the collector or commissioner; they were not required to yield their judgment to that of the Nicaraguan government. At another time Hughes pointed out that Hill was an appointee of the secretary of state and not a servant or employee of the Nicaraguan government. Memoranda of interviews between the Nicaraguan minister and Hughes, Mar. 3, 1923, and Mar. 15, 1923, Hughes papers, box 176, folder 93, Nicaragua.

detachments began landing in Nicaragua, financial interest in
that country was not large.

New York bankers in March, 1927, lent the Díaz government
one million dollars, secured by national bank and Pacific railway
stock, a lien on 50 percent of surplus revenues plus liens on new
taxes voted January 21, 1927, and on dividends declared by the
railway and bank.[13] The 6 percent interest plus 1 percent commission on the loan was not unreasonable under Nicaraguan circumstances, but the security, as Minister Eberhardt noted,
offered a wide margin of safety and put the bankers (J. & W.
Seligman and Company and the Guaranty Trust Company of
New York) in a dominant position for subsequent borrowing,
since the contract gave them first call on all foreign loans of
Nicaragua for the next five years. Eberhardt also feared that
pledging practically all government assets in the transaction
would prevent further borrowing until it was paid and that it
would interfere with maintenance of the national guard, paving
Managua streets, and sanitation programs which were largely
dependent on funds now pledged to the bankers.[14] Within a year
or so Nicaragua had paid this debt, freeing itself from bonded
indebtedness to New York.

Estimates of the total American investment in Nicaragua
varied from $9,600,000 to $24,000,000. In his financial survey of
1927–28 W. W. Cumberland set the figures at around $10,000,-
000, and a year later citizens of the United States led other
investors with $17,000,000.[15] Using the last figure (estimate of

[13] Eberhardt to Department of State, Apr. 2, 1927, 817.51/1786.

[14] *Ibid.* For the bankers' views see R. F. Loree to Stokeley W. Morgan,
Mar. 11, 1927, 817.51/1746.

[15] George J. Eder, chief, Latin American section, division of regional
information of Department of Commerce, to Stokeley W. Morgan, Latin
American division of the State Department, Jan. 8, 1927, 817.00/4841;
W. W. Cumberland, *Nicaragua: An Economic and Financial Survey*
(Washington, 1928), p. 15; Department of State to American diplomatic
and consular offices in Latin America, Mar. 6, 1930, Bluefields consular
post records, correspondence, 1930, VI, 850.31.

See also Max Winkler, *Investments of United States Capital in Latin*

December 31, 1928), the United States had less money in Nicaragua than in any other Latin American nation, with the possible exception of Paraguay. At times investors asked for protection, and during the revolutionary and bandit-disturbed years after 1925, they often asked for a warship and about as often received it. In 1931 when Stimson and Hoover, who were headed for withdrawal, delayed sending protection, protests and pressure came from some investors.

After the Stimson settlement of 1927, the two governments considered ways to bolster Nicaragua's economy because—as that nation's finance minister, F. Guzmán, said—political stability rested on economic stability.[16] Nicaragua wanted a large loan, and the Díaz administration was willing to initiate reforms making the nation practically a financial protectorate of the United States. Americans would extend their control to include not only customs but internal taxation; a board of estimate with a majority of United States citizens would prepare the nation's budget; an American comptroller would supervise expenditures. Included in Guzmán's proposal were a mixed claims commission and a loan expenditure commission, both headed by Americans whose votes would be necessary for any decision by the two bodies.

America (Boston: World Peace Foundation Pamphlets, 1928), who in appendix V lists investment in Nicaragua as $24,000,000 in 1929. According to Winkler's other statistics for the same year the United States had less invested in Honduras, El Salvador, Paraguay, and Dominican Republic. As of Jan. 1, 1931, Winkler lowered his estimate to $14,648,-700, making the investment lowest in Latin America except Paraguay. Winkler, "Investments and National Policy of the United States in Latin America," The American Economic Review, Supplement, XXII (Mar., 1932), 150. Part explanation for the variance in figures is what is included as investment. Eder, for example, points out that one lumber company listed itself as a $2,000,000 concern but had invested in Nicaragua only $30,000, the rest being in ships, warehouses in the United States, etc. Other sources of discrepancy are undeveloped concessions which one might list at actual price paid but which might be several times that value in the future.

[16] Guzmán to Stimson, May 14, 1927, 817.00/5910.

Some points of the proposal were especially attractive to Washington as aids in the free election of 1928. Dana Munro, chargé in Managua, suggested that internal revenues come under American control to prevent coercion of voters by discrimination in assessment and collection of taxes. McCoy agreed. Intermittent discussions on a financial plan continued, and other features in harmony with State Department ideas were evident. A loan could include funds for railways or roads into the disturbed areas of the north, giving military and political advantages to the Nicaraguan government. The plan could embrace provisions for the Guardia Nacional. Because of desire to include these ideas in any financial arrangement, Munro urged that the department rather than the bankers originate the financial plan, since it could then include provisions in addition to those merely safeguarding the loan.[17]

By October, 1927, the State Department decided in favor of a financial survey to determine the resources and needs of Nicaragua. W. W. Cumberland, who had been in Haiti as financial adviser and customs receiver, was to do the job. By March, 1928, Cumberland had finished his work and found the Nicaraguan government's finances satisfactory. He favored a collector-general of national revenue nominated by the secretary of state, a high commission to prepare a budget, and an auditor-general to check records and reports of government agencies, including the national bank. Important from the Nicaraguan standpoint was authorization to contract a loan for not more than $30,000,000, secured by all the government's revenues and receipts. He suggested that the loan be in series. The first would amount to $12,000,000—for revolutionary claims, the 1928 elections, public works, and refunding indebtedness.

The State Department, worried about political difficulties, had second thoughts concerning Cumberland's suggestions. Would the report's proposals not lay the department open to

[17] Munro to Department of State, Oct. 7, 1927, 817.51/1838.

charges that it was taking advantage of Marine occupation?[18] Washington wanted to consider the problem. The legation advised acceptance, or at least that the department take precautions concerning taxation, the bank, railroad, and Guardia, to make sure the Nicaraguan government did not misuse them; but Kellogg held off. After all, Cumberland had found conditions satisfactory. Much also depended on the bankers. In May, 1928, representatives of J. & W. Seligman and the Guaranty Trust Company came to Washington but talks were fruitless. The department objected to the bankers' proposal to lend only $3,500,000 in return for pledges on all revenues, internal and customs duties, railroad stock, and the national bank. Under that plan future advances would depend on the bankers, and there was no provision for payment of revolutionary claims.[19] The Nicaraguan loan floundered on this disagreement plus the bankers' desire to wait until after the election for a time when the securities market was more active. The bankers did not make the loan, nor any later loan.

The State Department tried to interest other lenders in reorganizing Nicaraguan finances. Moncada was fussing with bankers over the administration of the bank and the railroad. Disagreement led eventually to the retirement of the Guaranty Trust Company and J. & W. Seligman. The International Acceptance Bank became fiscal agent for Nicaragua and placed men on the boards of the railway and bank. The relationship was advisory and either party could end it.

Throughout the remaining years of the second intervention, Washington continued interest in Nicaraguan finances, although the matter was of even less importance in diplomacy than before. The department desired that the Nicaraguan government safeguard loans—now made mainly by the national bank—from poli-

[18] Department of State to Eberhardt, Apr. 19, 1928, 817.51/1912a.

[19] Department of State to Eberhardt, Aug. 3, 1928, 817.51/1973. See also memorandum of conference between State Department officials and bankers on June 13, 1928, 817.51/1949.

tics. The same concerns which bothered the department under Kellogg menaced the Stimson tenure—make sure the Guardia had money, discourage bribery in the elections of 1930 and 1932, protect Nicaraguan finances.

Thus financial matters were not the raison d'être of United States policy. Rather economics often became part of the search for stability or the means to achieve desired political ends. Assistant Secretary of State Robert E. Olds, in a memorandum on the Nicaraguan situation probably written early in 1927, frankly stated:

> Usually it has been sufficient for us to intervene on the sole *pretext* of furnishing protection of American lives and property. Naturally it is desirable wherever possible to confine the measures which we take within these limits. In this instance the measures would undoubtedly prove effective to stabilize the situation and insure the maintenance of the recognized government as against an ordinary revolt; but it is beginning to appear conclusively that they are not effective to accomplish the result in view of the substantial support which the insurrectionists are receiving from Mexico. The evidence now at hand indicates pretty clearly that unless we are willing to go beyond measures appropriate for the mere protection of American lives and property in the effected territory, there will be considerable bloodshed, and the government which we have recognized will be driven from power. This means that the Sacasa government, which we have refused to recognize, will take charge with the backing of Mexico.[20]

A much more important factor influencing American diplomacy was the idea of a Nicaraguan canal. Since 1849, Americans had considered such a waterway. Not until after the appearance of the United States as a world power and the urgent need for a "large policy" did the American government move ahead with the project. Although Panama won out, Nicaragua offered her

[20] Italics mine. Robert E. Olds, memorandum on the Nicaraguan situation, Jan. (?), 1927, 817.00/5854.

rivers and lakes as an alternative route. Nicaragua and the United
States culminated long discussion with the Bryan-Chamorro
Treaty of 1916, giving America an option on a canal route in
return for $3,000,000. This nation has never exercised its right
to build such a canal, but in the 1920's and early 1930's the
idea was much alive. In March, 1929, the United States Congress authorized a survey for the proposed interoceanic canal
through Nicaragua. For two and a half years the subject went
on, amid discussion of its feasibility, need, or justice. Some newspapers in Latin America pointed to it as evidence of plotting for
control of southern republics. John F. Stevens, former chief
engineer of the Panama Canal, argued there was no need for a
new waterway. The intriguing hustler of the Panama adventure,
Philippe Bunau-Varilla, found the suggested new route unfavor-
able. Then the Army engineers reported: Because of decreasing
world trade, the Great Depression, and operation of the Panama
Canal at only 50 percent of capacity, they recommended no
immediate construction of another canal.

Mexico was another consideration in United States-Nicaraguan
affairs. In the revolution after Chamorro's *golpe de cuartel* the
United States saw a threat from that nation. American officials
held that Bolshevist agencies in Mexico were partly responsible
for the Nicaraguan trouble and that the Calles government was
attempting to sit by while Mexico reached into the area near
the Panama Canal. The United States considered Central America and the Caribbean as a sphere of influence. From early days
this republic has been interested in the banana and sugar lands,
these close southern neighbors; Kellogg and Stimson were atten-
tive to them; the United States today is still interested. In 1927,
Robert E. Olds sized up the department's attitude when he
noted the importance of geography. Central America down
through the Isthmus of Panama constituted a legitimate area for
the United States, "if we are to have due regard for our own
safety and protection."[21] Mexico must not go into this area.

---

[21] *Ibid.* See also testimony of Kellogg before the Committee on Foreign
Relations of the Senate, Jan. 12, 1927, Kellogg papers, box 19.

The department received many reports of intrusion in Nicaragua. Although there was strong evidence that propaganda and arms for the Liberals and Sandinistas did come from Mexico, careful inquiries were not able to link aid to the government of that country. Dwight W. Morrow, our ambassador, found no connection. Even so, there was mutual distrust when the Calles government refused to recognize the American-backed Díaz regime and opened relations with the Sacasa group. The department regarded this action as a challenge to the continued influence of the United States in Central America. Mexican meddling was a matter of prestige. If Mexico won, Central Americans would believe that American recognition and support meant nothing. Until this time these nations believed the opposite—governments the United States recognized and supported stayed in power, those it did not recognize and support fell. Nicaragua was a test case; the department could not afford defeat. It made strong efforts to end the revolution and maintain Díaz in office until January 1, 1929.

During the Sandino affair some Americans again saw the hand of Mexican intrigue hindering United States efforts. Although there were in Mexico demonstrations and some vocal support of Sandino, the government's policies were not too unfriendly. As Minister Hanna observed in retrospect, the Mexican government did not give material support to Sandino's military operations and the living and travel expenses given the insurgent and his followers during their stay in Mexico facilitated their departure from Nicaragua, a trip welcomed by the United States.[22]

While Mexican interference seemed dangerous, that of Europe appeared only a remote possibility. European countries were interested in their nationals in Nicaragua and sometimes inquired of the United States about their safety. Once a British warship called at Corinto during troubled times, but it did not land troops or stay long. Later when Stimson and Hoover were attempting to disengage from Nicaragua and hesitated about sending ships to the east coast, Stimson was relieved that Britain

[22] Hanna to Department of State, Apr. 21, 1933, 817.00/7807.

did not raise the question of protecting life and property. The situation in Nicaragua did not primarily concern the Monroe Doctrine. Neither President Coolidge nor the State Department used it to explain United States actions in Nicaragua.[23]

In Congress, however, there were appeals to the doctrine. Senator Irvine Lenroot of Wisconsin asked how the nation could expect Europe to keep hands off if we did not protect lives and property in Nicaragua. Some legislators referred to a broadened doctrine under which the United States would protect Latin America from encroachments of other American nations as well as European states.[24] Other commentators dismissed the Monroe Doctrine as not pertinent to the Nicaraguan situation. Perhaps foreshadowing the famous Clark memorandum, Representative George Huddleston of Alabama decried the idea that Monroe or anyone of his time believed the 1823 dogma would be used for policing our southern neighbors. The Monroe Doctrine "claimed no superiority nor overlordship for ourselves, nor any greater right in any of the other countries than they had in our own."[25] But for those formulating our Nicaraguan policy the thoughts of Monroe apparently played little part. Actually, in the 1920's there was no one to challenge the United States on them.

American diplomacy toward Nicaragua also involved a quirk in recognition policy. This peculiarity of America's diplomacy embraced all of Central America. Hoping to curb revolutions in that area, the United States had encouraged these countries—

[23] Dexter Perkins, A History of the Monroe Doctrine (Boston, n.d.)—a revision of the book originally published under the title Hands Off: A History of the Monroe Doctrine—p. 337. In his testimony before the Senate Foreign Relations Committee, Jan. 12, 1927, Kellogg stated that "If we stay out entirely, they will go on with their revolution until they are financially and hopelessly ruined. They will default on their payments. They are necessarily bound to destroy American industries and properties, and you can gather as well as I can what foreign governments will say if we do not protect their citizens. 'We will do it ourselves.'"

[24] Congressional Record, 69th Cong., 2d Sess., vol. 68, part 2, 1404, 1563.

[25] Ibid., 70th Cong., 1st Sess., vol. 69, part 1, 1062.

Nicaragua, Guatemala, El Salvador, Honduras, and Costa Rica
—not to recognize governments coming to power in any of them
through coups d'état. First in 1907 and then 1923 these five Latin
American nations signed treaties to that effect. Although the
United States was not a party to the latter treaties, it sympa-
thized with their aims and the secretary of state presided over
the conference at Washington in 1923. The department followed
these special rules of recognition when dealing with Central
America. Washington had to do more than just decide which
government was in control; it had to determine the legitimacy
of the government. This burden complicated the recognition
process and continued the "moral diplomacy" of the Wilson
administration.

Emiliano Chamorro offered an important test to the 1923 treaty
when he skillfully maneuvered himself to power in 1925–26.
Chamorro's action helped bring out all the weaknesses of the
Central American recognition policy. How should the United
States handle Nicaraguan administrations which won elections
by a semblance of legality but ignored most of the constitutional
guarantees (as did every Nicaraguan president up to 1928)?
How does the opposition gain power if the "in" party denies
free elections? Will nonrecognition be the only sanction against
regimes such as Chamorro's? How can government get back on
the constitutional track? What if an outside nation interferes?

Knowing that, despite assurances to the contrary, the 1924
Nicaraguan election had been manipulated, American Marines
still withdrew in 1925 because Washington wanted to end the
first Nicaraguan intervention, which had begun in 1912. It was
not a well-planned withdrawal, for Nicaragua had taken only
haphazard measures for establishing a nonpartisan constabulary.
Within months American forces were back, facing full-scale civil
war. Washington threatened all-out intervention; but knowing a
small show of force was usually all that was necessary, the United
States then actually contemplated nothing more far-reaching.
The revolution ended. After promising a free election and saying
it would disarm those Nicaraguans who refused to stop fighting,

the department confronted the guerrilla warfare of Sandino. This warfare brought Nicaragua to the world's notice and brought to the United States a large measure of condemnation.

Thus the Central American treaty of 1923—in theory desirable, in practice a mixed, if not false, blessing—illustrates the dilemma of America's Nicaraguan policy. Emphasis on constitutional government, so dear to Anglo-Saxons, found less support in Middle America, where losers in elections were reluctant to turn government over to their opponents, since there was usually no way to regain power short of revolution. Under this recognition policy, then, the United States haltingly assumed obligations for free elections; otherwise it would be in the difficult position of maintaining in office a government which did not represent majority will. Supervised elections, of course, meant thoroughgoing intervention, an act fraught with pitfalls, as the Nicaraguan adventure attests. An opposite policy which might encourage revolution seemed as unacceptable as one discouraging revolution. A possible solution (one perhaps too often followed in American policy) was to back any strong man who came along who could preserve peace and order, but there was always the prospect of his fall.[26] In the early 1930's the United States adhered to the 1923 treaty when revolutions broke out in Guatemala and El Salvador, but after the Central American nations abandoned the agreement in 1934, the United States did likewise.[27]

Undoubtedly there were some intangibles affecting United States policy, subliminal reasons such as habit or the attitude of the white man's burden. Intervention had become a standard reaction to certain developments in the Caribbean area, and often a minor show of force was sufficient to bring satisfactory settlement. A warship at Corinto or Bluefields or Puerto Cabézas,

[26] For a discussion of the problem see memorandum from White to Grew, Nov. 7, 1924, White papers, box 3, Latin America, general folder.
[27] Robert Ferrell, *American Diplomacy in the Great Depression: Hoover-Stimson Foreign Policy, 1929–1933* (New Haven, 1957), p. 220.

a scant one hundred Marines in Managua had kept Nicaragua quiet for thirteen years prior to 1925. Such arrangements were not particularly desirable, but they were not too troublesome either. When Coolidge and Kellogg were confronted with the Nicaraguan situation in 1926, they reluctantly followed a familiar pattern which they felt would quickly stabilize the country. When results did not meet department expectations, Washington made a greater commitment, and what had begun as a relatively simple, seemingly normal response became a matter of national prestige. As Kellogg once noted in explaining his policy, "this has been the policy of President Taft, President Wilson, President Harding. . . ." Neither Kellogg nor Coolidge was ready to travel an uncharted course.

Another difficult-to-measure element that influenced United States-Nicaraguan relations was personnel. Many Americans serving in Nicaragua seemed to become too involved with various political leaders or factions. Undoubtedly the extreme partisan political atmosphere of Managua made charges of prejudice impossible to avoid. Nonetheless, the effectiveness of diplomats and soldiers was lessened because of it. Then, too, some Americans considered service in Central America undesirable and generally felt that Washington did not appreciate the importance of Latin America. One foreign service officer felt "it would help if men who specialized in Latin America knew they would not ordinarily be sent to posts like Buenaventura and Puerto Cortez where they would get no valuable experience. A man with the right spirit ought not to mind going to Managua or Tegucigalpa, if he knew that it was not necessarily a disgrace to be sent there."[28]

A combination of factors, then, embroiled the United States in the second Nicaraguan intervention: recognition policy, the Monroe Doctrine perhaps, Mexico, fear for the safety of the Panama Canal, the alternative Canal route through Nicaragua,

[28] Munro to White, Aug. 29, 1928, White papers, box 14, Munro file.

habit, and economics, although this last factor was not of primary importance.

But what were the alternatives to outright intervention? If it were possible to cut apart the processes of history—by some unhistorical time-stopping operation—so as to reorder events and reorganize results, could the United States in the uneasy months and years after the Chamorro coup d'état have followed any other course than open intervention? Perhaps nonintervention? Or multilateral intervention?

In the 1920's both of the latter policies appeared unwise. Total nonintervention seemed to lead nowhere except to chaos—a condition of course unacceptable to the United States. And after committing itself to the Díaz government, refusal to intervene further meant loss of prestige. Cooperation of Latin American nations with the United States would probably have been the best way to handle the Nicaraguan problem. During preparations for the 1928 election, Stimson had suggested something like this to Coolidge and the State Department. Nothing came of it, because members of the department feared complications which could obstruct what the United States was trying to do. The Latin American nations might well have been difficult to work with in the 1920's, for the true growth of Pan-Americanism did not come until the 1930's and the imminence of the Second World War. Still, multilateral intervention might have been the best course, had it been possible. Cooperating with the other republics of the hemisphere would have helped dispel the charges of imperialism leveled at the United States and might have provided the necessary restraint on American policy to avoid the embarrassing and damaging guerrilla war.

The intervention of 1925–33 did not go off easily, and it certainly brought increased pressure for the United States to change its policy in Latin America. America's actions in Nicaragua helped fan feeling all over Latin America, helped arouse distrust and hate for the yanqui; at least to Latin American satisfaction it proved the Anglo-Saxons were barbarians. The United States has had to contend with such feelings to the present day. Today

some Latin American authors honor Sandino as a voice of resistance against foreign aggression and the status quo. To them
Sandino is not an individual rebel but a symbol of all the down-
trodden—the peasant desiring land, the Indian experiencing
white exploitation, the mulatto suffering racial contempt.[29] Thus
the unpleasant experiences of the second intervention are used
to imply a connection between the United States and much that
is wrong in present-day Latin America.

Part of the American program in Nicaragua was establishment
of a nonpartisan national guard which, after Marine departure,
was the most powerful armed force in the country. Hoping that
the constabulary would perpetuate constitutional government,
the United States misjudged the Nicaraguan situation and in
fact created the vehicle Anastasio Somoza used to seize power
in 1936. This turn of events was not planned by the Americans,
as some Latin Americans have charged. Rather it reveals the
futility of attempting to impose from outside a political order
foreign to the recipient.[30]

Diplomacy with the southern neighbors now tries to avoid
intervention. Multilateral action through the Organization of
American States is the pattern for stability and well-being. Not
dead, however, is the idea that the United States may sometime choose to act alone. Cooperative action is complicated,
as Munro and McCoy knew when Stimson suggested Central
American participation in the 1928 election. One may ponder
what might happen if even today the United States felt its
interest imperiled in the Western Hemisphere and the O.A.S.
was hesitant to act. Presidents Eisenhower and Kennedy noted
obligations to protect our nation if the inter-American doctrine
of nonintervention should at any time conceal or excuse inaction.
In 1965, President Johnson did act alone, at first, in the Domini-

[29] Gregorio Selser, *Sandino, General de Hombres Libres*, I, unnum-
bered page of the "Del Prólogo a la Arenga," and II, 389, 392.

[30] Juan José Arévalo, *The Shark and the Sardines*, trans. June Cobb
and Raul Osegueda (New York, 1961), p. 171.

can Republic. Undoubtedly situations inviting intervention will arise again and the American people can hope their government will have good intentions, intelligence, and foresight for the complications of such a move. Perhaps the Nicaraguan affair may serve as a guide. It is clear from this episode in our diplomatic history that United States intrusion may end a crisis, but limited intervention and a few supervised elections cannot guarantee the political stability and well-being of a nation.

BIBLIOGRAPHICAL ESSAY

A generation has passed since American Marines withdrew from Nicaragua in 1933. Since that time much material relative to the period has become available. As a study of the development and execution of United States policy, this volume relies primarily upon Department of State files, records of the Marine forces in Nicaragua, and papers and diaries of several leading participants. The Nicaraguan archives were destroyed in the Managua earthquake and fire of 1931, leading Matthew Hanna to comment, "It may be said that the fire has literally destroyed the official sources of Nicaragua's history." Nonetheless, in Managua the Biblioteca Nacional and Archivo General de ¹a Nación have some materials pertinent to the study, mainly newspapers and periodicals.

1. BIBLIOGRAPHICAL AIDS

For United States diplomacy toward Nicaragua there are some special bibliographies. During the second intervention the division of bibliography of the Library of Congress mimeographed "Recent References on Nicaragua with Special Reference to Her Relations with the United States" (February, 1927). It includes, for the most part, magazine articles and refers to speeches in the *Congressional Record;* it lists some books. The following year the same source produced "United States Relations with Mexico and Central America." Van Lieu Minor compiled from material mostly in the University of Michigan library "A Brief Classified Bibliography Relating to United States Intervention in Nicaragua," *Hispanic American Historical Review,* XI (May, 1931), 261–277. Minor includes some public documents and books but mainly periodical literature. He also gives some

annotation. For a broader study of Central America there is William
J. Griffith, "The Historiography of Central America Since 1830,"
Hispanic American Historical Review, XL (November, 1960),
548–569. Griffith's essay includes mostly works published since 1920.
The author lists a number of titles on Sandino. He feels that the
history of Central America "offers a favorable and profitable field for
investigation" for historians. The *Handbook of Latin American Studies*, published from 1936 to 1947 in Cambridge, Massachusetts, and
then at Gainesville, Florida, is a cooperative annual volume offering
a guide to materials published in several fields—history, economics,
philosophy, music, literature. R. A. Humphreys, *Latin American History: A Guide to the Literature in English* (London, 1958), and
Richard F. Behrendt, *Modern Latin America in Social Science Literature* (University of New Mexico Press, 1949), give short listings on
Nicaragua with brief annotations.

Any student of American history is indebted to Oscar Handlin
and others for the *Harvard Guide to American History* (Cambridge,
Mass., 1955) although the listings are unannotated and include little
published beyond 1950. A major aid to historical researchers is Philip
M. Hamer, ed., *A Guide to Archives and Manuscripts in the United
States* (New Haven, Conn., 1961). Although it contains a few errors,
it is a monumental work. There is also the American Historical Association's *Writings on American History*; for the earlier volumes of this
series see the *Index to the Writings on American History, 1902–1940*
(Washington, 1956).

2. GENERAL WORKS

For full coverage of United States-Latin American relations from
almost the beginning of the nineteenth century until the early 1940's
there is Samuel Flagg Bemis, *The Latin American Policy of the
United States* (New York, 1943). The author finds that in spite of
some dark spots United States policy has been basically good. There
is also Graham H. Stuart, *Latin America and the United States*, 5th
ed. (New York, 1955). Julius W. Pratt, *America's Colonial Experi-
ment, How the United States Gained, Governed, and In Part Gave
Away a Colonial Empire* (New York, 1950), deals with Pacific affairs
as well as Latin American, from near the end of the nineteenth century. He notes that while American intervention in the Caribbean

helped governments financially, it made little change politically. Wilfrid H. Callcott, *The Caribbean Policy of the United States, 1890–1920* (Baltimore, 1942), found the United States developing a national conscience with regard to its southern neighbors. A full-length study of Kellogg's diplomacy based on private papers and archival material is L. Ethan Ellis, *Frank B. Kellogg and American Foreign Relations, 1925–1929* (New Brunswick, N.J., 1961). He finds that Kellogg, a second-rate secretary of state whose diplomacy lacked imagination, was overcautious and feared change. He sees, however, a foreshadowing of better Latin American relations. Norman A. Graebner, ed., *An Uncertain Tradition: American Secretaries of State in the Twentieth Century* (New York, 1961), includes an essay on Kellogg by Ellis. Jeanne Carol Traphagen, in an unpublished doctoral thesis on "The Inter-American Diplomacy of Frank B. Kellogg" (University of Minnesota, 1956), looks upon Kellogg's record as that of a competent, conscientious, industrious public official who performed his duty with credit to his country. The most recent work (1963) on Kellogg diplomacy is Robert H. Ferrell's volume (XI) on Kellogg and Stimson in the continuation volumes of the series, *American Secretaries of State and Their Diplomacy,* now edited by Ferrell. Mr. Ferrell believes that Kellogg showed up well as secretary of state, demonstrating intelligence and perception; he was a worthy successor to Charles Evans Hughes. *The Making of the Good Neighbor Policy* (New York, 1961), by Bryce Wood, has a chapter on the Nicaraguan experience.

The most authoritative study of Hoover-Stimson diplomacy is Robert H. Ferrell, *American Diplomacy in the Great Depression: Hoover-Stimson Foreign Policy, 1929–1933* (New Haven, Conn., 1957). The author believes that Latin America provided the one area of achievement during the period. A laudatory account of the same topic is William Starr Myers, *The Foreign Policies of Herbert Hoover, 1929–1933* (New York, 1940). Alexander De Conde, *Herbert Hoover's Latin-American Policy* (Stanford, Calif., 1951), believes Hoover's actions in this area were the real beginnings of the good neighbor policy.

Richard Current's *Secretary Stimson, A Study in Statecraft* (New Brunswick, N.J., 1954) is critical concerning Stimson as secretary of state. He also wrote the essay on Stimson in N. A. Graebner, ed., *An Uncertain Tradition.*

Another volume touching on United States-Latin American relations is Sumner Welles, *The Time for Decision* (Cleveland and New York, 1945) which notes that although Hoover desired to improve inter-American relations, he failed because of his high tariff policy. Laurence Duggan, *The Americas: The Search for Hemisphere Security* (New York, 1949) has a somewhat similar view stressing the work of Roosevelt and Welles on the good neighbor policy. Other studies are John Carter, *Conquest, America's Painless Imperialism* (New York, 1928) and A. Curtis Wilgus, *The Caribbean: Contemporary International Relations* (Gainesville, Fla., 1957), a series of essays. Germán Arciniegas, *The State of Latin America*, trans. by Harriet de Onis (New York, 1952) has a few pages on Nicaragua and is critical of the United States. A highly critical view which stresses the part played by the Wall Street bankers is John A. H. Hopkins and Melinda Alexander, *Machine-Gun Diplomacy* (New York, 1928). A more recent critical commentary on American policy is Juan José Arévalo, *The Shark and the Sardines*. The author uses Nicaragua as an example of his shark-sardine thesis.

Useful for development of the Monroe Doctrine is Dexter Perkins, *A History of the Monroe Doctrine* (Boston, 1955), a summary of Perkins' detailed studies on that dogma of American diplomacy.

Of histories of Central America, Dana G. Munro, *The Five Republics of Central America* (New York, 1918), although old, still has excellent comments and insights into some problems of these nations. See also his more recent *Intervention and Dollar Diplomacy in the Caribbean, 1900–1921* (Princeton, 1964). Hubert Howe Bancroft, *History of Central America*, 3 vols. (San Francisco, 1886–1887) provides information for the background of this essay. The volumes are part of his multivolume *History of the Pacific States of North America*. Bancroft used some of the materials of Ephriam G. Squier, whose *Nicaragua: Its People, Scenery, Monuments and the Proposed Interoceanic Canal*, 2 vols. in 1 (New York, 1856) gives an interesting account of early exploration of Nicaragua. Floyd Cramer, *Our Neighbor Nicaragua* (New York, 1929) is readable general history which goes back to Spanish colonial days. Other works which include chapters on Nicaragua are Frederick Palmer, *Central America and Its Problems* (New York, 1910); Charles W. Domville-Fife, *Guatemala and the States of Central America* (London, 1913); Wallace Thompson, *Rainbow Countries of Central America* (New York, 1927); Arthur

Ruhl, The Central Americans (New York, 1928); William Krehm, Democracia y Tiranías en el Caribe (Mexico, D.F., 1949). More recent is John D. Martz, Central America, The Crisis and the Challenge (Chapel Hill, N.C., 1959).

Charges of communism intruded upon the Nicaraguan question through activities of Sandino and Mexico. The small volume by Víctor Alba, Historia del Comunismo en América Latina (Mexico, D.F., 1954) contains a brief account of Sandino's relationship with the communists; there is also the more extensive work of Robert J. Alexander, Communism in Latin America (New Brunswick, N.J., 1957), which is based on interviews and much research in Latin America.

For geography there is a chapter on Nicaragua in August H. Keane, Stanford's Compendium of Geography and Travel: Central and South America, 2nd ed. (London, 1911), II.

Important parts of United States-Latin American diplomacy are trade and investments. Max Winkler discusses these in Investments of United States Capital in Latin America (World Peace Foundation Pamphlets, Boston, 1928). He points out that the large increase in United States trade and investment with its southern neighbors began during the First World War. See also his "Investments and National Policy of the United States in Latin America," The American Economic Review, Supplement, XXII (March, 1932), 144–151.

A policy of intervention in the Caribbean meant use of the Marine Corps. Clyde H. Metcalf, a Marine officer, traces the corps' history in A History of the United States Marine Corps (New York, 1939).

Useful annual surveys of foreign relations are Charles P. Howland, Survey of American Foreign Relations, 1928 (New Haven, Conn., 1929), published for the Council on Foreign Relations; and Arnold J. Toynbee, Survey of International Affairs, 1927 (London, 1929).

3. SPECIAL WORKS ON UNITED STATES-NICARAGUAN RELATIONS

The most interesting and readable account of American policy in Nicaragua is Harold Norman Denny, Dollars for Bullets: The Story of American Rule in Nicaragua (New York, 1929). Denny was a reporter for the New York Times and was in Nicaragua in the later 1920's. Many of his signed stories appeared in the Times during that period. Shorter but highly useful is Isaac Joslin Cox, Nicaragua and the United States, 1909–1927 (World Peace Foundation Pamphlets, Boston, 1927). Another work appearing at that time is Rafael de Nogales, The Looting of Nicaragua (New York, 1928). However, the author—a soldier of fortune or staff officer by profession, who served in the Turkish, Japanese, Spanish, and Venezuelan armies— presents little of value. He did raise the ire of Minister Eberhardt, who called the work a tissue of misstatements.

More recent studies include Charles Edward Frazier, Jr., "The Dawn of Nationalism and Its Consequences in Nicaragua," a Ph.D. dissertation completed at the University of Texas in 1958. It is a careful analysis stressing the Sandino affair as the focal point for the Latin Americans' dislike, jealousy, and distrust of the United States. William Russell, "Diplomatic Relations between the United States and Nicaragua, 1920–1933," a doctoral dissertation at the University of Chicago, 1953, is generally critical of American policy. Another work, well written, which emphasizes Sandino is Lejeune Cummins, Quijote on a Burro; Sandino and the Marines, A Study in the Formation of Foreign Policy (La Impresora Azteca, Mexico, D.F., 1958).

For studies of particular phases of American intervention see Roscoe R. Hill, Fiscal Intervention in Nicaragua (New York, 1933). Hill was a member of the high commission in Nicaragua at the time of the second intervention and does not feel that bankers were taking unfair advantage of Nicaraguans. John Milton Wearmouth, in his master's thesis, "The Second Marine Intervention in Nicaragua: 1927–1932," at Georgetown University, 1952, used Marine Corps records to reconstruct the military operations of the Marines. Neill Macauley's The Sandino Affair (Chicago, 1967) is a detailed description of the Marine campaigns against the Sandinista guerrillas. The author, keeping one eye on contemporary analogies, sees the possibility that the United States may have to face in Latin America what it now faces in Vietnam and earlier faced in Nicaragua. The story of the United States-created Nicaraguan national guard is found in Richard L. Millett's "The History of the Guardia Nacional de Nicaragua, 1926–1965" (Ph.D. dissertation at the University of New Mexico, 1966) based on research in Washington and Managua, including a large number of personal interviews. See also Major Julian C. Smith, et al., A Review of the Organization and Operations of the Guardia Nacional de Nicaragua (n.p., n.d.). Major Smith was at one time chief of staff of the Guardia.

A brief account (in part from the memory of a participant) of the Liberal revolution is found in Humberto Osorno Fonseca, *La Revolución Liberal Constitucionalista de 1926* (Managua, 1958).

4. AUTOBIOGRAPHIES AND BIOGRAPHIES

Sandino is the subject of some short works, most of which are adulatory. G. Alemán Bolaños, *¡Sandino! Estudio Completo del Héroe de las Segovias* (Mexico and Buenos Aires, 1932) quotes many letters and other writings of Sandino. Luis Felipe Recinos and Ruben Hernandez, *Sandino, Hazanas del Héroe* (San Jose, Costa Rica, 1934) is not of much value except as an example of the level on which many supporters put him. More useful because the author was an active politician and helped bring the Sacasa administration and Sandino to terms is Sofonías Salvatierra, *Sandino o la Tragedia de un Pueblo* (Madrid, 1934). See also the two-volume work by Gregorio Selser, *Sandino, General de Hombres Libres* (Buenos Aires, 1959); it is a repetitious eulogy to Sandino, a diatribe against United States intervention, but valuable for quoting a large number of Sandino documents. Anastasio Somoza's, *El Verdadero Sandino o El Calvario de las Segovias* (Managua, 1936) is a compilation of documents with brief commentaries attempting to show Sandino and his followers not as heroes but as people who burned, killed, and sacked. There is little relating to the Nicaraguan policy of the United States in *Somoza, Asesino de Sandino* by Ramón Romero (Mexico, 1959).

Biographies of American secretaries of state for the 1920's and early 1930's include Dexter Perkins, *Charles Evans Hughes and American Democratic Statesmanship* (Boston, 1956); David Bryn-Jones, *Frank B. Kellogg, A Biography* (New York, 1937); and Elting E. Morison, *Turmoil and Tradition, A Study of the Life and Times of Henry L. Stimson* (Boston, 1960), who makes use of the Stimson papers and diary as well as archival material. Written a short time after retirement in 1945 while "memory of important events was still alive" is Henry L. Stimson and McGeorge Bundy, *On Active Service in Peace and War* (New York, 1947).

Calvin Coolidge's *Autobiography* (New York, 1929) offers almost nothing on foreign affairs. William Allen White's *A Puritan in Babylon* (New York, 1938) makes only brief mention of Latin American affairs, while Claude M. Fuess, *Calvin Coolidge, The Man from Ver-*

mont (Boston, 1940) gives it very little more. The most recent biography is Donald R. McCoy, *Calvin Coolidge: The Quiet President* (New York and London, 1967). He finds that Coolidge's role in the conduct of inter-American relations was well played. "Indeed, it represented him at his best." Coolidge's choice for ambassador to Mexico had an excellent biographer in Harold Nicolson, *Dwight Morrow* (New York, 1935). Morrow was Kellogg's choice to be undersecretary when the latter came to head the State Department, but at Coolidge's insistence Joseph C. Grew was retained in that position until 1927. In Grew's diary (Walter Johnson, ed.) *Turbulent Era: A Diplomatic Record of Forty Years, 1904–1945*, 2 vols. (London, 1953), there are a few observations on Nicaragua. Herbert Hoover in his *Memoirs*, 3 vols. (New York, 1951–1952) briefly describes his postelection trip to South and Central America. He believes his administration established goodwill in Latin America under the term "good neighbor."

Willard L. Beaulac, who was assigned to the American legation in Managua in the early 1930's, has written an autobiographical sketch, *Career Ambassador* (New York, 1951). He reflects the growing department dissatisfaction with American intervention. He records his highly interesting experience in the Managua earthquake of 1931. Another American of later prominence, Matthew B. Ridgway, helped supervise the elections of 1928 and 1930. In his *Soldier: The Memoirs of Matthew B. Ridgway* (New York, 1956) he has little of importance on the elections but tells of his feats in hunting crocodiles in Nicaragua.

One of the foxiest and most intriguing of Nicaraguans during the American involvement was Emiliano Chamorro, who in 1960 gave way to entreaties of friends to give his views on the social and political happenings in Nicaragua during his lifetime; these observations appeared serially in "Autobiografía," *Revista Conservadora* (August, 1960, to March, 1962).

For flavor of the adventure which Nicaragua offered, Joseph Crad (pseudonym for Edward Clarence Trelawney-Ansell) tells in *I Had Nine Lives: Fighting for Cash in Mexico and Nicaragua* (London, 1938) of fighting for Sandino. William O. Scroggs, in his excellent biography *Filibusters and Financiers: The Story of William Walker and His Associates* (New York, 1916), related adventures of that extraordinary man.

5. NEWSPAPERS AND PERIODICAL LITERATURE

The New York Times gives wide coverage and is especially useful because of its index. It often printed foreign press comments. The United States Daily printed releases of government agencies and also had an index. In the United States, one may consult Nicaraguan newspapers for the period under study at the Latin American Library of Tulane University and at the Library of Congress. Such papers as El Diario Nicaragüense (Granada), El Centroamericano (León); La Noticia, La Prensa, La Tribuna, El Comercio (all of Managua) are available but the files are incomplete. In Managua the Archivo General de la Nación also has newspaper files, but again they are not complete. The researcher may also follow editorial opinion, both home and foreign, in The Literary Digest.

Periodical literature on American diplomacy toward Nicaragua, 1925–33, is large. Its intensity varied, naturally, with happenings in Nicaragua or Washington—a statement about Bolshevism, a coup d'état, supervised election, sudden attack by Sandino. The tone of the articles or editorials also varied with the political attitude of the periodical—for example, The Nation was one of the strong opponents of intervention. The more recent literature of scholarly journals is not large—a few articles on Sandino, election supervision, or the Nicaraguan canal.

Individuals connected with United States-Nicaraguan relations have written about observations or studies. The American commander of the Nicaraguan national guard from 1925 to 1927, C. B. Carter, gave his views in "The Kentucky Feud in Nicaragua," The World's Work, vol. 54 (July, 1927), 312–321; José M. Moncada, the Liberal general, supported American actions in "Nicaragua and American Intervention," The Outlook, vol. 147 (December 14, 1927), 460–462, 477. George T. Weitzel, former minister, and H. W. Dodds, Nicaraguan election expert, discuss their views in "The United States and Central America" and "The United States and Nicaragua," both in the Annals of the American Academy of Political and Social Science, vol. 132 (July, 1927), 115–126; 134–141. Dodds opposed American policy of constitutionalism in Central America. Also advocating recognition of de facto governments in Latin America was Lawrence Dennis, the American chargé who tangled with Chamorro. In "Revolution, Recognition and Intervention," Foreign Affairs, IX (January, 1931),

204–221, and "Nicaragua: In Again, Out Again," *Foreign Affairs*,
IX (April, 1931), 496–500, he asserted the United States could either
revert to general rules of international law regarding recognition and
let the factions fight it out or could continue the cycle of "in again,
out again."

Dana G. Munro examined motives for American intervention in
Nicaragua in "Dollar Diplomacy in Nicaragua, 1909–1913," *Hispanic
American Historical Review*, XXXVIII (May, 1958), 208–234, and
concluded that those persons directing American policy were less
interested in American investors than attainment of political objectives. See also Dana Munro, "The Establishment of Peace in Nicaragua," *Foreign Affairs*, XI (July, 1933), 696–705. Joseph O. Baylen,
too, thought that security was the primary object of American policy,
but it was marred by rising hatred for the *yanqui*. Note his "American
Intervention in Nicaragua, 1909–33: An Appraisal of Objectives and
Results," *The Southwestern Social Science Quarterly*, XXXV (September, 1954), 128–154. A. I. Powell, writing at the time of the
1928 Nicaraguan election, examined American policy in "Relations
Between the United States and Nicaragua, 1896–1916," *Hispanic
American Historical Review*, VIII (February, 1928), 43–64.

Contemporary articles of a general nature but not of outstanding
merit are: Lewis S. Gannett, "Dollars and Bullets: A History," *The
Nation*, vol. 124 (January 26, 1927), 89–90; "Big Brother or Big
Bully," *The Nation*, vol. 123 (July 14, 1926), 25; "Our Marines in
Nicaragua," *The Nation*, vol. 121 (August 26, 1925), 243–244. See
also "Cabbages and Kings Country," *The Living Age*, vol. 327
(November 14, 1925), 343–345, a journalistic treatment of the raid on
the International Club in 1925. Carroll Binder, "On the Nicaraguan
Front," *The New Republic*, vol. 50 (March 16, 1927), 87–90,
believed most Nicaraguans did not care whether Marines were there
or not. Writing for the same periodical, Linton Welles in "Our Coming Intervention in Nicaragua," (May 11, 1927), 322–324, asserted
that the United States was political policeman of Central America.

Charles W. Hackett discussed American intervention several times
in *Current History*: "Intervention in Central America," XXXIV
(June, 1931), 434–440; "Rival Governments in Nicaragua," XXV
(February, 1927), 734–736; and "United States Intervention in Nicaragua," XXVI (April, 1927), 104–107. For a brief summary of Nicaraguan history from Spanish times until 1929 see James E. Edmonds,

"Nicaragua's Centuries of Strife and Bloodshed," *Current History*, XXXI (November, 1929), 286–293.

Sandino was an enigma. During the height of the trouble, Carleton Beals took a trip to Nicaragua to interview him. "With Sandino in Nicaragua" appeared in six installments in *The Nation*, vol. 126 (February 22, 1928, to March 28, 1929). Beals's articles were friendly. He also wrote "This Is War, Gentlemen!" *The Nation*, vol. 126 (April 1, 1928), 404–406. A Nicaraguan who lauded Sandino was Salomon de la Selva, "Sandino," *The Nation*, vol. 126 (January 18, 1928), 63–64. More recently Joseph O. Baylen has studied Sandino. His "Sandino: Patriot or Bandit?" *Proceedings* of the South Carolina Historical Association (1950), pp. 30–48, found Sandino a revolutionary in a patriotic cause and not a bandit. The same article expanded appears in the *Hispanic American Historical Review*, XXXI (August, 1951), 394–419. Baylen has also written about the struggle between the Sandinistas and the Somoza-led Guardia in "Sandino: Death and Aftermath," *Mid-America: An Historical Review*, XXXVI (April, 1954), 116–139.

The other Nicaraguan whose name was probably best known to outsiders was Emiliano Chamorro. Walter Scott Penfield, onetime legal adviser to the Nicaraguan legation at Washington and in Nicaragua during Chamorro's 1925 coup, discusses the coup d'état in "Emiliano Chamorro, Nicaragua's Dictator," *Current History*, XXIV (June, 1926), 345–350. He thought Chamorro should retire. William C. Carey, "Emancipated Nicaragua," *The Living Age*, vol. 328 (February 20, 1926), 415–418, described in a journalistic, humorous way the first session of the Nicaraguan Congress after Chamorro seized power. Analysis of Central American press comment is in "After Our Marines Left Nicaragua," *The Literary Digest*, vol. 87 (December 12, 1925), 21. Carleton Beals looked at the Conservative general in "Chamorro, the Strong Man of Nicaragua," *The Nation*, vol. 126 (April 18, 1928), 430–432.

Regarding the Stimson mission and United States policy in general see Stimson's articles, "American Policy in Nicaragua," *Saturday Evening Post*, vol. 200 (October 1, 1927), 8–9; (October 8, 1927), 20–21; (October 15, 1927), 18–19. Reportedly, Secretary Kellogg was delighted about the articles. Charles W. Hackett, in "Nicaraguan Civil Strife Ended by United States Ultimatum," *Current History*,

XXVI (July, 1927), 634–637, recited the then known facts of the mission.

As for free elections, Virginia L. Greer gives a careful, well-documented analysis in "State Department Policy in Regard to the Nicaraguan Election of 1924," *Hispanic American Historical Review,* XXXIV (November, 1954), 445–467. H. W. Dodds describes 1928 in "American Supervision of the Nicaraguan Election," *Foreign Affairs,* VII (April, 1929), 488–496. For broader analysis of the State Department's use of elections in dealing with Latin American nations see Theodore P. Wright, "Free Elections in the Latin American Policy of the United States," *Political Science Quarterly,* vol. 74 (March, 1959), 89–112.

Some Marine officers have described their experiences. Colonel H. C. Reisinger, "La Palabra del Gringo!: Leadership of the Nicaraguan National Guard," United States Naval Institute *Proceedings,* vol. 61 (February, 1935), 215–221, told of generally good relations between Marine leaders and Nicaraguan troopers of the Guardia. Similar is Captain Evans F. Carlson, "The Guardia Nacional de Nicaragua," *The Marine Corps Gazette,* XXI (August, 1937), 7–20. Marine patrols were not easy. Captain Merritt A. Edson writes of "The Coco Patrol," *The Marine Corps Gazette,* XX (August, 1936), 18–23; (November, 1936), 40–41; XXI (February, 1937), 35–43. *The Marine Corps Gazette,* during the late 1920's and early 1930's, published a number of articles by Marine officers on operations in Nicaragua.

The location of Nicaragua and possibility of an interoceanic canal were important considerations in State Department policy. See Nicholas J. Spykman, "Geography and Foreign Policy," *American Political Science Review,* XXXII (February, 1938), 28–50; (April, 1938), 213–236. The author did not call geography a determining factor but found it conditioning. Note also Spykman and Abbie A. Rollins, "Geographic Objectives in Foreign Policy," *American Political Science Review,* XXXIII (June, 1939), 391–410; (August, 1939), 591–614. Whiting Williams in "Geographic Determinism in Nicaragua," *Annals* of the American Academy of Political and Social Science, vol. 132 (July, 1927), 142–145, examines geography and Nicaraguan troubles. The idea of a Nicaraguan canal came to life in the late 1920's when Congress authorized a survey. John F. Stevens in "Is a Second Canal Necessary?" *Foreign Affairs,* VIII (April, 1930), 417–429, argued against another canal. Roscoe R. Hill, "The Nicaraguan Canal Idea to 1913," *Hispanic American Historical Review*, XXVIII (May, 1948), 197–211, traces the idea for approximately a hundred years up to the Bryan-Chamorro Treaty. Thomas A. Bailey in "Interest in a Nicaraguan Canal, 1903–1931," *Hispanic American Historical Review*, XVI (February, 1936), 2–28, brings the story up to the early 1930's. See also Percy F. Martin, "The United States and Nicaragua," *Fortnightly Review*, new series, vol. 121 (April 1, 1927), 476–480.

For the United States-Mexico conflict over Nicaragua, Carleton Beals, "The Nicaraguan Farce," *The Nation*, vol. 123 (December 15, 1926), 631–632, gives the Mexican view, as does Pedro D'Alba, "Mexico and Nicaragua," *The Living Age*, vol. 332 (February 1, 1927), 204–206. Charles W. Hackett in "The Mexican Crisis and Intervention in Nicaragua," *Current History*, XXV (March, 1927), 870–877, notes the lack of evidence for Kellogg's charges of Bolshevism. Also concerned with the topic of these charges is "Mexico and Central America," *Current History*, XXV (February, 1927), 763–764.

6. PRINTED SOURCES AND GOVERNMENT PUBLICATIONS

The United States is more nearly current than any other major government in publishing its diplomatic papers, now up to the middle 1940's with the series *Foreign Relations of the United States*. Material on Nicaragua is in the series for each of the years 1925 to 1933. Although the volumes contain only a fraction of material relating to any one country, the selection is good. During the second intervention the State Department twice published accounts of United States-Nicaraguan relations—*A Brief History of the Relations Between the United States and Nicaragua, 1909–1928* (Washington, 1928) and *The United States and Nicaragua, A Survey of the Relations from 1909 to 1932* (Washington, 1932). Another department publication is J. Reuben Clark, *Memorandum on the Monroe Doctrine* (Washington, 1930), a collection of documents and statements with commentary. In the covering memorandum to the Secretary of State, Clark separated the Roosevelt Corollary from the Monroe Doctrine. Note also the Department of State's weekly series, *Press Releases*, in which the department, beginning in October, 1929, printed the daily mimeographed releases.

At the request of Nicaragua, the Department of State in 1927 appointed W. W. Cumberland to make a financial and economic survey of Nicaragua. The following year he published his *Nicaragua, An Economic and Financial Survey Prepared, at the Request of Nicaragua, under the Auspices of the Department of State* (Washington, 1928). The year before, Harold Playter and Andrew J. McConnico made a useful study—*Nicaragua, A Commerical and Economic Survey* (Washington, 1927)—for the bureau of foreign and domestic commerce of the Commerce Department.

For valuable statistical information the *Report of the High Commission* and *Report of the Collector-General of Customs* were published annually in Managua. When Irving A. Lindberg became both collector-general of customs and high commissioner in 1928, he combined the reports.

Annual Reports of the Navy Department for 1925 through 1932 provide information on ships and personnel in Nicaraguan waters and ashore. The reports of bureaus and offices of the Navy Department were not printed for 1933 for reasons of economy.

Henry L. Stimson's *American Policy in Nicaragua* (New York, 1927) contains the author's story of the Stimson mission and thus can be considered a printed source. Much of what President Coolidge told reporters appeared in the newspapers as remarks from "the White House Spokesman." About one-sixth of President Coolidge's press conference material (the more important comments and statements) appear in Howard H. Quint and Robert H. Ferrell (eds.), *The Talkative President: The Off-The-Record Press Conferences of Calvin Coolidge* (Amherst, Mass., 1964). There are a few comments on Nicaragua. *Addresses Delivered During the Visit of Herbert Hoover, President-Elect of the United States to Central and South America, November-December, 1928* (Pan American Union, Washington, 1929) is what the title describes. Hoover stopped at Corinto for a short visit.

Concerning the Denver conference for reconciliation between Liberals and Conservatives, José Barcenas Meneses, *Las Conferencias del "Denver," Actas Autenticas de las Sesiones, con introduccion y lijeros comentarios* (Managua, 1926), is important, although it gives the Conservative viewpoint. For congressional reaction to events in Nicaragua and American diplomacy toward that country there is the *Congressional Record*. *Parliamentary Debates, House of Commons*, vol. 251 (London, 1931) records British government reaction to Stimson's attempts to keep marines from the Nicaraguan interior. For background I used William R. Manning, ed., *Diplomatic Correspondence of the United States, Inter-American Affairs, 1831–1860* (Washington, 1933), III, and his *Diplomatic Correspondence of the United States Concerning the Independence of the Latin-American Nations* (New York, 1925), II.

7. MANUSCRIPT SOURCES

A. ARCHIVES

For a general guide to the material in the National Archives see Philip M. Hamer, *Guide to the Records in the National Archives* (Washinton, 1948); note also his more recent *A Guide to Archives and Manuscripts in the United States.*

As in its policy of publishing diplomatic papers, the Department of State is liberal in making its records available to researchers. Records through 1936 are in the "open period" and are available with few restrictions. After 1936 and up to the mid-1940's is a limited-access period for which the researcher must make application and submit notes for review. Again the policy is liberal.

Sometimes overlooked are consular post records. For Nicaragua, those of Bluefields and Corinto are available. They are mostly on trade and economic conditions, but some are on politics, especially reports from Bluefields. The diplomatic post records for Managua show evidence of the Managua earthquake and fire of 1931. With these records there is a small bound volume, "American Foreign Service Legation, 1909–1933, Hanna Papers," which carries the following explanation: "The documents here bound were left in the legation at Guatemala by the late Matthew E. Hanna, who died while serving as American minister at that post." Much of this material is in regular State Department files.

Through preliminary inventory number 76 on "Records of United States Participation in International Conferences, Commissions, and Expositions" (Washington, 1955), compiled by H. Stephen Helton, the researcher can find descriptions of records of United States electoral missions to Nicaragua in 1928, 1930, and 1932.

The Navy branch of the National Archives offers material for study of the intervention in Nicaragua. There are a few folders of correspondence in the secretary's files, record group 80. See also general records of the Navy Department, general correspondence, 1926–1940 (record group 80); United States Marine Corps, adjutant and inspector's office, general correspondence, 1913–1932 (record group 127); naval records collection of the office of naval records and library, subject file, 1911–1927, WA-7, Nicaragua (record group 45).

The Navy branch also has records of Marine detachments in Nicaragua, 1928–1932. There are one hundred forty-seven steel filing trays of this material which includes correspondence, personnel files, intelligence reports, engagements with Sandinistas. There is no arrangement by boxes, but within any single tray the material is usually chronological by topic. The naval records management center, historical branch, records and research section in the Navy Annex at Arlington, Virginia, has thirteen boxes and twenty-three microfilm reels of records on Marine Corps units in Nicaragua, 1927–1933. There is a file guide to the boxed material.

B. Personal Papers

Chandler P. Anderson MSS. and diary. Library of Congress. Anderson was counsel for the Nicaraguan government in the 1917 boundary mediation with Honduras before the Department of State. He was later legal adviser to the Nicaraguan legation while Emiliano Chamorro was minister in Washington. Friendship between Chamorro and Anderson continued after the minister left. The diary is a good source for the Nicaraguan topic because Anderson had access to the secretary of state, and it also gives Chamorro's point of view. Anderson corresponded with several people about Nicaraguan affairs.

William E. Borah MSS. Library of Congress. It is a huge collection but does not contain much on Nicaragua.

Wilbur J. Carr MSS. and diary. Library of Congress. Carr was assistant secretary of state from 1924 to 1937. The collection has approximately five thousand items, including letters, diaries, speeches, articles, and scrapbooks. Most of the material deals with administration of the State Department. In his diary there are comments about national politics and department policies. A few entries relate to United States-Nicaraguan relations.

Calvin Coolidge MSS. Library of Congress. This is a large but disappointing collection, because Coolidge desired his personal papers destroyed and apparently most of them were. There are few letters by Coolidge; most are staff replies to incoming mail.

Charles Evans Hughes MSS. Library of Congress. These papers were particularly useful for the earlier portion of this work.

Frank B. Kellogg MSS. Minnesota State Historical Society. Most of the papers cover his tenure as secretary of state. There is not much on Nicaragua.

Frank R. McCoy MSS. Library of Congress. A rather large collection of ninety-five boxes, some of which have material on supervision of the 1928 election, including clippings and pictures. Correspondence to his family contains interesting off-the-record views of the work in Nicaragua.

David Foote Sellers MSS. Library of Congress (Naval Historical Foundation Collection). As commander of the special service squadron, Sellers corresponded with General Logan Feland and the chief of naval operations. Many of these dispatches show Navy sensitiveness about Nicaragua.

Henry L. Stimson MSS. and diary. Yale University Library. The index to these papers is what any researcher would wish. One volume of Stimson's diary records events of his mission to Nicaragua in April-May, 1927. Other volumes for 1930 and 1933, when he was Hoover's secretary of state, contain scattered references.

Francis White MSS. National Archives. White was assistant secretary of state for most of the period covered by this volume. These papers are a collection of memoranda and letters (forty-two boxes). While most of the material can also be found in the State Department files, there are some personal letters which help explain aspects of our Nicaraguan diplomacy.

INDEX